CRISIS AT THE BAR

CRISIS AT THE BAR

*Lawyers' Unethical Ethics
and What to Do about It*

Jethro K. Lieberman

W·W·Norton & Company·Inc·
NEW YORK

Copyright © *1978 by Jethro K. Lieberman.* Published simultaneously in Canada by George J. McLeod Limited, Toronto. Printed in the United States of America.

ALL RIGHTS RESERVED

FIRST EDITION

Library of Congress Cataloging in Publication Data

Lieberman, Jethro Koller.
Crisis at the Bar.

Includes bibliographical references and index.
I. Legal ethics—United States.   I. Title.
KF306.L53   174'.3'0973   77-25492

ISBN 0-393-05644-9

1 2 3 4 5 6 7 8 9 0

For   S. E. V. L.

No one can have been for twenty years in active and varied legal practice without becoming convinced that the profession to which he belongs harbors within itself examples of as base, deliberate and ingenious depravity as any that, less favored by fortune or cunning, have gravitated into the penitentiary. He finds, moreover, on the part of those numerous members of the bar who cannot look upon meanness with any degree of allowance, and on the part of the bench which is nominally charged with the regulation of the officers who come before it, a half-sad, half-humorous *consensus,* as to the existence of such baseness and as to the perpetration of specific offenses, and an altogether sad acquiescence in them, as beyond the inadequate power of penal process to correct. Yet it may fairly be doubted whether all the unpunished rascalities of pettifoggers, shysters and barrators, all the devices of trials at *nisi prius,* all the bullying and tricking of witnesses, all the affidavit-mongering of the special-motion room, so much discredit in public opinion those lawyers who are innocent of them, as the principles which distinguished jurists have sometimes avowed as the proper basis for professional conduct.

—*Theodore Bacon, 1882*

Contents

The Fine Print: A Disclaimer
and Some Acknowledgments

This book is critical of lawyers. Because individual remarks, not to mention a general tone, can be misunderstood, I wish to make a disclaimer at the outset. I do not hate lawyers, nor undervalue the worth of their services or the importance of their social function. Neither do I abhor law or legal institutions. One who has been trained in the law, who has worked side by side with lawyers, and who spends his professional time talking to and about lawyers cannot have an unsophisticated animus against the fundamental process and values they represent.

But this book is not a history of law or of the bar, nor an analysis of how legal institutions work (or how they ought to work) in a democratic society. The book has a much narrower, hence more intense, focus than that. I deal here with a cluster of serious problems that lawyers have largely brought on themselves. This cluster carries the label "ethics." I contend that the ethical system is in complete disarray. No attempt is made to provide a history of the good things that lawyers in fact have done.

Moreover, reams have been written about the issues discussed, and this book should not be read in the expectation of finding a summary of the literature. Nor, though the book does discuss the crisis in lawyers' ethics, does it pretend to be a lawyer's analysis, with each lawsuit and argument laid out in catalogue order.

Many people have given me their time, thought, and opinions. Some are mentioned in the text or notes and to them I am grateful. But I do wish especially to thank Monroe H. Freedman, Ruth Hochberger, Joel F. Henning, C. Russell Twist, and Thomas S. Johnson for their advice or other aid. Of course the opinions expressed in this book are mine and should not be imputed to them or to others. Thanks also to Bonnie Nelson and Elizabeth K. Lieberman for their typing services and to Jessica D. Lieberman for indexing help. And special thanks to Edwin Barber, editor nonpareil, and the efficient but invisible staff of W. W. Norton & Co. Finally, I am pleased to acknowledge the kindness of the Michie Publishing Co. for permission to reprint pp. 30–31, 48 of Monroe H. Freedman, *Lawyers' Ethics in an Adversary System* (Bobbs-Merrill, 1975); and the American Bar Association's Section of Criminal Justice for permission to reprint pp. 8–10 of "Standards of Conduct for Prosecution and Defense Personnel: A Symposium," in *American Criminal Law Quarterly,* vol. 5, Fall 1966.

J.K.L.

Hastings-on-Hudson
November 1977

CRISIS AT
THE BAR

CHAPTER 1

An Ethics Quiz

From the shadows of the Sunday pulpit and the twice-weekly philosophy classroom, the problem of unethical conduct has burst into the
glare of daily headlines. The news stories have not been confined to
any one group: politicians, public administrators, business executives,
and others have been subjected during the 1970s to intense public
abuse for acts that they had routinely (but often secretly) practiced
for years. The public outrage is due largely to our suddenly finding
out what those acts consisted of.

But one group—the lawyers—have practiced their craft openly and
with a well-developed set of publicly proclaimed ethical principles. No
profession on earth, not excluding the ministry, has today as comprehensive and publicly articulated a code of ethics as the lawyers. The
bar's written canons have been buttressed since the early years of this
century by an interpretive gloss of Talmudic dimensions. Yet, for all
that, lawyers have not been immune from public criticism. To the
contrary, they have felt more heat than all the others.

That lawyers have been marked for public contempt may be ac-
counted for by their general failure to abide by their self-professed
principles. But I submit—and it is the burden of this book to show
—that the public contempt for lawyers stems rather from their adher-

ence to an unethical code of ethics, paradoxical though that may seem.

A code of ethics ought to be a forthright instrument. Do right by one's client. Avoid conflicts of interest. Uphold the law. Such precepts ought to be clear to anyone, but especially to lawyers, given the very nature of their profession. But are they clear? The following quiz may help to answer that question.

1. You are the salaried attorney for an automobile insurance company. One of the provisions in its standard insurance contract guarantees to supply a lawyer at no charge to policyholders whenever they are sued in connection with an accident covered by the policy. As the company's lawyer, is it ethical for you to serve as defense counsel?

Yes____ No____

2. You are a private practitioner. You represent buyers and sellers of houses. As part of your representation of home buyers you arrange for title insurance policies to cover the sale. These policies provide your clients with insurance to cover losses in the event that title to the property is later proven defective. Your client pays a one-time-only charge for the policy. The title insurance company offers you a percentage of this premium as a "commission" for bringing it the business. May you ethically accept the commission?

Yes____ No____

3. Your city bar association decides to establish a legal aid program for people who cannot afford lawyers' regular fees. Under the program a reduced schedule of fees is in effect. To qualify, the client must earn no more than an established maximum salary. May the bar association ethically advertise this program in newspapers and on radio and television?

Yes____ No____

4. A man comes to your office and says that his invention of a better mousetrap has been pirated by a large national manufacturer. This invention, he claims, is worth a lot of money. He wants to sue the manufacturer for a percentage of its profits, but until he wins the case he cannot afford to pay you. May you ethically take on the case in return for a promise that the client will pay you one-third of all future royalties if you win?

Yes____ No____

5. You practice in a small Western town. There are fifteen other lawyers in the community; no other lawyers are available for a radius of at least 150 miles. One day a man of Oriental appearance comes to your office and asks you to file suit against the town's largest employer, a factory, for unlawfully refusing him a job. There is considerable anti-Chinese feeling in the community. The man tells you that he has talked to all the other lawyers in town and they have refused to help. You are the last lawyer to whom he can feasibly look for assistance. He offers to pay you your regular fee. You have never been employed by the factory. May you ethically refuse to represent him?

Yes____ No____

6. You are the salaried attorney for a bank. The president of the bank hits on an ingenious scheme to lure customers away from his competitors. He offers to have the bank's trust department prepare free wills for anyone depositing $5,000 or more. He asks you to supervise the drawing of the wills. May you ethically participate in this plan?

Yes____ No____

7. You are asked to represent Equality Now, an activist women's rights group, on an ongoing basis. EN wants you to tour your state, making speeches to other women's groups, urging them to bring test cases against practices that appear to discriminate against women. You are permitted to offer the services of EN, yourself included, in filing such suits. As part of your campaign you prepare handbills

explaining EN's position and its commitment to file suits and asking for donations. You list yourself as director of the litigation project. May you ethically act as the attorney for clients who are induced to come forward in such a manner?

Yes___ No___

8. You are a recent law school graduate. You are concerned that a large number of people in your town cannot afford the customary fees of lawyers in the community. You conclude that your bar association's legal aid program is not working properly. You decide, therefore, to establish a "legal clinic," which will process a high volume of cases requiring relatively simple services, like uncontested divorces and simple wills, for a low fee. You refuse to take on as clients people making more than an established maximum salary, but you cannot and do not police this salary requirement. May you ethically advertise your clinic on television, listing your fees?

Yes___ No___

9. You decide to take the patent case in Question 4. As you begin to research the case, you discover that it involves extremely complex laser technology. Without the help of several laser experts, you have no hope of winning. But your client cannot afford to pay the experts. He suggests making the same arrangements with them that he has made with you: to pay a percentage (smaller than yours!) of all future royalties if the suit is successful. May you ethically approve of and cooperate with such an arrangement?

Yes___ No___

10. A sensational murder trial has just ended in a guilty verdict, though the defendant stoutly maintained his innocence and gave what sounded like a convincing alibi to the jury. The judge sentences him to life imprisonment. You have been following the case closely because a good friend has been conducting the defense (although you have never spoken to him about the case or the defendant). Several

weeks after the defendant loses his final appeal and is carted off to
prison, a nervous-looking man whom you have never seen before
comes to your office and begs to consult with you professionally. You
agree to listen to his problem. You close the door and instruct your
secretary to hold all calls. Your new client then blurts out that he is
the actual murderer. He asks whether he is safe from prosecution now
that someone else has been convicted. You verify his story. It becomes
clear to you that the person in prison has been framed. You advise
your client to give himself up but he adamantly refuses. May you
ethically contact your friend, the lawyer for the man who has been
wrongly convicted, to tell him of this startling development?

Yes____ No____

Answers: Questions 1–5: Yes.
Questions 6–10: No.

If you answered all the questions correctly, either you peeked or
you are a lawyer in desperate need of rethinking some fundamental
ethical questions. If you answered one or more incorrectly, congratu-
late yourself, because you evidently possess a consistent mind and an
honorable disposition.

The ten quiz questions come from common situations in legal
practice and from debates that have recently exercised the legal community. If you remain confused over the answers, explanations (such
as they are) follow.

1. Normally a lawyer may not accept payment from anyone other than
his client because the client's interest and the employer's interest may
differ. A conflict of interest contradicts the entire purpose of the
lawyer-client relationship. There happens to be a potential conflict of
interest between the insurance company and the driver, but the ethics
committee of the American Bar Association has ruled that it is nevertheless permissible for insurance company lawyers to represent

policyholders on the ground that there is no actual conflict of interest.

2. As long as you tell your client that the title insurance company pays a commission and obtain your client's permission to take the fee, it is ethical to do so—again, even though the payment comes from someone other than the client. According to the bar, consent cures all problems.

3. Although advertising has long been considered a grave impropriety, the bar may ethically advertise its legal aid program because it is performing a public service in doing so, even though individual participating lawyers may profit from the ads.

4. Long-standing tradition forbids lawyers to buy into lawsuits. But there is an exception to the general rule for the so-called "contingent fee" whereby the lawyer is paid only if he wins the case. Even though the contingent fee arrangement may pose a conflict between the client's interest (a smaller, but quicker settlement) and the lawyer's interest (a larger, farther-off judgment after trial), it is justified on the ground that without it many people would be unable to afford legal counsel at all.

5. Although the legal profession claims a duty to serve the public, an individual lawyer may refuse to represent anyone. The canons of ethics state explicitly that the decision to accept a client is solely for each lawyer to make. Otherwise, presumably, false claims would be constantly pressed.

6. The bank's lawyer may not draw wills for depositors. Doing so would violate the rule against being paid by someone other than a client.

7. Soliciting clients is reprehensible because the lawyer has a duty not to stir up litigation. However, the Supreme Court has ruled that the

bar may not constitutionally prevent a lawyer from participating in a plan to alert people to their civil rights and to help them secure those rights. So the Equality Now lawyer can stump the state and solicit plaintiffs. But the constitutional right to do so does not make it ethical for the lawyer to print her (or his) name on a handbill. Solicitation, unless done by the bar itself, can be undertaken only for the people's advantage, not for the lawyer's.

8. Until 1977 the lawyer could not ethically advertise his law clinic. In June 1977 the Supreme Court ruled that a lawyer has a constitutional right to advertise fees for routine services. But that ruling has not prompted the bar to more than grudging acquiescence, and every sign suggests that the bar will resist any liberalization of the Court's rather narrow decision, which did not by its terms extend to television.

9. Although the lawyer may represent the inventor on a contingent fee basis, he may not arrange for the client to pay the expert witnesses in the same manner. Because the experts would be paid only if the client wins the case, a contingent fee arrangement might induce the experts to lie. (But if a large corporation puts an expert on retainer, so that he will testify when necessary, that is ethically permissible, even though the expert might come to enjoy his regular payments and feel a similar compulsion at least to shade his testimony in favor of his employer.)

10. A lawyer may never reveal the confidences of a client, even though an innocent man may languish in prison. The lawyer's fidelity to client must be total.

These answers are not my invention. They are the ones commonly given by lawyers who have the power to make such pronouncements officially, either as judges or as members of ethics and disciplinary committees of state bar organizations. But the answers are no more defensible for that. They betray an inconsistency that runs deep through the lawyers' code of ethics. They also betray a faulty moral tone: for the pre-eminent public profession in America to have ethical guidelines that violate the United States Constitution is astonishing.

But change is afoot. Of late lawyers have been challenged to answer many of the same quiz questions in court. And they have scored badly, occasionally even flunking. It is this failure, prompting a crisis throughout the legal profession, that I will chart in the present book.

CHAPTER 2

The Bar as Unindicted Co-Conspirator

The Art of Lying

That particular lawyers behave improperly should be no occasion for wonderment. We all behave improperly now and then, and any group of people has its minority that behaves unscrupulously most of the time. Lawyers who steal from clients or represent them in a shoddy manner are not the focus of this book. Everyone, including those who commit them, acknowledges that these acts are reprehensible. The present concern, rather, is with the sins of those who profess to be doing right. Lawyers parade their code of ethics as the standard, if not the guarantor, of public virtue. But too often the code serves as a convenient cloak for dubious behavior. The confusion that arises when lawyers profess as proper a course of conduct they do not really wish to follow is best illustrated by the problem of lying.

If the justice that lawyers are sworn to serve consists in a search for truth, lying ought to rival incest as the foremost taboo. And so it does, in a formal sense. Catch a thoughtful lawyer in an unguarded moment, and he will want you to believe that he and Immanuel Kant share the same moral imperative: that telling a lie is absolutely wrong no matter the circumstances and that the consequences that the liar intends from his untruth are irrelevant in judging the rightness or wrongness of the act. In other words, ends do not justify means.

The testimony of many lawyers could be summoned to support this belief, and it is not for lack of respect that I cite only the following:

> No man can be either too honest, too truthful, or too upright to be a thoroughly good lawyer, and an eminently successful one. A lawyer does not acquire valuable clients by getting a reputation for being willing to practice any kind of chicanery in their behalf. It is too apt to occur to the good client that the lawyer who, when "in a corner" or "on the spot," will lie for him, may, in a similar corner, lie *to* him for the lawyer's own advantage.
> A lawyer need never lie for his client.[1]

This forthright homily on lying is that of Henry S. Drinker (1880–1965), who wrote the first modern "treatise"* on legal ethics.[2] Sometime head of the Philadelphia bar's grievance committee and chairman of the American Bar Association's prestigious Committee on Professional Ethics and Grievances† (1944–1953, 1955–1958), Drinker was a senior partner in Drinker, Biddle & Reath of Philadelphia, the quintessential Main Line law firm.

He was always sensitive to criticism of lawyers and the bar. In an article that Drinker took to be an attack on the profession, Charles P. Curtis, a Boston lawyer, suggested that under certain circumstances a lawyer "is in duty bound to lie." In response, Drinker protested:

> I am indeed glad that fifty-one years ago, when I was wavering between law and medicine, this article was not given me by one on whom I relied, as a fair statement of the ethics of advocacy. Had I then read and believed it, I might not have chosen a

---

*"Treatise" may be a misnomer, for the book (first published in 1953) is less an analysis of the purpose of ethics in a professional system than a compilation of bar association and judicial rulings about specific factual situations—in other words, a lawyer's book, in which the panoply of learning substitutes for the core of insight.

†Now known as the Committee on Ethics and Professional Responsibility.

profession which, as misrepresented by Mr. Curtis, I could never respect. I would thus have been denied the joy and deep satisfaction of a life whose primary interest and activity has been the practice of a profession of which I have never for an instant been ashamed; but which, as the years go by, I regard with increasing love and reverence. For has it not produced, for five hundred years, a far greater number of wise and trusted advisers, advocates, and public servants than any other calling?[3]

This is a fair sample of one level of argument that often passes for lawyers' logic—ad hominem, non sequitur, ahistorical. It reminds me of the public official who admits that yes, in theory, political corruption is possible but that in fifty-one years at the highest councils of the nation he has never glimpsed it. Of course Drinker did not allude to his intimate role in the construction of the 1927 Pennsylvania "preceptor" plan, which successfully aimed at reducing the number of Jewish immigrants admitted to practice. In those days, Drinker complained of "Russian Jew boys" who came "up out of the gutter . . . following the methods their fathers had been using in selling shoe strings and other merchandise."[4] Some would call this a lie, others a wild exaggeration.

But the lies that Drinker excoriated were adversary lies, those a lawyer may wish to make in the heat of defense at trial. It is less honorable to lie on behalf of one's client than on behalf of one's status, Drinker seems to be telling us.

Consider some cases.

CASE I. A DIRECT LIE TO A POLICEMAN.

A lawyer is called on the telephone by a former client who is unfortunately at the time a fugitive from justice. The police want him and he wants advice. The lawyer goes to where his client is, hears the whole story, and advises him to surrender. Finally he succeeds in persuading him that this is the best thing to do and they make an appointment to go to police headquarters. Meanwhile the client is to have two days to wind up his affairs and make his farewells. When the lawyer gets back to his office, a police inspector is waiting for him, and asks him whether his client is in town and where he is. Here are questions which the police have every right to ask of anybody, and even a little hesitation in this unfortunate lawyer's denials will reveal enough to betray his client. Of course he lies.[5]

Charles Curtis, who posed this case, explained the result by noting that "the relation between a lawyer and his client is one of the intimate relations. You would lie for your wife. You would lie for your child. There are others with whom you are intimate enough, close enough, to lie for them when you would not lie for yourself. At what point do you stop lying for them? I don't know and you are not sure."[6]

Nonsense, Drinker retorted. The relationship with a client neither entitles nor requires the lawyer to lie. The clever lawyer will find another way to accomplish the same end. Since the lawyer has an obligation to keep confidential what he hears from his client, he must simply refuse to answer the question. Thus, writes Drinker, "when the police officers asked the lawyer, there was no necessity for him to lie. He should have said: 'If I knew, my duty as a lawyer would forbid my telling you.' "[7] Note that Drinker used the subjunctive, thus subtly suggesting to the police inspector that he did not in fact know. "If I *knew* . . ." he recommends that the lawyer say, rather than, for example: "Even though I may *know* . . ." or "I may know or I may not know but in either case . . ." Is Drinker's way a means of telling a lie without somehow actually doing so? A way of sitting on the line between truth and falsehood? We need not impute a sneaky motive. Drinker may simply have been in the habit of talking that way. Let us turn, instead, to

CASE 2. AN INDIRECT LIE TO A JUDGE.

Everyone agrees that it is wrong to tell a bald-faced lie directly to a judge sitting during a court proceeding (note the qualifiers: there are

plenty of outs). Even Curtis says flatly: "I take it that it is inadmissible
to lie to the court. A lawyer's duty to his client cannot rise higher than
its source, which is the court."[8] But what is a lie? Is a misleading
impression created in the mind of a judge, when a lawyer could easily
correct it, the same kind of linguistic monster?

The standard example is that given by Samuel Williston in his
memoirs of Boston practice. Long a professor at Harvard Law School
and regarded as one of the leading legal scholars in the nation, Williston (1861–1963) told of being retained to help defend a Pittsburgh
boiler manufacturer in the early 1900s. Rather than taking a commission, the company's Boston selling agents were entitled to pocket the
excess of the sales price over the manufacturer's cost. Eventually a
dispute arose as to how the cost figure was to be determined, the
agents claiming that they had been underpaid. The decision would
turn on how the contract between them defined "cost," and this was
none too clear. As Williston tells the story:

> There was a vast amount of correspondence between the parties
> during the years covered in this dispute. We had sent to us from
> the defendant's office a large box full of the plaintiff's letters and
> also many press copy books which contained copies of the de-
> fendant's replies. Most of these letters had no pertinence with
> reference to the dispute, but occasionally there was a sentence
> that seemed relevant. We went through the whole correspon-
> dence and had typewritten copies made of everything that
> seemed relevant. These copies were arranged in chronological
> order, and at the trial we had them on the counsel table before
> us.
>
> The case was tried before Chief Justice Knowlton. I opened
> the case at some length and I also made the preliminary part of
> the final argument. The Chief Justice decided promptly in favor
> of the defendant [Williston's client]. . . . The plaintiffs either did
> not have so full a file of their correspondence with the defendant
> as we did, or it had not been so carefully examined by their
> counsel, for we had letters in our file that would have been useful

to them. They did not demand their production and we did not feel bound to disclose them. In the course of his remarks the Chief Justice stated as one reason for his decision a supposed fact which I knew to be unfounded. I had in front of me a letter that showed his error. Though I have no doubt of the propriety of my behavior in keeping silent, I was somewhat uncomfortable at the time.[9]

If Williston's discomfort was temporary, at least he felt a twinge. The bar's ethics committee does not. Although there is some authority[10] for the proposition that a lawyer must inform the judge of a law or other legal precedent that the judge seems to have overlooked, no rule requires the lawyer to hand over facts, even where the judge possesses only a false version of them.

This is a troublesome conclusion. What is the difference between a false statement and a silence that cloaks an untruth? Henry Drinker thinks[11] there is an important distinction between Williston's silence, which let the judge assume something that was not so, and his saying: "Your Honor has stated all the facts correctly, at least insofar as I know them to be." Of course, the attorneys for the other party could have had the knowledge that remained in Williston's possession had they been clever or diligent enough to ask for the correspondence during pretrial maneuvers. And it may be inefficient to run a legal system in which one's lawyers must look out for the other fellow's interests. But that implies, at the most, that the lawyer need not rush to disclose evidence damaging to his client. It does not imply that the lawyer may stand by idly while falsehoods are uttered in court. Yet here is an adversarial misrepresentation (by silence) that Henry Drinker—and the bar—approve of.

CASE 3. A DIRECT LIE TO THE COURT.

There is another type of lie that happens every day in courtrooms across the United States. It takes place during the ritual that follows the successful "plea bargain," the deal struck between prosecutor and criminal suspect. The prosecutor has too many cases to try. If each defendant insisted on a full trial, the public might actually have to pay for a criminal justice system. The defendant, of course, wishes to avoid a lengthy stay in jail. So they make a deal. If the defendant will agree to save the prosecutor the trouble of proving anything (and thus risk losing altogether), the prosecutor will see to it that some of the many charges hanging over the defendant's head will be dropped (or reduced in severity) and a ceiling will be placed on the length of the sentence.

This seems a reasonable trade. Often it *is* a reasonable trade, for some people *are* guilty, and the legislative judgment that, regardless of the circumstances, a man who stole may be sent away for a quarter or more of his life is simply outrageous. So the plea bargain is understandable, reasonable, and justifiable.

But in the courtroom, plea bargains remain a dirty secret. No one owns up to the negotiation over a plea. Instead, a ritual is enacted denying that negotiations ever took place. An extract of dialogue that George V. Higgins sets forth in *The Friends of Richard Nixon* gives the flavor and the method of the lie. Judge John Sirica has just refused to accept E. Howard Hunt's request to plead guilty to only half the counts of the Watergate indictment in which he was named, despite a deal with the prosecutor to permit him to do so. Hunt is forced to give in and plead guilty to all. Sirica is now interrogating Hunt as to his motives in pleading guilty (the interspersed comments are Higgins's):

> "Has your guilty plea," Sirica said, "to the six counts that I have mentioned been induced by promises or representations by anyone as to what the sentence will be, imposed by this Court?"
>
> Of course it had been. "No, your Honor," said Hunt.
>
> "Has anyone threatened or coerced you into making this plea of guilty," Sirica said, "the plea of guilty to these counts?"
>
> Silbert [the prosecutor] had assured Bittman [Hunt's lawyer]

that Hunt would probably get considerably more time in jail if he demanded a needless trial, and Bittman, cognizant of Sirica's reputation as Maximum John, earned by the imposition of heavy sentences, agreed with him. Bittman certainly told Hunt.

"No, your Honor," Hunt said.

"Has any promise of any kind been made to induce your plea of guilty?" Sirica said.

Silbert had promised to recommend lenience if Hunt cooperated and pleaded guilty. Bittman certainly reported that promise to Hunt. "No, your Honor," Hunt said.

"Are you entering this plea voluntarily," Sirica said, "of your own free will, because you are guilty, and for no other reason?"

Perhaps. "Yes, your Honor," Hunt said.[12]

And what does lawyer Bittman do while this charade is being played? Does he ask Judge Sirica for leave to speak, mindful of an obligation that this farce be brought to the court's attention? Does he say, "Your Honor, I was there. I, the defendant's lawyer, arranged with the prosecutor who now stands before you that my client would plead guilty in return for a lesser sentence, and I so advised my client"? Of course he did not, nor do the thousands of criminal defense attorneys who stand before like-minded, if less prepossessing, judges every day. And neither do the prosecutors.

What are we to make of this? A committee of lawyers could say several things (their formal opinions are silent, so we shall have to surmise). One, they might note that, as in Williston's case, the lawyer did not himself actually say anything, that the misrepresentation, if any there be, lies rather in silence. We have already dealt with this response. And here the misrepresentation was not inadvertent but stimulated: the client was coached—by the lawyer—to say the lie.

Two, they might retort that no perjury has actually been committed, since the lawyer always reminds his client that the judge is not bound to accept the deal (as Judge Sirica demonstrated when he refused to accept Hunt's deal to plead guilty to only three of six counts). But this is a disingenuous argument. The lawyer knows that the judge will be lenient, and so informs his client (else the "system" would break down). The plea bargain is not made in a vacuum but in the dense reality of a jail or D.A.'s office. There, the metaphysics of an ethics committee is unknown.

Three, our ethics committee might note that this is not really a lie but rather a legal fiction, through whose offices the law always progresses. Yes, some lawyers really say such things.

Four—and now it gets nasty—our committee might wish to let the defending lawyer twist slowly in the wind (as lawyer John D. Ehrlichman once suggested for lawyer L. Patrick Gray). In other words, they might wish to pin the blame on him and cut him loose from the legal system. "Well, yes," they might phrase it, "Bittman did it, and so do other lawyers, but that doesn't make it right." But it is just this that ethics committees have never done. Though lawyers routinely coach their clients on how to lie under these circumstances, the bar has not condemned the practice but tacitly endorsed it. That the misrepresentation is not particularly serious scarcely answers Drinker's comment that a lawyer "need never lie for his client."

Somewhat bewildered by the examples just pondered, I decided to probe the leadership of the ABA, to see whether, despite its prevalence, lying falls in the category of regretted evil and not sanctioned good. I journeyed to Philadelphia, to the old law offices of Henry S. Drinker. He is no longer there, of course, but a senior partner in his firm, Lewis S. Van Dusen, Jr., is chairman of Drinker's old ABA committee. (Van Dusen's succession is reminiscent of the French family that for seven generations served the kings of France as state executioners.)[13]

Van Dusen was sixty-five years old at the time of my interview, tall, lean, craggy-faced, crisp, blunt, and sporty in a seersucker jacket in the heat of a July day. With a crowded daily calendar, Van Dusen nevertheless let me put some logical, some impertinent questions to him for an hour and a half. At the very end, I asked point-blank whether it was ever proper for a lawyer to lie. I wanted to know, I explained, because it seemed to be a topic in the news of late. Van Dusen's answer was a short and unambiguous no. He thus upheld the philosophical purity of his distinguished predecessor. Lying is ungentlemanly, unlawyerlike; those who lie act wrongly. The bar is pure.

Since a sweeping answer to a sweeping question can always stand closer scrutiny, and not at all because I distrusted his answer or his intentions, I narrowed the focus. Suppose, I continued, a lawyer is negotiating on behalf of a client wishing to purchase something. The client says he will pay up to one million dollars but instructs his lawyer to obtain it, if he can, for much less. Mindful of these instructions, the lawyer proceeds to dicker with the seller's agents, telling them at one point in his most sincere voice that his client will not allow him to offer more than half a million dollars. This kind of thing happens all the time. Clearly the lawyer has told a lie. Has he done wrong?

"Oh," said Van Dusen, "that's different."

"Different? What is it if not a lie?"

"Tactics," replied the master.[14]

Mea Culpa

The lawyer's ability to make, and believe in, distinctions without a difference is what finally led to the bar's criminal prosecution. In June 1976 the United States Department of Justice filed suit in a Washington, D.C., federal district court naming me—and 210,000 other lawyers—unindicted co-conspirators. My colleagues in this prosecution include former Watergate Special Prosecutor Leon Jaworski, former Attorney General Elliot L. Richardson, and others of eminent stature. Even Gerald R. Ford, who became the second unindicted co-conspiring president in history.

This is not, let it be said, a partisan prosecution, at least in the usual sense. The Justice Department is itself peopled mainly by lawyers. Nor have these earnest government attorneys been prompted by masochistic urges. The explanation is more mundane: they did it out of chagrin. During the last several years the Justice Department had already sued real estate brokers, various engineers, and undertakers and for some time it had been issuing pointed warnings to lawyers to clean house. But lawyers are paid to sweep the floors of others, and we found it rather more difficult to turn our attention to our own. Because we were unwilling or unable to act, the government has now done it for us, by formally suing the American Bar Association.

These 210,000 lawyers share only one bond—membership in the ABA. We stand accused of following—or, to make a distinction for which we lawyers are justly famous, of agreeing to follow—the ethical precepts of our profession, and thereby violating the Sherman Act, bedrock of the nation's antitrust laws. The government alleges that by promising to adhere to the ABA's model code of ethics (adopted in varying degrees in each state), we had formed an agreement in restraint of the trade of lawyering.

Specifically, the prosecution concerns the right to advertise. The problem is, as I have already noted, that lawyers don't allow themselves to do it—not the way our more forthright business clients do it, at any rate. The theory is that advertising is hucksterism, which would deceive and injure the public. So the ABA code of ethics more or less prohibits it.

Now, it is certainly clear that if all the automobile manufacturers assembled in a room and said, "This advertising thing is getting too expensive; let's all agree to wind it down," an antitrust conspiracy in restraint of trade would thereby have been hatched. But lawyering, so the lawyers say, is different; it's a profession, and professionals have different concerns from business people. (This is also what the undertakers told the Justice Department, to no avail.) And that's what the argument is all about: not only, or even mainly, advertising, but whether professionals may regulate all aspects of their professions in ways not entrusted to common folk.

Most lawyers know little of the ABA. Only half of all American lawyers join it, and those who do become members do not do so for the position it takes on world events. They do not sign up to interject themselves into the bar's antic politics. Few care about the appointments of dozens of obscure committees or about annual floor debates over the United Nations genocide convention. All of that is for aging campus politicians, with which the ABA is well stocked.

No, most lawyers belong to the ABA to purchase cheap insurance (a program now under investigation by the Internal Revenue Service) and to subscribe to bar journals and other legal periodicals.* The members' connection with forming, forcing, or enforcing a code of ethics is as remote as Richard Nixon's name was from the 1976 Republican Convention. Indeed, in 1970, the sixty-two-year-old canons of ethics were junked by a special committee and replaced with a "Code of Professional Responsibility" that looked, at least on paper, wholly different. But none of us whose pledges to abide by the code had been signed before 1970 ever had a chance to vote on the new set of ground rules. Quite probably, most of us haven't even read the fifty-plus pages of fine print that purport to govern the subject matter of this book.

So, while the leaders of the bar will argue on "technical" (i.e., legal) grounds that the bar is innocent of antitrust violations, we mere citizens of the bar may argue even more broadly and plausibly that we are innocent, period.

This gets to the heart of the matter. We *are* innocent, but we are not without sin. Our innocence is that of Adam and Eve before the Fall, not of the saint who stared down temptation and refused to give in to it. We are innocent, in short, because we are ignorant of what ethics is truly about. And this is as true of the public at large as it is of lawyers. Our new status as unindicted co-conspirators is thus closer to the mark than many of us would ever have dared to contemplate.

---

*To be fair, an important minority is active in matters of some substance: monitoring court decisions, administrative regulations, and legislation, and advocating and lobbying for changes. But it is a minority.

To assume that one knows without reflection the sum of ethical conduct is itself ethically suspect. But for years this was a widespread belief—that what is right and wrong is plain to see—and it deterred law schools from giving any serious consideration to the subject. Law students received no sustained instruction in ethics until the advent of "post-Watergate morality" (in Spiro T. Agnew's waspish phrase), because it was presumed that their morals, good or bad, were fixed before matriculation.

If ethics were confined to the domain of gross immorality, this assumption would be correct. We know it is unethical to steal, for example, because theft is unlawful and has been regarded as a crime in most cultures from time immemorial. But what is right and wrong in a professional sense is not so obvious. What about the use of blue calling cards? What about working as a salaried attorney on behalf of union members? The answers (the bar has said no to both) do not spring immediately to mind. And because they do not, there is today a crisis at the bar, requiring each of us to rise when the roll of unindicted co-conspirators is called.

There is more to it. Since 1973, American lawyers have taken an awful beating. The long simmering public discontent with lawyers and their methods was brought to a boil in that year by the dreadful revelations that certain lawyers had been committing crimes and taking other dubious actions at the highest councils of the United States government. (More than twenty-five lawyers were formally named as defendants or co-conspirators in Watergate and related criminal proceedings.)

The issue is not, to repeat, as many bar leaders foolishly believe, that there are good and bad people in any walk of life. That other, virtuous lawyers fought the malefactors does not tell us why the President of the United States and his chief advisers went wrong. As bar leaders are fond of remarking when seeking to justify the monopoly they hold as a profession, lawyers are supposed to be better than the common run of men and women. Lawyers are specially selected, specially trained, and specially paid. Their character is supposedly investigated and certified. They are subject to sanctions not employable against the lay public.

The bar's response to Watergate is thoroughly characteristic of the institutional mind, which prides itself on the lengths of the leaps it can make from one end of a tautology to the other. General Matthew B. Ridgway's suggestion was that the way to remedy the Army's failure to abide by the code of West Point is to continue to teach the code at West Point.[15] Lawyers have their own tautology: that all would have been well if these miscreants had followed the code of professional ethics. If the disease is unethical conduct, prescribe ethics. Watergate, in other words, was *their* Watergate, not ours.

For too long we unindicted co-conspirators (and other lawyers) have allowed this answer—at once a false diagnosis and disingenuous apologia—to stand in place of truth. The plain, sad truth is that *the Watergate crowd acted as they did rather more because they were generally abiding by the profession's ethical system than because they were traitors to it.* These men of small mind were not markedly dissimilar from most members of the American bar. Indeed, they were of it: they came from good law schools, good practices, decent communities. That the bar sincerely believes the system is noble is why this system's rot is now stinking across the land. For unlike the ambulance chasers at the turn of the century whom the bar's elite held in low repute, it is today this very elite that is perceived as having violated canons of decency and propriety. The crisis of the bar springs from the inefficacy of the formal rules in curbing the worst instincts of the best lawyers.*

For lawyers, Watergate posed a double fright. The lesser evil,

---

*The failures are not confined to lawyers; all professionals show similar lapses. When revelations of massive fraud in the Medicare and Medicaid programs were aired in August 1976, medical leaders did not rise up to condemn doctors who were reported to have been kicking back a substantial part of their fees to landlords, a practice severely condemned by both lawyers and doctors in their formal ethics.

though it seemed larger at the time, was the damage that the scandal could wreak on the image of the profession. This is not such a useless preoccupation with surface image as it may sound. Damage to the reputation of the bar is a real concern and a genuine danger, because no Western democracy can do without law or lawyers to operate the necessary legal system. Contempt for lawyers, ultimately reflected in strict public controls, can only undermine the civil liberties of the people. So this was a legitimate concern and it received the major public attention (and still is receiving it).

But there was another horror—more private, hence not discussed. This was the quick, internal doubt (as when one wakes up from a bad dream still supposing it to be real) whether I the honest lawyer who condemns Richard Nixon and his cabal of counselors would have done any differently in his or their place. It is easy to read the newspaper commentators and nod in agreement, feeling the exaltation of moral fervor. Would any of us have had the nerve to stare down Haldeman, however? To quit before the papers were shredded, the tapes altered or destroyed? No one on Nixon's staff did, though the subsequent revelations paint plenty of private reasons to have done so. Are we so much more virtuous? This is an uncomfortable question.

In 1973, I spent many a long summer night sitting with a number of other lawyers watching installments of our favorite television rerun: Senator Ervin, the great constitutionalist (who spent much of his public life battling against the rights of blacks), and his colleagues questing after the riddle of Watergate. We were smug; our talk was the usual blather, a recital of Nixon's sins. "How could they do that? Such stupidity!" But the more we insisted, the more I withdrew into doubt, recalling a recent incident from my own career.

A partner in the law firm for which I once worked asked me to prepare a memorandum on some esoteric point of law. His purpose —hence mine—was to permit us to avoid moving ahead on a lawsuit we were defending. Our client, a large, well-known organization, wanted to delay. After an appropriate amount of research, I came back with an answer rare in law: an unambiguous negative. We could not do what the partner had proposed. We didn't stand a chance; the argument was unsound. Naturally the partner didn't like my memo. He came down to my office to ask me, politely, to go back to the books, to find *any* plausible argument that could be made along the lines he had earlier outlined. I explained why I thought that any further research would simply be a waste of time and money. The partner smiled and said that any argument whatsoever would do if it could be made to look tenable. Maybe, he suggested, I could find what we needed by simply looking through all prior cases ever decided by an American court on the subject. And then he said this: "After all, we don't need to win the point; we're only doing this for the purpose of delay."

Rarely is the matter put so nakedly. In the best law firms—and this was one of them—you do not talk, or need to talk, about delay for delay's sake. You speak, rather, of the client's need for an all-out defense, of his right to raise every legitimate point in his favor. It is the judge's job, after all, not counsel's, to decide whether the defense will stand up; if you forgo a possible defense, then you are not serving your client with that fidelity that the independent bar in the United States is equipped to give. But delay? Unfortunately, delay for delay's sake is a violation of both the code of ethics and the Federal Rules of Civil Procedure. A lawyer who permits his conduct to be so guided by his client's only real defense—bankrupting his opponent—is guilty of a woeful breach of ethics.

What should I have done? I am still not sure of the answer. I now know that the problem is more difficult than it seemed at the time. The partner was my boss; I was only a salaried associate. In most cases, and this was one of them, that is the only consideration. I went back to the books, spent several more hours, ransacking every case I could find, to no avail. Having now let the client's meter run far beyond the value of the service, I redrafted my memo, reiterating the opinion that our position on this minuscule point was hopeless. I did not hear from the partner about this problem again. He reassigned it —a third take—to another associate. Delicacy prohibited me from inquiring where it came to rest. But it didn't seem to matter; at least I had not participated in a fraud on the court.

Or did it matter?

Where did my responsibility as a lawyer lie? Should I have gone further? Should I have protested to a committee of the partners (none existed for the purpose of receiving such complaints)? To one other partner? Should I have refused to work on the problem? Should I have resigned?

Like most situations out there in the world, the circumstances dictated my response. I had joined the law firm less than half a year before. I was new at law practice. The point at issue was trivial, and even if it had been asserted in court, was one the judge would quickly have rejected. The client hardly objected to the money we were billing it for time spent; it had plenty of money for this purpose. The few discussions at law school about ethical matters never came close to this. If I had run to someone else, would he have interceded? If I had quit, could I ever hold a job longer than the first time an uncomfortable situation arose?

Needless to say, these thoughts, if I entertained them at all, did not consume much of my time. I went along. There seemed no reason not to. I had not been asked to engage in active fraud with the client to achieve some illegal goal. I was not participating in an incipient perjury. I was asked neither to lie nor to be involved in any conflict of interest. What is the problem, then?

This: from precisely such insignificant occurrences, the seeds of large-scale violations of law and ethics are planted. Not the petty fraud that any big-time lawyer would abhor and shun, but the subtle and continuing erosion of ethics that characterizes modern law practice. Two years after I turned in my second memo and stopped working for the client that wanted to delay, it gained sudden notoriety as a participant in the widening circle of events known as Watergate.

Would a "proper" code of ethics have prevented Watergate? Perhaps not. It is true that formal codes are not self-enforcing. If it can be demonstrated that the guiding formal philosophy of lawyers is corrupt, does it not follow that the only way to overcome that corruption is to regulate lawyers directly through the organs of government?

Not, I think, unless it can be shown that real reform is impossible. For an ethics that is felt is self-enforcing, and an ethics that is actually enforced will ultimately be felt. Had the right code existed and been taught, Watergate might have run a shorter course, with lawyers saying much earlier on, "This I cannot do." But no ethic in a modern society can be viscerally grasped; it must be stated, dissected, and justified. Until this preliminary series of steps is taken, we cannot conclude that reform is impossible or that lawyers are unethical by nature or by inclination.

We come, then, to our task: to investigate the problems of the ethic that governs lawyers and to inquire about prospects for change. Thus shall I do penance for being an unindicted co-conspirator. But the task of reform is always a collective undertaking. This book is intended to incite that undertaking, so that lawyers may recover the respect among their neighbors that their position in a democracy ought to entitle them to, and once did.

CHAPTER 3

Writing the Ten Commandments

In a 1906 *Atlantic Monthly* article promoting the idea of a national code of ethics, David J. Brewer, associate justice of the U.S. Supreme Court, wrote that the ideal lawyer "ever sees on the lofty summits of Sinai the tables of stone chiseled with imperishable truth by the finger of God."[1] But the formal code of ethics of the American legal profession was not handed down from on high. It was written by three Confederate army colonels from Alabama during the 1880s. They plagiarized much of their text from a short treatise by a Pennsylvania judge.*

Ethics connotes immutable moral principles, a body of common rules to which civilized communities will always be drawn. That is how the bar generally speaks of its ethical precepts. The real truth is that for centuries lawyers adhered to unwritten traditions—part social manners, part fraternal etiquette, part ethics proper. When these were finally transcribed by a self-conscious bar in 1887, the tables of stone did not endure unmarred. They were soon worn thin with erasures that continue to this day: the truths of legal ethics appeared to be more perishable than a cut flower on a summer day.

Justified as protection for the public, the formal code came into

*This technique is known in law as "precedent."

being as a means of assuring lawyers professional autonomy—freedom from state interference. How and why this happened is the subject of the present chapter.

The Legal Profession: An Overview

The traditions of the bar emerged centuries before the modern concept of individual freedom. The idea of supplying a service subject to no outside scrutiny or control was simply unheard of. For centuries before the bar had any consciousness of itself as a brotherhood of practitioners, the craft guilds had been organized as monopolies that strictly regulated price, quality, and product. Lawyers themselves were not called into being because people needed help against the barbarisms that passed for criminal law in those days.* The professional impetus came instead from the growth of royal administration. As the kings slowly extended their rule throughout the land, a professional class became necessary to conduct the sovereign's affairs.

England has the only relevant professional history for Americans. We may, according to Professor David Mellinkoff, mark 1292 as "a good point of departure."[2] In that year Edward I issued a writ "calling for the justices to assure a supply of lawyers to serve the king and his people." Unlike the profession here, the legal profession in England never was and still is not monolithic. It comprised a number of specialists who retained a monopoly over quite different aspects of practice; for example, the act of writing out legal documents was claimed as the exclusive right of the scriveners. By 1402, Henry IV required prospective attorneys to be "examined by the justices" and to be "sworn well and truly to serve in their offices, and especially that they make no suit in a foreign country."[3]

*The law tried offenders not by argument and evidence but by ordeal: pressed under heavy weights or tossed into lakes and rivers, the survivors were adjudged innocent or guilty through the hand of God.

The centuries that followed witnessed the transformation of a rude profession to a highly organized body whose most distinguished members were educated at the great universities and rose to prominent positions in government and on the bench. During this time also there were epochal changes occurring in the fabric of the society the lawyers served. England became a nation-state; the monarch the center of authority. Law and administration from London began to replace the private law and policy of the manorial lord. And entirely apart from the king and Parliament, a vast body of legal principles—the common law—grew out of the arguments of lawyers before the judges of the King's Bench.

Though the common law is often called judge-made law, because it was announced from the bench and sanctified on appeal (instead of being proclaimed by king and consented to by Parliament), it would be more accurate to call it lawyer-made law. The rights of Englishmen, at least of those Englishmen who had access to the courts (considering the population as a whole, the principles of the common law dealt with but a narrow segment),[4] were established in the fray of courtroom battle, inch by inch. There was no grand declaration of the law governing land transactions or contracts or all the rest: a specific case would be brought to court and the contentions of each side would be argued out by the lawyers before the judges. From the early days, the judicial opinions (despite their erratic publication) served as precedent for subsequent cases.

This process of lawmaking was coincident with the growth of the national economy and the emergence of a middle class. As the traditionalism of the feudal period gave way, as land became alienable, as commerce and manufacturing grew, the frictions of daily life increased. No longer were families isolated in the manors; cities played a greater role in the life of the nation; interdependence of all the people became everywhere more obvious. The old ways would no longer suffice; custom could not harden quickly enough to guide the multiple affairs of the citizenry without some more authoritative guidance. This could be found only in government. Consequently, men of affairs more and more had to resort to the courts for interpretations of contracts, for enforcement of bargains, for judgments about land ownership, and the like.

This growing complexity and consequent enlargement of the common law had, not surprisingly, enormous ramifications for the bar. For our purposes, the most important of these were two: an increasing professionalism of the lawyer and increasing vilification of the profession by the public.

By the seventeenth century, when the first ships set out to colonize the New World, the common law judges had spread their decisions in the court yearbooks for more than three hundred years. The mass of opinions, though slight by our own standards, was nevertheless accumulating into a verbose library. Moreover, the common law was exceedingly technical: over the course of centuries it had hardened into formulas no less arid than those of witch doctors. Incanting the wrong phrase in court pleadings could lead to dismissal of the suit. And the phrases, learning, and judgments were not entirely in English; they consisted of the odd mixture of vernacular, Latin, and a peculiar "law French" that in diluted form remains with us still.

To cope with all this demanded considerable literacy and forensic skill. Since it was not the lawyer's fault that he needed this arcane learning, could he really be blamed if he did not exert himself or exhort his brethren to simplify? The learned have always made great sport of displaying erudition to those of lesser understanding, and not simply from cynical or hypocritical motives. There is genuine delight in showing oneself to be educated, and the elegance of ritual phrases has always cast a mysterious spell that suggests to the habitual user the necessity of continuing without deviation. More litigation bred more opinions, more citations, more learning, more ritual.

So the bar's very professionalism contributed to its loss of public esteem. In the days of technical pleadings, great causes could turn on utter irrelevancies, but irrelevancies for which many lawyers were highly paid. No wonder Benjamin Franklin japed in the 1737 *Poor Richard:* "A Countryman between 2 Lawyers, is like a fish between 2 cats."

But the professional attitude was scarcely free of cynicism. As the law grew more complex, it bred a consciousness of economic benefit to be derived from keeping itself mysterious. Lawyers fought to defend the law's verbosities and intricacies.

An early biography of an American judge revealed how lawyers in 1774 viewed the introduction of Blackstone's *Commentaries,* the four-volume summary and synthesis of the common law of England that provided American lawyers during the last quarter of the eighteenth century and the first half of the nineteenth with most of their book learning:

> When Parsons came to the Bar [in the mid-eighteenth century], in every case of importance, all was thought to depend on the learning, sagacity, cunning and eloquence of counsel. It would have been in vain for any one man to have attempted a reformation, for most practitioners at that period would have united against a change, from the mistaken idea that business depended on giving an air of mystery to the proceedings of the profession; forgetting that no science, however difficult to attain, has any mystery in its farthest reaches or in its remotest principles. It can hardly be believed at this day [1821], but it is fact, that many old lawyers, who were in full practice when Blackstone's *Commentaries* first appeared in this country, were frequently heard to regret and complain that he should have so simplified and arranged his subject, and so clearly explained the principles of law, that the same amount of knowledge, which had cost them many years to collect, might be obtained in a short time.[5]

Despite their best efforts, however, lawyers could not prevent the public from discovering the vapid quality of legal science or keep doubters from heaping scorn upon it. As one Philadelphia newspaper put it in 1736: "When you find out how little there is in a Writing of vast Bulk, you will be as much surpriz'd as a Stranger at the Opening of a Pumpkin."[6]

Conditions in the New World gave birth to a native distrust of lawyers as a class. Here there were no rigid distinctions between peoples, no long established aristocracy. As Daniel Boorstin has written: "The American uncertainty as to what really made a man a 'gentleman' had blurred all the lines between high-tone 'professions' and other occupations."[7] Every man was considered capable of handling his own affairs, and in a frontier country he pretty much would have to.

Almost from the first, the American distrust of lawyers showed through. As early as 1658 a Virginia statute provided that no lawyer should "pleade in any courte of judicature within this collony, or give councill in any cause, or controvercie whatsoever, for any kind of reward or profit."[8] Landowners and the clergy persuaded Massachusetts, New York, and Pennsylvania to promulgate similar provisions.[9]

Throughout the eighteenth century, the average lawyer continued to be held in dreary contempt. Just three weeks after the Declaration of Independence was proclaimed, the president of Yale College, Timothy Dwight, denounced the profession to the graduating class in terms that echo familiarly across two centuries:

> That meanness, that infernal knavery, which multiplies needless litigations, which retards the operation of justice, which, from court to court, upon the most trifling pretences, postpones trial to glean the last emptyings of a client's pocket, for unjust fees of everlasting attendance, which artfully twists the meaning of law to the side we espouse, which seizes unwarrantable advantages from the prepossessions, ignorance, interests and prejudices of a jury, you will shun rather than death or infamy.[10]

After the Revolution, the general revulsion against lawyers intensified. Charles Warren, the historian of the American bar, noted that many of the pre-eminent lawyers of the period had been royalists who had left the country or retired. Most of the remaining "better" lawyers were in government, the army, or on the bench. "This left the practice of the law very largely in the hands of lawyers of a lower grade and inferior ability."[11]

But it was what these lawyers were called upon to do that set the tone: "The chief business . . . was the collection of debts and the enforcement of contracts; and the jails were filled to overflowing with men imprisoned for debt under the rigorous laws of the times."[12] Shortly after the war, there were in Worcester, Massachusetts, then a rural area with less than 5,000 residents, more than 2,000 lawsuits on the court dockets. No wonder the people called for a halt—militarily, as Daniel Shays attempted in his aborted rebellion; and civilly, as in 1786 the citizens of Braintree near Boston resolved at a town meeting: "that there may be such laws compiled as may crush or at least put a proper check or restraint on that order of Gentlemen denominated as Lawyers, the completion of whose modern conduct appears to us to tend rather to the destruction than the preservation of the town."[13]

In 1787, John Quincy Adams, then a senior at Harvard College, wrote his mother, Abigail: "The mere title of lawyer is sufficient to deprive a man of the public confidence. . . . The popular odium which has been excited against the practitioners in this Commonwealth prevails to so great a degree that the most innocent and irreproachable life cannot guard a lawyer against the hatred of his fellow citizens."[14]

In that same year, H. St. John Crevecoeur, in his famous *Letters of an American Farmer,* put the case against lawyers bluntly:

Lawyers are plants that will grow in any soil that is cultivated by the hands of others, and when once they have taken root they will extinguish every vegetable that grows around them. The fortunes they daily acquire in every province from the misfortunes of their fellow citizens are surprising. The most ignorant, the most bungling member of that profession will, if placed in the most obscure part of the country, promote litigiousness and amass more wealth than the most opulent farmer with all his toil. . . . What a pity that our forefathers who happily extinguished so many fatal customs and expunged from their new government so many errors and abuses both religious and civil,

did not also prevent the introduction of a set of men so dangerous. . . . The value of our laws and the spirit of freedom which
often tends to make us litigious must necessarily throw the greatest part of the property of the Colonies into the hands of these
gentlemen. In another century, the law will possess in the North
what now the church possesses in Peru and Mexico.[15]

The professional class that arose in the face of this extreme antipa-
thy was neither highly organized nor specialized as was the bar in
England. The few early attempts to divide legal work functionally
between barristers (courtroom lawyers) and solicitors (office counselors) failed completely. Of the guild-like power that the bar exerted
over its English members during the eighteenth century there was
none in the colonies. "There was no American London where lawyers
could consolidate their monopoly."[16] Far from consolidating, they
could not even attempt it: the monopoly over law that lawyers held
in England and that they now hold in America simply did not then
exist.

Because there was no professional monopoly, knowledge of law was
widely diffused among the educated. "In no country," wrote Edmund
Burke in an oft-cited passage, "perhaps, in the world, is the law so
general a study."[17] Although today we characterize a significant proportion of the Revolutionary leaders as lawyers—25 of the 56 signers
of the Declaration, 31 of the 55 members of the Constitutional Convention, and 10 of the 29 senators and 17 of the 65 representatives in
the first Congress were lawyers—they were unlike the modern professional. "Contrary to common belief," Boorstin explains, the prevalence of lawyers in public affairs "does not show the importance of a
specialized learned profession in the making of our nation. The
American experience had not bred awe for the learned specialist in
law or in anything else. . . . What it does show is the pervasiveness
of legal competence among American men of affairs and the vague-
ness of the boundary between legal and all other knowledge in a fluid
America. How little does it tell us about Jefferson—a self-trained

lawyer with a brief apprenticeship . . .—to say that he was a 'lawyer by profession.' "[18]

There were, to be sure, great lawyers, especially during the first half of the nineteenth century. Some advocates, like Daniel Webster, have probably never been surpassed. But lawyers did not conceive of themselves as belonging to or restrained by any formal group.

By the 1830s, most bar associations had all but died out. In 1800, 14 of the then 19 states and territories required some period of training for admission to the bar. In 1840, the number had dwindled to 11 out of 30 and by 1860 to 9 out of 39. In some states, the training requirements were simply ignored; in others, like New Hampshire, Maine, and Wisconsin in the 1840s, the legislatures expressly abolished all requirements. Every resident over twenty-one was permitted to practice law without more. In still other places, the examination was cursory at best.[19] Seeking admission to the bar in the District of Columbia in 1829, Salmon P. Chase, who was later to become Chief Justice of the United States, presented himself to the federal court for examination. As he later recalled:

> I answered as well as I was able—how well or how ill I cannot say—but certainly, I think, not very well. Finally the Judge asked me how long I had studied. I replied that, including the time employed in reading in college and the scraps devoted to legal reading before I regularly commenced the study, and the time since, I thought three years might be made up. The judge smiled and said, "We think, Mr. Chase, that you must study another year and present yourself again for examination." "Please, your honors," said I, deprecatingly, "I have made all my arrangements to go to the western country and practice law." The kind Judge yielded to this appeal, and turning to the Clerk said, "Swear in Mr. Chase." Perhaps he would have been less facile if he had not known me personally and very well.[20]

The Jacksonian populism was by no means confined to freeing up the practice of law. From the 1830s to the 1870s (a period Roscoe

Pound characterized as the "era of decadence" of the bar), entry into all professions was free. The only exceptions, in fact, and these were limited, were for law and medicine. The prevalent view was that expressed by Lemuel Shattuck in his 1850 *Report of the Sanitary Commission* (of Massachusetts): "Anyone, male or female, learned or ignorant, an honest man or a knave, can assume the name of physician and 'practice' upon any one, to cure or to kill, as either may happen, without accountability. It's a free country."[21]

In the face of such sentiments and of such openness, formal organizations of lawyers could not survive. With them went any pretense of formal ethics and formal sanctions for their violation.

This did not mean that there was no sense of professional propriety or that lawyers did exactly as they pleased. "Pressure to conform to group standards . . . made itself felt in the long discussions and exchanges of professional talk as horses stumbled or wagons bumped their way over the indifferent roads between courthouses; pressure . . . was expressed through the mock courts that were held of an evening at the tavern, to call one of the brethren to account for conduct that day in court."[22] The sense of intimacy that touched those who saw themselves toiling at a common task served to check many excesses that might have occurred had lawyering been a more private occupation.

An even more basic tradition—that of fidelity to client, regardless of consequences—was also nurtured during this period. The classic statement of the conflict between client and community and of the lawyer's duty under the circumstances was Lord Brougham's celebrated defense of Queen Caroline of England in divorce proceedings brought by King George IV in the House of Lords in 1820.

George had secretly married a Catholic widow, Maria Fitzherbert, in 1785. But his father, King George III, had not consented to the union, and under British law the marriage was therefore void. Had the marriage been legal, moreover, the younger George would have forfeited his title to the crown because no heir to the throne could lawfully have a Catholic spouse. So George deserted Mrs. Fitzherbert and in 1795, unable to make good on sizable debts, married his cousin Caroline on his father's promise that if he did so his debts would be settled. Caroline and George lived together little more than a year, the time it took to produce an heir. Twenty-four years later, George, now king, brought his suit for divorce.

Addressing the Lords on behalf of Queen Caroline, Brougham said:

> An advocate, by the sacred duty which he owes his client, knows in the discharge of that office but one person in the world—that client and no other. . . . Nay, separating even the duties of a patriot from those of an advocate, and casting them if need be to the wind, he must go on reckless of the consequences, if his fate it should unhappily be to involve his country in confusion for his client's protection.[23]

The words seem unrelated to the case, except as a bold but general declaration of the advocate's duties. But to a few they had a very definite meaning. As Brougham explained years later: "The statement was anything rather than a deliberate and well-considered opinion. It was a menace, and it was addressed chiefly to George IV, but also to wiser men, such as Castlereagh and Wellington. I was prepared . . . in case the Bill passed the Lords . . . to dispute the King's title. . . . What I said was fully understood by George IV; perhaps by the Duke and Castlereagh, and I am confident it would have prevented them from pressing the Bill beyond a certain point." Brougham's point, which succeeding generations of the bar have accepted, is that duty to client is paramount, no matter what the consequences for others, even though the entire nation may become embroiled in bitter controversy and the government weakened.

This adversary ethic was admirably suited to the political, economic, and social conditions of frontier America. In early laissez-faire days, comparatively few interactions among people led to disputes serious enough to require courts to resolve them. When disputes that could not be compromised did arise, moreover, they almost always pitted one man against another; strangers to the immediate transaction were rarely affected by the quarrel or its settlement.

The private adversarial system was thus the most economic method of resolving disputes. The public had to fund courts, but it did not need to pay for elaborate bureaucracies that might serve as a standing body of mediators waiting for cases. Whenever necessary, the independent lawyer was ready to hire out his services.

The adversarial legal system thus mirrored and supplemented the underlying adversariness of a people not bound to timeless traditions. Where freedom of contract replaces status of birth and where the contract itself usually deals with material gain for both parties, the desire to win becomes nearly an end in itself. The tradition of the advocate who would use every artifice he knew for the benefit of his client was far more a reflection of clients than of lawyers.

The development of a professional ethic at this stage of the culture, therefore, was naturally built around an adversarial model of litigation. Lawyers worked for individual clients, and the arena of that work was mostly in the courtroom, or else preparing documents (like wills and contracts) that would have to withstand the rigors of the courtroom if challenged at some later date.

But the time was coming when these conditions would no longer apply. The Civil War was the watershed. When the questions of slavery and secession had at last receded, industrialization and urbanization became potent forces. The business corporation spread its organizational logic nationwide. Where states once required that every corporate charter be enacted by special act of the legislatures, they now permitted entrepreneurs to incorporate simply by filing the requisite papers and paying the nominal fees.

The lawyers followed these changes—and helped to bring them about. New institutions of government required lawyers to help control and direct the explosion of business; new institutions of business required lawyers to help guide them around the rules of government and to direct their increasingly complex relationships with distributors, retailers, manufacturers, transporters, and others who bore significantly on the doing of business. Corporate and financial interests were in the cities; there, too, the lawyers went.

The urban lawyers who now worked exclusively or predominantly for business clients stayed put in law offices and did not ride circuit from court to court. Instead of stopping for the night with other lawyers from distant parts of the state, they stayed by themselves in libraries. (Not that libraries were devoid of human contact: Felix Frankfurter and Franklin D. Roosevelt first met in the library of the Association of the Bar of the City of New York in 1906.)[24] The feeling of community that tends to exist in any group of people small enough to know each other either personally or by reputation—and the control that goes with it—quickly gave way.

Moreover, when lawyers went to work for the expanding corporate interests, they forsook the courtroom to which the adversarial ethic was adapted. In the courtroom both parties were represented by lawyers. Outside, only one—the corporation—was, and the effects of its transactions spread far beyond those immediately concerned. The perception that the corporations were a pernicious influence in American life would come to be attributed to the lawyers who labored for them.

Not surprisingly, the first move toward a remedy for the dissipation of the legal community came from leading lawyers in the nation's largest metropolis, New York. They were especially alarmed at the rife judicial corruption in the city that Boss Tweed then dominated. In February 1870 the Association of the Bar of the City of New York, the first modern bar association, was brought to life on the call of 235 of the city's 4,000 lawyers.

At its charter meeting, one lawyer lamented the loss of independence: "We have become simply a multitude of individuals, engaged in the same business. And the objects and the methods of those engaged in that business are very much dictated by those who employ them. [Lawyers] . . . are and do simply what their employers desire."[25] To counteract this tendency, the constitution of the association provided, among other things, that "the Association is established to maintain the honor and dignity of the profession."[26]

The old guild mentality, the belief that the profession had or ought to have a kind of corporate existence, thus began to stir across the land. Implicit in the call for association was the creation of an ethical code.

Between the chartering of the Association of the Bar and the formation of the American Bar Association eight years later, sixteen city and state bar associations came into existence in twelve states. One of these was Alabama, and it is here that the first formal code of ethics was adopted in 1887.

Formalizing the Code

How this came to be is a story briefly told.[27] In 1881, Thomas Goode Jones of Montgomery, chairman of the state bar's Committee on Judicial Administration and Remedial Procedure (and later a federal judge), recommended the adoption of such a code, a matter that he had contemplated since his first introduction to Justice George Sharswood's *Essay on Legal Ethics* in his night law school courses during the late 1860s. Published in 1854, this was the first American book on legal ethics (though an earlier lawyer, David Hoffman [1784–1854] published his "50 Resolutions" early in the century).[28] Sharswood (1810–1883) was appointed to the Pennsylvania Supreme Court in 1867 and became chief justice in 1879. His essay was to be the model for all subsequent codes—ironically, because the frontier homilies that he espoused were unsuited to the changed conditions that made a formal code seem imperative.

Jones's recommendation met with the approval of the association, though it would take six years to be adopted. In 1883, a special committee was created to draft the code. Jones and two others were appointed—all had been colonels in the Confederate army. Owing to the press of work (Jones, who did the drafting, had become Speaker of the Alabama State House) and to a mishap (part of the draft blew out the window in 1886 shortly before it was to be read to the association's delegates), the code was not adopted until December 1887. Only one of the canons that Jones proposed was rejected. It read: "An attorney should not conduct his own cause." It was defeated after a member of the association objected that "it is one of the American privileges to make a fool of yourself and it is guaranteed by the [state] constitution, and I do not see anything wrong with it." As for the rest, most were copied verbatim from Sharswood's book.

The final text contained fifty-six canons. Most resembled more a code of etiquette than a code of ethics. An attorney should be punctual (canon 6), should not display temper (canon 7), should uphold the honor of the profession (canon 8), should not stir up prejudice against the profession (canon 9). Preserving the image of the bar as the bar would like to see itself will, if it can be done, be a decided factor in professional cohesion, but such rules have little or nothing to do with professional tasks of the lawyer.

There were, to be sure, a host of rules that with age seem obvious and unexceptional: the attorney must preserve the confidences of his client (canon 21), "must not be a party to oppression" (canon 14), may not represent conflicting interests (canon 25), must respect the client's money "as a sacred fund" (canon 37). Interestingly, canon 16 specifically permitted advertising ("newspaper advertisements, circulars, and business cards, tendering professional services to the general public are proper; but special solicitation of particular individuals to become clients ought to be avoided"). This sanctioning of advertising was tempered by the rule against stirring up litigation (canon 20), "except where ties of blood, relationship or trust make it an attorney's duty."

Only once, in canon 10, did the code come to the nub of the lawyer's task, and even then it articulated its concept of the lawyer's duty in bombastic ambiguity:

An attorney "owes entire devotion to the interest of his client, warm zeal in the maintenance and defense of his cause, and the exertion of the utmost skill and ability," to the end, that nothing may be taken or withheld from him, save by the rules of law, legally applied. No sacrifice or peril, even to loss of life itself, can absolve from the fearless discharge of this duty. Nevertheless, it is steadfastly to be borne in mind that the great trust is to be performed within and not without the bounds of the law which creates it. The attorney's office does not destroy the man's accountability to the Creator, or loosen the duty of obedience to law, and the obligation to his neighbor; and it does not permit, much less demand, violation of law, or any manner of fraud or chicanery, for the client's sake.

The canon conveys the already dying vision of the lawyer who is primarily occupied with representing the client in court. Litigation is the only context; on the many other roles the lawyer was to play (and was already playing)—drafter, negotiator, spokesman, lobbyist, business adviser—the code is silent. The revolution in law—its coming penetration into every facet of business life and most facets of personal life—was not yet felt or acknowledged.

All in all, the 1887 code was a potpourri of manners (don't sue a client—canon 47), tactical advice ("duty not to be over solicitous about comfort of jurors"—canon 54), fraternal concern ("services to the family of deceased attorney should be rendered without charge" —canon 52), and ethics proper (rules relating to the attorney's obligation toward client). The Alabama code stood as a statement of the rules of the game that a family of professionals—like the weavers and tanners and fullers of yore—adhered to in recognition of their commonalty and because it might, by forcing an affiliation, help keep them out of trouble.

By the turn of the century, the practice of law in the United States had been transformed. The age of corporate organization had given birth to the corporate law firm. The lawyers who inhabited these firms were not merely comfortable and did not merely have the good esteem of their townsmen: they had the potential of becoming millionaires, and the community in which they moved was national. Some of them became heads of the industrial giants, like United States Steel and the Union Pacific Railroad.

But to go to these law firms one had to have certain qualifications. Large sums of money and huge responsibilities are not handed out to any new boy on the block. If you were white, Protestant, native-born, preferably with a British surname, and had attended the best law schools, like Harvard or Yale or Columbia, then you had an excellent chance of prospering among the bar's elite. Catholics, Jews, blacks, and women were automatically excluded.

This exclusion was necessary to the elite bar's sense of identity. Any fraternity is defined not only by whom it accepts but also by whom it excludes. The growing anonymity of the bar was thus compensated for by a tightly knit circle of lawyers who knew each other personally through practice or the bar association. Even when the number of lawyers grew beyond the point of instant recognition, each person could nevertheless be instantly pegged and understood through identification with his firm. A telling, though later (1940), example was the time "when an opposing counsel charged one of [John W.] Davis's partners with making a fraudulent contention in argument. Immediately, the judge interrupted him. 'Wait a minute, counsel,' he said. 'The firm you're talking about is Davis, Polk, Wardwell, Gardiner & Reed [now Davis, Polk & Wardwell]. You can't charge them with fraud!' "[29]

But this change in the conception of how the best lawyers conducted their practices came at a price. Many doubted that the new corporate lawyer was a worthy successor to his ancestor, the circuit-riding generalist, and public attacks were frequent. The rawest was that of a former Columbia law student, Theodore Roosevelt, then president of the United States.

Speaking at Harvard in 1905, Roosevelt denounced the new-style lawyer: "Many of the most influential and most highly remunerated members of the bar in every center of wealth make it their special task to work out bold and ingenious schemes by which their very wealthy clients, individual or corporate, can evade the laws which are made to regulate in the interest of the public the use of great wealth."[30] Judging by the American Bar Association's twitch, Roosevelt had plunged deeply into a nerve. Henry St. George Tucker, president of the ABA that year, appointed a committee to ponder the establishment of a national code of ethics. Members included Tucker, Supreme Court Justice Brewer, Thomas Goode Jones of Alabama, and Alton B. Parker, Roosevelt's Democratic opponent in the 1904 election.

The following year the committee reported that a code of ethics was advisable, practicable, and "of very great importance." In words that did not seem to contradict President Roosevelt, the committee declared:

> Our profession is necessarily the keystone of the republican arch of government. Weaken this keystone by allowing it to be increasingly subject to the corroding and demoralizing influence of those who are controlled by graft, greed and gain, or other unworthy motive, and sooner or later the arch must fall.

Continuing, the committee said:

> We cannot be blind to the fact that, however high may be the motives of some, the trend of many is away from the ideals of the past, and the tendency more and more to reduce our high calling to the level of a trade, to a mere means of livelihood, or of personal aggrandizement.

This was precisely the criticism that Roosevelt and many others had leveled against the corporate bar.

But in a vertiginous pirouette, the committee suddenly made it plain that others would have to take the blame:

> With the influx of increasing numbers, who seek admission to the profession mainly for its emoluments, have come new and changed conditions. Once possible ostracism by professional

brethren was sufficient to keep from serious error the practitioner with no fixed ideals of ethical conduct; but now the shyster, the barratrously inclined, the ambulance chaser, the member of the Bar with a system of runners, pursue their nefarious methods with no check save the rope of sand of moral suasion so long as they stop short of actual fraud, and violate no criminal law. These men believe themselves immune, the good or bad esteem of their co-laborers is nothing to them, provided their itching fingers are not thereby stayed in their eager quest for lucre. Much as we regret to acknowledge it, we know such men are in our midst. Never having realized or grasped that indefinable something which is the soul and spirit of law and justice, they not only lower the morale within the profession, but they debase our high calling in the eyes of the public. They hamper the administration, and even at times subvert the ends of justice. Such men are enemies of the republic; not true ministers of truth, honor, and integrity. All such are unworthy of a place upon the rolls of the great and noble profession of the law.[31]

It was as though when John Dean said that he was startled at finding so many lawyers on his list of those embroiled in Watergate, John Mitchell or Richard Nixon were to have commented: "You're right. We have to do something about those lawyers who insist on defending the Black Panthers and war resisters and other radicals so obstreperously."

The ABA adopted the essence of the Sharswood code. In so doing the association pinned the stigma of immorality on the "lower" class of lawyers and allowed the bar to avoid (that is, to ignore and conceal) its obvious racial, religious, and class prejudices. For it was no accident that the "shysters" were Jewish, Catholic, and other immigrant lawyers who talked, dressed, and acted differently.

The upper classes, the ABA members, had no need to violate canons proscribing the advertising of one's availability as a lawyer or one's specialty, or the solicitation of business, or the stirring up of litigation, or the acquiring of an interest in a client's legal claim—the corporate bar has rich, enduring clients who largely pay their attorneys to keep them out of litigation, not to stir it up. The corporate clients knew their attorneys' specialties or could easily find out. These clients would not lightly change their lawyers; it is expensive and time-consuming to educate a new firm to the details of the business.

The young attorney from the best law schools could wholeheartedly agree with Sharswood's dictum to "let business seek the young attorney, and though it may come in slowly, still, if he bears in mind . . . that he should especially cultivate . . . habits of neatness, accuracy, punctuality, and despatch, candor toward the client, and strict honor toward his adversary, it may be safely prophesied that his business will grow as fast as it is good for him that it should grow."[32] This certainly would be true in their experience because the clients were already there when they arrived fresh for their first day's work. But the less advantaged lawyers, the "shyster" and the "barratrously inclined," had no such luxuries. As Jerold S. Auerbach has noted:

> Sharswood's safe prophecy may have comforted a young nineteenth-century attorney in a homogeneous small town, apprenticed to an established practitioner, known in his community, and without many competitors. It could hardly reassure his twentieth-century counterpart, the new-immigrant neophyte in a large city where restricted firms monopolized the most lucrative business and thousands of attorneys scrambled for a share of the remainder. He could draw scant comfort from Sharswood's confident assertion that some preordained rule determined that his practice grew no faster than was good for him. He either hustled or starved.[33]

The canons had still another effect: they made it as difficult as possible for the vast bulk of the population to obtain legal counsel for the increasing number of injuries to which they were subjected in a rapidly industrializing nation. Such obstructions, not surprisingly, were welcome to the clients of the same attorneys who drafted the Ten (actually thirty-two) Commandments, those Sinai tables of stone which Justice Brewer hymned.

With the adoption of the canons of ethics in 1908, the American Bar Association gave to a small elite an instrument of considerable power with which to control the entire profession. Since the 1890s, state after state had turned to occupational licensing laws for an expanding list of professions, including law. Though it never had quite the power of organized medicine to reduce to a minimum the number of new entrants, the bar nevertheless could and did use the canons of ethics, together with bar examinations, increasingly stringent educational requirements, and character committees to limit the admission of would-be advocates and to lift the practice of law outside the rules of capitalism. The free market for which the lawyers so passionately contended was for their clients, not for themselves. Antitrust laws prohibiting agreements in restraint of trade were for businessmen; antitrust was certainly not to be applied against lawyers (nor, until 1975, was it).

In its own way, the code's development made sense. The purpose of a professional code of ethics is to protect the public from the rule of *caveat emptor*—let the buyer beware. But *caveat emptor,* though a rule of the marketplace, is at least subject to the discipline of the marketplace. Remove the market, deny that law is a business, and some other discipline must be found. But since law entails a specialized body of knowledge—that's why lawyers are required to be licensed, after all—no one except the professional can know enough to impose that discipline. It follows, therefore, that only the lawyers can be entrusted with such a delicate task.

The canons of ethics were the perfect device to accomplish this end. They freed the elite bar from any restraints whatsoever, since the canons had no bearing on the way the elite practiced. At the same time, the canons gave the elite bar the power to regulate those who it claimed were giving the profession a black eye. Thus the canons helped crush competition, enhanced the position of elite clients, and ensured that the lower stratum of the bar would never be able to dictate to those in charge. It was a masterly strategy and it worked. Jacksonian populism was dead. The bar became a monopoly.

The Code of Ethics: A Preview

The ABA canons were schizophrenic. They stood in two distinct traditions: brotherhood of the bar and laissez-faire (or adversarialism) for the public. They asserted a need for lawyers to cooperate with one another but assumed that clients would act in a dog-eat-dog fashion toward each other and allowed the lawyer to act on that assumption. For all that the canons required, the lawyer could avail himself of an emptier set of scruples than the client, as long as the lawyer honored canons prohibiting certain specific acts.

Interestingly, a draft version of one canon had said: "A lawyer should not do for a client what his honor would forbid him to do for himself." It was pointed out that such a rule might collapse the entire administration of justice in the country: "No man of honor would defend a righteous claim against himself by pleading the statutes of frauds, of usury, or of limitations. Is an attorney, therefore, justified in refusing to set them up for himself?"[34] If so, what would become of Lord Brougham's menace? The draft version was deleted.

With two major exceptions the canons were virtually identical with the 1887 Alabama code. The two exceptions, however, are noteworthy.

Canon 27 reversed the permission granted to lawyers to advertise. "The most worthy and effective advertisement possible, even for a young lawyer, and especially with his brother lawyers, is the establishment of a well-merited reputation for professional capacity and fidelity to trust. This cannot be forced, but must be the outcome of character and conduct," it opined. What was permissible for lawyers in rural Alabama where the quiet and slow "establishment of a well-merited reputation" was possible was now denied to lawyers in urban areas for whom such establishment was impossible. So much for Justice Brewer's "imperishable truth by the finger of God."

The other change was the addition of a final section (canon 32) entitled "The Lawyer's Duty in Its Last Analysis":

> No client, corporate or individual, however powerful, nor any cause, civil or political, however important, is entitled to receive, nor should any lawyer render, any service or advice involving disloyalty to the law whose ministers we are. . . . Above all a lawyer will find his highest honor in a deserved reputation for fidelity to private trust and to public duty, as an honest man and as a patriotic and loyal citizen.

These reassuring words are virtually meaningless. How can one remain faithful both to "private trust and public duty" if they conflict? What must the lawyer do to remain "patriotic and loyal" as a citizen? Can his duties as citizen conflict with his duties as a lawyer? In setting out such ambiguous standards, the canons thus gave the interpreters ample scope to stifle only those lawyers whose approach to law practice they chose to view as wrong.

By the 1960s, it had become patent that the canons were faulty. Indeed, it had been evident since 1928, when thirteen of fifteen additional canons were adopted. Significantly, the last two canons, dealing with lawyers advertising their services to other lawyers and with preventing "unauthorized practice of law," were adopted during the Depression (in 1933 and 1937).* Occasional amendments, hundreds of oracular interpretations by the ABA's Committee on Professional Ethics and Grievances, and dozens of undefined terms only added to the confusions.

In 1964, Lewis F. Powell, Jr., then president of the association and

---

*Six of the fifteen additional canons dealt with fees or the appropriate forms of employment relationships. Five concerned non-fee obligations to clients. Three dealt with advertising. One proclaimed the obvious: that as far as the ABA was concerned, the canons applied to all lawyers equally, regardless of specialty.

now an associate justice of the Supreme Court, called for a searching re-examination. A special committee was appointed, consisting of two law professors, two former judges, and eight men whom their chairman, Edward L. Wright of Little Rock, described as "general practitioners." Two of these were former presidents of the ABA, one a chairman of the ethics committee. All these "general practitioners" were members of substantial law firms; most concentrated their efforts on corporate clients. No women served on the committee, or blacks, or Jews. Most went to top-ranked schools. None was then serving in government, although some had served previously. None had been legal aid attorneys, although through their firms the private practitioners were involved in *pro bono* work. In short, all were members of the bar's elite, though the ABA had grown from less than 2,000 members at the time the first committee began its work in 1905 to some 120,000, or 60 percent of the entire profession, by the mid-1960s.*

From the staff work and the committee's deliberations during the period 1965–1969 a complete revision of the canons emerged. Renamed the Code of Professional Responsibility (CPR), it is divided into three parts: (1) nine *canons,* "statements of axiomatic norms" or broadly worded duties of lawyers; (2) *ethical considerations* that are "aspirational in character" and that relate to each canon; and (3) mandatory *disciplinary rules* that "state the minimum level of conduct below which no lawyer can fall without being subject to disciplinary action."

The new canons are a partial break from the Sharswoodian mood and rhetoric. There is even some innovation in the recognition of duties that the profession as a whole owes the public; for example, canon 1, which states that "a lawyer should assist in maintaining the

---

*Concerned about the lack of representativeness, the committee stated in its foreword to the new code that it "has held meetings with 37 major units of the profession and has corresponded with more than 100 additional groups. The entire committee has met a total of 71 days and the editorial subcommittee of three members has met 28 additional days [and certain other named individuals, representing the American Bar Foundation, and ABA committees on discipline and enforcement and availability of legal services] attended many of our meetings."

integrity and competence" of the profession, and canon 2, which holds that a "lawyer should assist the legal profession in fulfilling its duty to make legal counsel available." The new code is more subtle, more modern, and also more long-winded (in a standard textbook, the forty-seven old canons require fourteen pages, whereas the new code takes up fifty-eight pages).[35]

But the change was more of form than of substance. As we will explore in detail in the following chapters, the code remains confusing, ambiguous, and inconsistent. Before we turn to the bill of particulars, however, one deep-rooted flaw in the present code should be set forth.

In 1966, John F. Sutton, Jr., reporter of the ABA's Special Committee on Evaluation of Ethical Standards, said that the 1908 code "has often been criticized—and I think justly so—for its great attention to the work of the trial lawyer and its neglect of other areas,"[36] like those of the prosecutor and the corporate lawyer. The new code is subject to the same criticism. It lights the way with buoys in waters that fewer and fewer are traveling on. Though there is an occasional nod to other roles, the canons still assume that by and large the bar is homogeneous. It is not. In fact, the American bar comprises four very different types of practitioners, and it is well to see those differences from the start. They are:

The personal lawyer. This is the attorney who writes your will, gets you a divorce, sues your neighbor when a fence is wrongly built through your front lawn, helps you adopt a child, prepares the papers when you buy a house. He deals with your domestic legal problems. Since none of the four bars has impermeable boundaries, many personal lawyers may do business law as well. Usually, however, this will consist of work for small family businesses managed in the main by their owners. The personal lawyer is the general practitioner of old, the prairie lawyer of Abraham Lincoln's time. Perhaps half the bar today—some 200,000 lawyers—would fit somewhere within this tradition.

The institutional lawyer. This is the business lawyer who works in a private law firm, a corporation, or any of a number of other institutions. He may handle personal problems—fancy law firms will do "matrimonial" work, for example, but only as an accommodation for clients whose more lucrative corporate business they wish to retain. The institutional lawyer deals with "big" problems and organizations —with antitrust, corporate law, securities, taxes, real estate and zoning on a large scale, and dozens of other complex and expensive matters. The institutional lawyer is often in federal court; the personal lawyer rarely. Even when he is dealing with individual clients, the institutional lawyer is usually asked to further the client's business or institutional interests; for example, the business investments of a movie star or a superbowl quarterback.

The criminal lawyer. This is a hybrid type. Many personal lawyers practice low-grade criminal law, bailing out a client's teen-ager who has just been arrested on a marijuana charge or defending the client himself on any of a number of driving offenses. Some institutional lawyers occasionally find themselves involved with white-collar criminal matters—securities fraud, for instance. But there is a definable class of attorneys whose principal work is criminal law only—from capital crimes to shoplifting, from income-tax evasion to private swindling. This is not to say that all criminal lawyers will accept any criminal case; there is sub-specialization in this branch of law as elsewhere. But the techniques and procedures are generally the same no matter what the crime.

The public service lawyer. This too is a hybrid, for many personal and institutional lawyers drift in and out of government service, and some even carry on private practices while serving in government. Nor do public service attorneys necessarily work for government; there are many self-styled "public interest" lawyers who work for private law firms and for other groups that serve interests until recently unrepresented.

Of these four types of lawyers, the work of only the first and third falls within the conventional model. The personal lawyer, who operates from his own office, usually by himself, although sometimes associated with one or two partners, and who carries on a diverse practice that frequently takes him to court, is the model known to the bar in the last century when the code of ethics was formulated. By extension, the criminal lawyer fits within the model, for he is a specialist who (usually) finds it convenient or profitable or enjoyable to spend his full time handling criminal cases when he could, if he chose, devote part of his professional life to civil litigation as well.

The second and fourth types fall outside the conventional model. Neither the large private institutions nor regulatory government figured in the development of the lawyers' code. These institutions pose a whole new range of problems. Though the conventional ethic has plenty of cracks in it, it is here, in the institutional realm, that the code falls apart altogether. To these flaws and failures we now turn.

CHAPTER 4

"Keeping It for Ourselves":
The Bar vs. the Public

A Responsibility to Serve

From time to time I have had occasion to upbraid a department store, airline, or merchant who has done me grave injustice (like dunning me for something I have already paid for or tricking me into a smoking section of a congested airplane). Usually I demand some form of relief, and I always place my demand, neatly typed, beneath a letterhead that says "attorney at law." Because I am licensed to use these words, I sometimes get satisfaction by return mail. What a pity that everyone cannot be furnished with such a letterhead; it would be so much cheaper than hiring someone for his engraved stationery.

But legal stationery cannot be printed up indiscriminately because lawyers possess a professional monopoly. Since the classic tendency of monopolies is to hold back on services in order to drive prices up, a professional ethic ought to counsel service, as the code does.

The lawyer's first duty, says the current code, is to make legal services available to the public. "A lawyer should not lightly decline proffered employment. . . . A lawyer [should accept] his share of tendered employment which may be unattractive both to him and the bar generally."[1] So speaks the code. But on this test of lawyers' ethics, the bar flunks. There are two reasons, both stemming from the nature of modern legal practice.

In the old days, the lawyer was a jack-of-all-trades. That model lawyer, Abraham Lincoln, was the exemplar of this tradition in the 1850s. "As an all-purpose attorney, Lincoln argued cases that ranged across the entire legal spectrum, from divorce, murder, and rape cases to contests involving disputed wills, maritime law, the right of way of railroads, actions for injunctions, foreclosures, debts, trespass violations, slander suits, and patent infringements. And in criminal cases he could 'stoutly argufy' on either side of the law, serving one day as defense counsel and another day as court-appointed prosecutor."[2]

Today no lawyer could handle such a range of cases. The law is too complex to allow any one person to be good at such a variety of problems; besides, there is more to be earned by becoming excellent in one rather narrow branch of law. And the lawyer who specializes —a large part of the bar does—will "decline proffered employment," not lightly but for the sensible reason that he is not competent to handle the ordinary affairs of life.

The second reason for the lack of services follows: lawyering costs too much. Statistics collected in an American Bar Foundation survey from 1974 to 1976 confirm that for the middle class, at least, lawyers are too expensive to use. As one prosperous corporate attorney bewailed in 1975: "If you earned $75,000 a year you couldn't afford my fees. Things have gotten so bad I can't afford my own fees. It scares me."[3]

High fees that price legal services beyond the reach of most people do not result only from an overt conspiracy. Lawyers have discovered that specialization is financially rewarding, and if the lawyer can find clients who pay him well, the canons do not require him to forfeit their business in order to serve the poor. To the contrary, "a lawyer is under no obligation to act as adviser or advocate for every person who may wish to become his client," says one of the code's ethical considerations.

Chesterfield Smith, the voluble former ABA president from Lakeland, Florida, who enraged many members of the bar in 1973 and 1974 when he blasted President Nixon for dishonoring the law, says he thinks that lawyers will have to be forced to serve the public. "I see the time coming," in the 1990s, he says, "when some lawyer will be disbarred for sitting in his office all day examining title abstracts"[4]— hence for merely making money instead of devoting his talents to those in need.

I think this is a mistaken view of a lawyer's responsibilities. It serves to mask what is truly unethical about the bar's organization for service—namely, its penchant for placing incredible obstacles in the path of those seeking legal assistance.

The duty to make legal services available, it seems to me, is society's. The bar's duty is not to impede the rendering of service.

In restricting entry into the legal profession, society has not been overcome by a charitable impulse to do lawyers a favor. The impact of its requirement that a person be licensed falls on every person, limiting the ability of each to pursue the calling of his choice. This is done in the public interest to ensure qualified representation. The tendency of the licensing requirement is, of course, to create a monopoly, but no individual lawyer can be blamed for that. Freedom requires that individuals—even lawyers—not be treated as public utilities.[5] If society wishes a service, then society ought to be willing to pay for it. So, while lawyers may individually have a moral duty to help those in need, even those unable to pay, it would be unfair to impose a legal requirement on the bar collectively to do so.

But this does not mean that lawyers are home free to do as they please. Unfortunately, despite their exhortations to the contrary, lawyers have gone out of their way to place impediments in the path of those seeking counsel. How lawyers organize themselves to avoid serving is a serious ethical lapse. Here we can condemn the bar collectively, for as we will see in this chapter, lawyers are adept in placing formidable obstacles in the way of potential clients and of untraditional lawyers willing to carry out their moral duty to serve.

Group Practice and Its Enemies

One obvious solution to the costliness of seeking out an independent lawyer with an office and considerable overhead is to put him on salary. This will assure the lawyer of a steady income and will free him from the anxieties that afflict the independent practitioner. Because he is more secure, he can afford to accept less for each case. And if people in a group know that they are entitled to avail themselves of his services by sharing the cost of his salary, each person is insuring himself against the risk of a much higher cost in the event of later legal catastrophe. In 1913 a modest program like this started up in Illinois, and here's what happened.

Coal mining is a hazardous occupation, and it is not rare for a miner to be hurt on the job. Under a state law enacted in 1912, an injured miner receives worker's compensation from a fund that the coal companies pay into. To collect his compensation, a miner would have to hire an attorney and file papers with the state Industrial Commission. The company would then either offer a settlement or take its chances with the Commission (a gamble the worker could also take). Retaining a lawyer could be expensive; in the early days most would charge between 40 and 50 percent of the recovery. Since most of the legal work was routine, it was a lucrative business for the bar.

Shortly after the worker's compensation law went into effect, the United Mine Workers' Illinois branch decided that the private bar was making too much money. So it instituted a program whereby a union legal department would help the union members. For half a century, the union operated this legal department.

In 1963 the Illinois union hired an attorney and put him on an annual retainer of about $12,000. The work did not overly burden the union's lawyer, for he was a state senator and carried on an active private practice at the same time.

At the beginning of his employment, the union gave him a letter that read in part as follows: "You will receive no further instructions or directions and have no interference from the District, nor from any officer, and your obligations and relations will be to and with only the several persons you represent." The union and attorney frequently advised its members that he was there to be consulted but that no member was bound to seek his help over any other attorney. Usually, injured miners did use his services.

From 1963 to 1966 he collected more than $3 million for his clients, charging the union only his annual $12,000 retainer. Had he been a private attorney, his percentage would have amounted to between $500,000 and $1 million, money that would have come directly out of the pockets of the clients. The union lawyer rarely spoke to the miners, most of his work consisting of filling in blanks on legal forms for submission to the Industrial Commission.

This arrangement pleased everyone but the local bar. After all, $500,000 is a lot of money to be forfeiting to an interloper. So in 1966, acting under authority delegated to it by the state, the Illinois Bar Association filed suit to enjoin the union and the lawyer from conducting their legal assistance program.

The state bar charged that the lawyer was violating canon 47, which prohibited any lawyer from permitting "his professional services, or his name to be used in aid of, or to make possible, the unauthorized practice of law by any lay agency, personal or corporate." "Unauthorized" practice was an ingenious doctrine that the bar solemnly adopted in 1937 when the rigors of the Depression had become too great to tolerate new forms of competition. Canon 47 supplemented a 1928 canon, which banned the practice of law by "intermediaries" or by lawyers retained by them.*

_____

*Canon 35, as amended in 1933, read as follows: "The professional services of a lawyer should not be controlled or exploited by any lay agency, personal or corporate, which intervenes between client and lawyer. A lawyer's responsibilities and qualifica-

The ethical fear is not entirely groundless. Whoever pays your salary has the right to demand services in return. If the association or corporation directs its lawyer (an employee) to represent its members or employees or customers, then the lawyer has a potential conflict of interest, for the employer may not wish to have the client pursue some cases. The intermediary may therefore try to limit the lawyer's independence, to the client's detriment.

At most, however, the conflict is only potential. The "intermediary" is not practicing law or representing clients; the lawyer is. As long as the lawyer is *in fact* independent and acting only for the individual clients, where is the harm?

The blanket and anomalous prohibition against "unauthorized practice of law" by a licensed lawyer is a characteristic of one broad class of ethical rules, a characteristic we will call *overkill.* It says in essence: What you are doing may or may not be proper, depending on the circumstances, but we can't take any chances with the public well-being, so we will condemn the beneficial as well as the harmful.

The rule against lay intermediaries is deeply rooted. In 1925, before the existence of canons 35 or 47, the ABA Committee on Ethics and Grievances condemned attorneys who received a salary from an automobile club. The club's money came from the members' dues, and membership entitled them, among other things, to free legal counsel in connection with certain driving offenses and traffic accidents. Citing no written canons to buttress its arguments against the arrangement (for there were none), the committee concluded with a flourish: "The furnishing, selling or exploiting of the legal services of members

---

tions are individual. He should avoid all relations which direct the performance of his duties by or in the interest of such intermediary. A lawyer's relation to his client should be personal and the responsibility should be direct to the client. Charitable societies rendering aid to the indigent are not deemed such intermediaries.

"A lawyer may accept employment from any organization, such as an association, club or trade organization, to render legal services in any matter in which the organization, as an entity, is interested, but this employment should not include the rendering of legal services to the members of such an organization in respect to their individual affairs."

of the Bar is derogatory to the dignity and self-respect of the profession, tends to lower the standards of professional character and conduct and thus lessens the usefulness of the profession to the public."*[6]

The opinion was, and remains, hogwash. Far from "lessening the usefulness of the profession," the practice made it more useful. And who can honestly suppose that members of the automobile club or outsiders thought less of the bar because free services were available? Lawyers are not statistical-minded, so in imposing their rule of overkill they can have no way of knowing whether they have eliminated a great amount of good to forestall a little evil or vice versa. It is instructive that the 1925 opinion was not prompted by complaints from clients.

Neither was the action against the Mine Workers' attorney in 1966. Indeed, the arrangement was clearly beneficial to the union member clients. There was no showing that the union interfered with its lawyer's representation of members. In other words, he retained his independence. Nor was he sloppy or dishonest. He achieved results for the members at a cost many times less than the "independent" bar would charge for this relatively routine work.†

The state bar did not prove to the contrary; it just mindlessly repeated the precedential hogwash. Just how vapid the lay intermediary doctrine is can be seen clearly from the provision that allowed "charitable societies" to hire lawyers to serve the poor. The relationship between client and lawyer in the union arrangement is identical with that in the charitable society. In either situation the lawyer is paid by someone other than the client. The lawyer is as susceptible to direction by one not his client in the one situation as in the other. The true difference is that the charitable society lawyers do not com-

*Three years later, to cover its embarrassment in having a formal opinion on an ethical matter to which no canon applied, the ABA adopted canon 35, which simply restated the language of the committee's opinion. Interestingly, the ABA's official compilation of its ethical opinions claims that the opinion just cited is an "interpretation" of canon 35—a neat trick, under the circumstances.

†Justice Harlan thought the evidence showed that the attorney *might* have been too quick to settle with the coal companies and that the relatively low average recovery indicated the attorney had no incentive to spend a great deal of time on any one client.

pete against the private bar for clients, because indigents do not otherwise hire lawyers. What is ethical, therefore, is any arrangement that does not steal clients away from those apostles of free enterprise, the independent practitioners. Or, as one former member of the ABA's Unauthorized Practice of Law Committee put it, "We're keeping it for ourselves."*[7]

Notwithstanding the transparent hypocrisy, the argument against lawyers salaried to "lay intermediaries" impressed the lawyers who sat as justices of the Illinois Supreme Court. The court ruled that the lawyer would have to sever his relationship with the Mine Workers.[9]

Luckily, the union appealed the case to the United States Supreme Court at exactly the right moment in history, and it then became apparent that the Illinois bar had committed a major tactical blunder on behalf of the entire American legal monopoly. For the Supreme Court ruled that it was *unconstitutional* for the profession, through the courts, to prohibit the union's salaried lawyer arrangement.[10]

Building on cases decided a few years earlier, Justice Hugo L. Black, for an eight-man majority, wrote that Illinois's interference with the union's legal program was a violation of the First Amendment right of all persons to form associations to protect their legal rights. As Justice Black had put it in one of the earlier cases: for the lay public "to associate together to help one another to preserve and enforce rights granted them under federal laws cannot be condemned as a threat to legal ethics."[11]

Though clearly foreshadowed in the earlier cases, the Court's decision, handed down in December 1967, shook the organized bar, for in recognizing a right to associate to enforce rights under *state* laws, it threatened a radical reorganization of the delivery of legal services in the United States. That such a reorganization has not yet come to be,

---

*So ludicrous is the reach of the unauthorized practice of law doctrine that lawyers who work for accounting firms are barred from representing the firms' clients before the Internal Revenue Service, though the service and ethic of each group at this junction of the professions is identical.[8] The doctrine also prohibits the lawyer who is, say, also an accountant (or a marriage counselor or psychologist or whatever) from practicing as both.

a decade later, is testament to the bar's ethical insensitivities. The story is instructive.

Eighteen months after the Supreme Court decision, the ABA approved its new Code of Professional Responsibility, complete with all its Ethical Considerations and Disciplinary Rules. Significantly, canon 2 ("a lawyer should assist the legal profession in fulfilling its duty to make legal counsel available") contains no rules instructing lawyers on what they must do to ensure that their services are available to the many who need them. Instead, the lengthy disciplinary rules tell lawyers (in maddening sentences full of double negatives) how not to provide counsel to the public.

The crucial rule began by saying that with certain narrow exceptions, a lawyer could not work for an organization that pays him to do legal work for someone else. One of the exceptions, aimed directly at the Supreme Court threat, read as follows:

> [A lawyer may work for a nonprofit organization] but only in those instances and to the extent that controlling constitutional interpretation at the time of the rendition of the services requires the allowance of such legal service activities.[12]

This confusing prose says that an attorney may not ethically work for an organization that pays him to do legal work for someone else unless a court has first ruled that the bar cannot stand in his way. It put such attorneys at a serious disadvantage, for the Court had actually ruled only in the Mine Workers case. Who could know what deviations from the precise scheme that the Mine Workers had set up would be tolerated? The net effect, though no one ever stated that this was the intention, was to bar lawyers from even taking a risk. Unless already approved, the decision to accept a salary from the group would be unethical.

Nor was this all. The new ABA code placed further restrictions on the group's lawyer. The group could not have been formed for the purpose of rendering legal services (a restriction resembling the airline "affinity" rule that precludes an association whose members meet each other only on cut-rate charters from qualifying for charter status). The group must exist for some other primary purpose (which, of course, the Mine Workers did). The code also said that the legal services must be "incidental and reasonably related to" the group's underlying purpose. In other words, a stamp collectors' club could not sign up a lawyer to help its members defend against automobile accidents.

This grudging recognition of a decision of the United States Supreme Court debased the very meaning of a code of ethics. It was disingenuousness cubed, amounting as it did to a statement by the bar that "we, the organized profession of lawyers, will do everything we can to circumvent the ruling of our nation's highest court on a constitutional question concerning access to legal services because we are unhappy with it." Ethical behavior is not so stingy.

For it had been clear all along that without these "ethical" obstructions, many organizations—unions, churches, professional associations—could rather quickly begin to provide legal counsel to a vast number of Americans. And it was just such a specter that the bar feared (more accurately, one strong element of the bar, for some dissenters made their position known).

The new Code of Professional Responsibility went into effect in 1970, two years after *United Mine Workers*. In 1971, the Supreme Court had occasion to consider another group legal services case.[13] The facts were similar to those in the Illinois case. As Justice Black summed them up: "The Michigan State Bar brought this action in January 1959 to enjoin members of the Brotherhood of Railroad Trainmen from engaging in activities undertaken for the stated purpose of assisting their fellow workers, their widows and families, to protect themselves from excessive fees at the hands of incompetent attorneys in suits for damages under the Federal Employers' Liability Act." The union recommended a certain number of lawyers, who in return agreed to charge no more than one-quarter of the amount they recovered. Despite the 1967 decision, the Michigan Supreme Court issued the injunction.

The Supreme Court reversed. In sweeping language, the Court said "that collective activity undertaken to obtain meaningful access to the courts is a fundamental right within the protection of the First Amendment. However, that right would be a hollow promise if courts could deny associations of workers or others the means of enabling their members to meet the costs of legal representation."

The game was almost up, but lawyers are expert at stalling.

Three years later, in 1974, the ABA once again changed its code. (Those tables are wearing thin.) The disingenuous language quoted above disappeared. In its place, however, the bar continued to make a distinction that hampered the full flowering of group legal services.

This was the distinction between the "open panel" and "closed panel" plans. The closed panel is the union legal service plan. It is called "closed" because, in return for the members' dues, the salaried lawyer is the only one who may be consulted for free. If the injured worker chooses to retain another lawyer, the union will not pay for it; the client will have to use his own funds. By contrast, the open panel is an arrangement whereby a subscriber to the legal service is free to select any attorney he desires (or, more commonly, any attorney on a list of participating attorneys who have agreed to the plan's fee schedules). Under the open panel, the subscriber pays an annual premium, like medical insurance, and can look to the "prepaid insurance plan" (the insurance carrier) to pay his lawyer's fees.

The bar obviously liked the open panel better because it meant that the general practitioners' business would not be lost to a group of potential clients already captured by a salaried lawyer.* So the ABA added a provision stating in effect that open panels were now ethical whereas closed panels were not. Various state bar associations began

---

*Again, typical of the inconsistencies of the code, the legal assistance offices of the military—a closed panel—were exempted from the ethical prohibitions. Of all possible legal service arrangements, this was perhaps the least defensible, for the military is the one institution which has a strong enough force (the unit's commanding officer) with the power and motive to press the lawyer to act against the best interests of his client in order better to serve the command.[14]

scrambling, following the lead of the Shreveport, Louisiana, bar association in 1971, to set up citywide or statewide prepaid insurance packages operated through the associations.

In 1975, the bar finally relented and amended the code anew. This time the grand distinctions on which the ethical character of a lawyer had depended only the year before vanished. Not at all coincidentally, Congress in that year passed a law allowing unions to bargain for prepaid insurance as an employee benefit; the law explicitly forbade bar associations to interfere with the process.

In 1976, Congress removed certain income-tax impediments, and the prepaid insurance revolution is now well launched. Within the next few years, group legal services will become a major means of delivering legal counsel to the nation. Thanks to the bar? In part, of course, yes, because wherever there is a major crisis, lawyers will be found on both sides. Some lawyers took risks and cooperated with prepaid plans early on, while those activities were regarded with great suspicion. But the bar as a whole deserves little credit: its instinctive reactions held the revolution back at least ten years, and forestalled a sensible and orderly evolution for more than half a century.

"Like Being against Vietnam in 1960": Sins of Self-Promotion

In 1972, two young Los Angeles lawyers, Leonard D. Jacoby, 30, and Stephen Z. Meyers, 29, decided that it was time to break loose from the standard law practice to which they had become accustomed since their graduation from law school five years before. Young lawyers do this all the time: spend a few years with established practitioners, learn the ropes, make their mistakes at someone else's expense (like interns in hospitals), and then face the world as entrepreneurs, maybe even bringing along a client or two to ease the pain of independence. If Jacoby and Meyers had played the conventional game, they would have rented a room or two in an office building downtown, stocked it with furniture as expensive as they could afford, put a rug on the floor, bought a potted plant, installed a secretary behind a desk near the front door of their suite, and printed up stationery boldly proclaiming their new partnership: "Jacoby & Meyers, attorneys at law."* Then they would have waited for people with problems to call.

Unlike a firm of interior decorators or private investigators, the new law firm could not place ads in the local paper or have the neighborhood kids stick red and yellow broadsides under the windshields of automobiles in supermarket parking lots. The lawyers could send a somber (and expensive) card around to other lawyers announcing the formation of their firm. If they were discreet, they could also phone their friends to say they were now in business and if a will was the thing, why, hop on over. But aside from that, they would have had to wait—or visit the criminal courts and hunt up some assignments to represent indigents.

Jacoby and Meyers did it differently. They rented a storefront brick and glass office in a middle-class suburban shopping center in Van Nuys. In block letters about one foot high, the glass front proclaimed something new: "Legal Clinic of Jacoby & Meyers." Inside, the office was sparsely furnished. The sign on the door gave unusual office hours: in addition to the normal work week, it said, the lawyers would be available on Saturdays and in the evenings. Clients were invited to use their Master Charge cards.

The two proprietors hired a small staff, consisting at the outset of three so-called "paralegal counselors." Like a paramedic, the paralegal is not a licensed professional but has pertinent skills that can relieve the attorney of much routine work. The original paralegals were law students.

The clinic opened in September 1972 with a routine that is simplic-

---

*Or, perhaps, "Jacoby & Meyers, P.C.," meaning "professional corporation." Until recently, it was unethical to incorporate; law firms were always partnerships. But there were tax and other advantages to incorporating, so the bar found a graceful way to amend holy writ.

ity itself. Clients were greeted by one of the counselors, who charged a fifteen-dollar initial consultation fee (to recapture some expenses and to ensure that people who just wanted to chat would not take up valuable time). They handed out a blue-backed brochure that described the clinic's methods and typical fees, all of which were considerably lower than the local bar association's then prevailing minimum fee schedule. For an uncontested divorce, for example, the clinic would bill the client $100. For the same service, the private bar would charge $400. Jacoby & Meyers wanted $300 for a business bankruptcy; the other lawyers in the area twice as much. The clinic, said the brochure, was "a common sense approach to providing high quality, low cost legal services."

The paralegal counselor discussed the case initially with the client, ascertaining that the case was one that the clinic could realistically handle and jotting down the relevant facts on forms that Jacoby and Meyers had specially prepared, making it simple to track the case from start to finish.

"We're capitalists," says Stephen Meyers.[15] Like all capitalist organizations, the idea is to work efficiently and to realize as much as possible the economies of scale. The ordinary practitioner who takes a divorce case must charge more because when he goes to court considerable time is lost waiting for the case to be called. Court calendars are crowded; dozens of cases can be on the docket on any one day. Time in court is time away from the office and from other clients' problems. But the "simple economics of a high-volume business" with a low overhead, Jacoby says, allows the clinic to accumulate a number of nearly identical cases and schedule them all for the same day in the same court. Waiting time for each case is reduced drastically.

The theory corresponds to reality: within six months the clinic was handling 1 percent of all divorce work in Los Angeles County. In June 1973, Jacoby and Meyers opened a second office. By then the two clinics together had a staff consisting of four full-time attorneys, nine part-time specialists, and several paraprofessionals. "People are willing to save some money not to have plush carpeting or sit on an attorney's lap," Jacoby noted.

But by then, also, the clinic had encountered opposition from the state bar. In March 1973, Jacoby and Meyers were formally charged with violating the state code of ethics. The charges were couched in particularly severe language. The two lawyers were accused of having conducted themselves dishonestly, corruptly, and with "moral turpitude." Any one of these charges, if sustained, could have brought disbarment.

The basis for the charges was twofold. The first allegation was that in using the words "legal clinic" the lawyers were practicing under an "assumed" and "misleading" trade name. The second allegation, that Jacoby and Meyers had unethically advertised for business, grew out of an open house the night of September 13, 1972, at the clinic offices.

Maurice Mayesh, then president of the Consumer Legal Action Council and head of a Consumer Federation of California task force to study legal services, hosted the evening affair. He invited a few members of the press. Discussion centered on the theory and operation of the new clinic. Within the next few days and for several weeks thereafter, several reporters called on the lawyers for interviews. Among the reporters were those from the *Los Angeles Times,* the *Los Angeles Herald Examiner,* the *Los Angeles Daily Journal, Newsweek,* the *Christian Science Monitor,* and San Francisco radio station KCBS. Jacoby and Meyers cooperated with these journalists, speaking freely and, on one occasion, at least, posing for photographs outside their office. Not surprisingly, the clinic attracted the bar's attention, and the charges were lodged.

Subsequently, in response to still more inquiries from the press, Jacoby and Meyers distributed a "press kit" to reporters who called. The press kit told about the clinic and responded to the bar's allegations of unethical conduct.

The California bar's disciplinary process is a protracted one. A local committee of three private practitioners hears the initial charges.

The committee's findings and recommendations are then forwarded to a statewide committee, which is free to disregard what the local committee decides. These findings and recommendations in turn are submitted to the California Supreme Court, which has the last word. In Jacoby's and Meyers' case, the local committee held hearings on twenty-one separate days, commencing in March 1974, one year after the initial allegations were filed, and stretching on until August of 1975. During that time, some peculiar things happened.

In the month the hearings got under way, James D. Fellers, ABA president-elect, said "legal clinics" had the "greatest potential for effective and efficient legal services for low- and middle-income Americans."[16]

In December 1974, the ABA's Special Committee on Delivery of Legal Services held a two-day meeting on legal clinics—named as such—in New Orleans. Representatives of five legal clinics, all established after the Van Nuys clinic had become a going concern, were invited. Jacoby and Meyers were not. The chairman of the ABA committee was then Stuart L. Kadison, a member of the California state bar's board of governors, under whose aegis the investigation of Jacoby and Meyers was being conducted.

Far from condemning the idea, the committee unanimously agreed that the legal clinic deserved a trial run. The committee's own clinic, though; not the Legal Clinic of Jacoby & Meyers. The committee decided to seek $250,000 to fund a "model" clinic under bar auspices for a two-year period. Why a model clinic? "To see if there really is a demand for this type of service," said one of the committee members. Never mind that by then Jacoby and Meyers had six full-time lawyers, four part-time lawyers, twelve paraprofessionals, and had worked their way through 5,000 cases.*

On the day before Halloween in 1975, the local administrative committee of the state bar announced its findings and recommendations in the matter of Leonard D. Jacoby and Stephen Z. Meyers. By a

---

*At this writing, in the summer of 1977, the ABA model clinic has been operating in Philadelphia for just about a year. It calls itself a "legal clinic."

two-to-one vote, it found them guilty of unprofessional conduct. The committee recommended that the pair be suspended from practice for forty-five days and that they be ordered to remove the words "legal clinic" from their offices.

The committee did acquit them, however, of the serious charges of "moral turpitude," dishonesty, and corruption. "The Committee is greatly influenced by the mitigating circumstances of Respondents' honest belief in the social desirability of the legal clinic approach," the majority opined. Nevertheless, the two-man majority found that the lawyers' motive in talking to the press and in using the name legal clinic was to "generate business" for their law practice. This conclusion was reached despite the lawyers' "honestly held belief that the financial success of their law firm was necessary to prove the practicability of the 'legal clinic' concept."

Jacoby and Meyers had argued that they had a constitutional right to discuss the concept of their legal clinic and to speak out about the investigation in which they had become embroiled. *The majority agreed.* Astonishingly, however, it concluded that the constitutional right was outweighed by their intention to "generate law business" and must yield. In short, the committee said that you may exercise your constitutional rights if you are an attorney but only as long as you exercise them in an ethically approved manner (a term left to the bar to define).

Aside from the name on their glass office front, Jacoby and Meyers did not "advertise" in the usual commercial sense. They "went public" only by talking to the press. That the California bar reacted as it did is not surprising, for there is a deeply ingrained belief that any lawyer who talks to a journalist is unethically seeking publicity. But when establishment lawyers have a point to make, they are not shy about seeking out those who can transmit their words to a larger public.

In the spring of 1976, for example, I received a call from a public relations firm inquiring whether their man could bring Milton Handler by my office. He had several things he wanted to say, the PR man told me, about a pending antitrust bill in the Senate. Handler is senior partner in Kaye, Scholer, Fierman, Hays & Handler, and as a professor of law at Columbia Law School for fifty years is considered by many the dean of the antitrust bar. When Milton Handler asks to call upon a reporter, something *must* be on his mind. Which, of course, there was.

He was personally upset, Handler said when we met, about the nature of the antitrust bill (which subsequently was enacted into law). He was especially concerned about a provision in it permitting state attorneys general to file massive antitrust suits against private corporations on behalf of the citizens of the state. The potential for blackmail was high, Handler warned, because a state attorney general with his eye on higher office would not exactly be upset at headlines about his crusade against corporate America. (There may be truth in what Handler said; we should be suspicious of all prosecutors, after all, not merely of those who go after political minorities.) At any rate, what was interesting was that Handler was making the rounds of various news offices with his PR man in tow.

Later that afternoon I talked by phone about it with the PR man and Handler. They both assured me that Handler was doing this out of personal conviction, not at the behest of a client. I assume that he was not acting in his capacity as counsel or advocate for any client. But, by and large, Handler's clients do not disagree with his antitrust views. In publicizing his personal criticisms of the pending legislation, Handler inevitably suggested to potential clients that here is a lawyer with their interests at heart.[17]

Nevertheless, Handler was clearly within his rights to do as he did. The question was intensely political even while it bore intensely on the pocketbooks of many of Handler's clients. The right to talk as Handler did is what free speech is for. But it seems to me equally clear that what Handler did was in no significant way different from what Jacoby and Meyers did. If anything, Handler initiated the conversations with journalists to a greater extent than did the California lawyers. Neither ought to be characterized as "advertising."

As for the use of the term "legal clinic," close inspection will reveal a considerable amount of hypocrisy. How does a reputable group of lawyers refer to itself? Well, the very most reputable lawyers refer to themselves by the names of dead men. A very few use the names of deceased presidential candidates, who were founders or late partners in the firms. Other companies of lawyers, there being few presidential candidates, use the names of their own more private but no less distinguished guiding spirits. Aren't these "misleading trade names"? Are not potential clients affected by an implicit boast that community pillars serve as partners? If the bar wishes to take no risks in deception, ought it not require law firms to use the names of those actually in practice? No, says the ABA's ethics committee; it would, after all, be rather awkward for a firm to have to change its name every time one of its titled partners passes on. Old customs are thus approved, new ideas rejected, without apparent consistency. Like law, ethics is a complex science.

Entrenched interests charge that young lawyers use the term "legal clinic" to imply that they are "virtuous."[18] That is misleading, they say, because there is nothing to back up the claim but the name. Throughout the country, however, there are lawyers who were once on the bench but who resigned either to go into politics or to make money. They continue to use the title "judge." Yes, they *were* judges, but what subtle virtue is conveyed by their clinging to the title? What influence or extra knowledge are they trying to hint at?

The case against Jacoby and Meyers made its way through the administrative appeal process during 1976. In November the case came before the California Supreme Court, a majority of the bar's statewide disciplinary committee having rubber-stamped the local committee's forty-five-day suspension recommendation of one year earlier. At the supreme court hearing, counsel for the state bar repeated the arguments against the use of the term "legal clinic." He did not mention to the justices that the governing body of the state bar had, shortly before, executed a complete about-face and recommended a change in the California code of lawyers' ethics to permit the use of those forbidden words.

Why do lawyers press for things that their own clients have already repudiated? Leonard Jacoby put his finger on it in 1975, when the state bar announced it would consider the question of reforming the rules: "It's like being against Vietnam in 1960."[19] Jacoby and Meyers had simply come out for reform ahead of conventional wisdom, and were now paying for their foresight. The bar's prosecution of them was the predictable response of traditionalists unable to persuade themselves that times have changed. Defenders of the disastrous course can always be found, right up to the last minute and probably even beyond.

In May 1977, a little more than four years after charges were first pressed, the California Supreme Court ruled against the state bar and exonerated Jacoby and Meyers. It is unconstitutional, the court said, to discipline lawyers for giving interviews about the delivery of legal service in America."The First Amendment protects the freedom of expression of all citizens, including lawyers," the court declared. Jacoby and Meyers, it said, "have a right not only to respond to questions from the media on important issues but also a right to seek out the media to express their views." The court also noted that in its 210-page brief the state bar failed even to discuss whether the term "legal clinic" was in fact deceptive. It was not, the court concluded.[20]

"The American People Are Like Children": The Ethics of Advertising

Commercial advertising of legal services, properly speaking, began on February 22, 1976, when the Legal Clinic of Bates & O'Steen inserted in the *Arizona Republic* the ad pictured complete below. The newspaper circulates throughout Arizona and in several communities outside the state.

But much had gone before. In March 1974, John R. Bates and Van O'Steen, both 1972 law school graduates, had started a legal clinic modeled closely on that of their California counterparts. Because of

Jacoby's and Meyers' problems, Bates and O'Steen carefully refrained from talking to the Phoenix press; there was no open house, no press kit, and even reporters from afar were treated warily. The Arizona state bar left the clinic alone. It operated quietly, serving a few hundred clients but making little money.

In June 1975, the Supreme Court issued its *Goldfarb* decision, declaring that lawyering is a business subject to the antitrust laws. The implications were broad: private restraints on lawyers' economic activities—like, for example, the bar's rules against advertising—might be unlawful. That same month, the Court also ruled that the First Amendment protects not only political speech (like newspaper columns or my opinions in this book) but also commercial speech, including advertising. (The case involved a Virginia weekly newspaper that carried an advertisement for a New York abortion clinic at a time when abortions were unlawful in Virginia. The state prosecuted the newspaper, but the Court threw the case out.)

In February 1976, in response to pressures these cases were generating, the ABA relaxed somewhat its tight restrictions on lawyer advertising (page 99). Bates and O'Steen decided to test the waters.

When the ad appeared, the Arizona state bar pounced. Within two months the board of governors recommended to the state supreme court that the two Phoenix lawyers be suspended from practice for one week each. An administrative committee had advocated suspensions of six months each, but the board of governors concluded that Bates and O'Steen had run the ad in good faith as a test of the Arizona code of lawyers' ethics.

In May, the U.S. Supreme Court decided another advertising case, this one a little closer to Bates' and O'Steen's home. The Court voided rules of the Virginia Board of Pharmacy that forbade druggists to advertise drug prices. The Court explicitly left open the question of whether the ruling would apply to lawyers, doctors, and other professionals.

In August of 1976, three months later, the Arizona Supreme Court brushed aside all legal arguments against the code, declining to apply the Virginia pharmacy case. But the state court did rescind the one-week suspensions in favor of official censure (*i.e.*, a tongue-lashing). Bates and O'Steen appealed to the U.S. Supreme Court.

Let us pause to consider the arguments against lawyer advertising.

> The traditional ban [says Ethical Consideration 2–9] is rooted in the public interest. Competitive advertising would encourage extravagant, artful, self-laudatory brashness in seeking business and thus could mislead the layman. Furthermore, it would inevitably produce unrealistic expectations in particular cases and bring about distrust of the law and lawyers. Thus public confidence in our legal system would be impaired by such advertisements of professional services. The attorney-client relationship is personal and unique and should not be established as the result of pressures and deceptions. History has demonstrated that public confidence in the legal system is best preserved by strict, self-imposed controls over, rather than by, unlimited advertising.

This sweeping set of generalizations is perhaps the most extraordinary collection of non sequiturs in the entire Code of Professional Responsibility. (1) It neglects the informational value of advertising. (2) It assumes that all advertising is deceptive. (3) It ignores the higher public interest rooted in the First Amendment. (4) It overlooks the vast ground between "self-imposed controls" and "unlimited advertising."

The phraseology is not a result of muddleheadedness, however. It is deliberate. It is a further illustration of the lawyer's propensity to rules of overkill. If advertising were allowed, they reason, then some ads will be bad; therefore, ban all ads.

Advertising is one of those prickly subjects on which most Americans have a ready opinion. Advertisements are the butt of jokes. Some hold that advertising is profoundly manipulative; others that most or all advertising is deceptive. But it is astonishing that lawyers who spend much of their professional lives representing corporate clients whose very existence depends on advertising can so harshly denounce it.

In December 1975, the ABA held a conference in Chicago for the heads of all the state and large metropolitan bar associations to present and discuss a draft of new rules that would permit extensive lawyer advertising. The rules were prepared by the ABA's ethics committee in response to pressures from the Antitrust Division of the Justice Department in Washington. The overwhelming consensus of the delegates (among whose clientele numbered all sorts of advertisers) was that the rules were bad, that advertising is bad, that the leadership of the ABA had gone a little crazy. The predominant cry was that when lawyers start to advertise they will inevitably deceive, dupe, and delude the public, that all the worst qualities that the public imputes to lawyers (and that lawyers are constantly at such pains to deny) will be shown to be true. Advertising, they feared, would allow lawyers to mulct their clients through dazzling or tantalizing come-ons about services and benefits that can never be guaranteed.

Hundreds of lurid examples were proffered to show how raucous and rancid the air would become if lawyers could advertise. Here are two taken from the dissent of S. White Rhyne, Jr., to a District of Columbia ethics committee report advocating drastic liberalization of the rules:

> Lawyer C has an office with his name and the words "Attorney at Law" in the front window in two-foot-high flashing neon letters. On top of the building is a billboard with a picture of the blindfolded goddess "Justice," holding scales in one hand, a large illuminated dollar sign in the other. Beneath the picture is the legend, "Lawyer C for Big Judgments." On weekends, C's employees walk the streets, handing out balloons and bumper stickers with the same legend, and an airplane writes it in the sky. Lawyer C later begins practicing under the trade name, "Big Judgments, P.C."
> The law firm of D and E advertises "You saw your doctor and

you still hurt? See us and perhaps we can help relieve the pain. Our prescriptions can restore your wealth if not your health." On radio and television, the same message is preceded by a dulcet voice crooning "Zap your M.D., hire D and E."[21]

What a poor opinion Rhyne has of the average lawyer's ethics and of the public's judgment. The fulminations against advertising are indicative of a fear by the establishment that lower-class lawyers will be carried away. "We know," the leaders of the bar seem to be saying, "what lust we have for 'filthy lucre.' We know we represent clients we would never in our right minds associate with outside the office (or, if we do associate with them, we do so only because it is politic, not because we like to).* We do that, we know, because we are well paid for it. We know we spend our lives in pursuit of obscure things because we are paid well. We also know that we are the cream of the profession. Imagine what those lawyers with thinner blood would do given half a chance."

But the code of ethics forbids deception and misrepresentation. It also enjoins the lawyer to be competent. Permitting advertising would not restrict or abolish these rules. To the contrary, according to expert witnesses at a trial of the advertising issue in Virginia, "remedies for deceptive or misleading statements by lawyers would be more easily enforced if the statements are made in published form rather than orally in the privacy of an office consultation."[23]

But there is more to the opposition than that. Lawyer advertising would communicate that which is now unspoken. One important thing now unspoken is that the lawyer performs many needless services for relatively high fees (see Chapter 5). Advertising may help to

---

*In perhaps the most forthright statement on this point ever made, Chesterfield Smith, ABA president in 1973–1974, testified to the Senate Subcommittee on Representation of Citizen Interests (the Tunney Subcommittee) in February 1974: "I have represented some of the greatest cruds of all Florida."[22] His point was that the views of one's clients should not be imputed to oneself because lawyers often represent those with whom they disagree. But Smith's characteristically pungent way of expressing this point speaks volumes about the nature of the lawyer's practice. This is not to demean Smith, who is undoubtedly one of the most progressive and fearless of the recent leaders of the bar.

make this clear. Hence advertising will be a catalyst for drastic reform of the general style of practice. Legal clinics will no longer be novelties; they will be hard commercial necessities. That is all to the good as far as the public is concerned, but undeniably it will make the lawyer's life more harried and bothersome.

These considerations help explain the glaring contradiction in the code of ethics that prohibits on the one hand sensible, easily obtained directories of lawyers and, on the other, permits directories and even ratings of lawyers under bar auspices. The code of ethics of every state permits, as the CPR puts it, "a listing in a reputable* law list or legal directory giving brief biographical and other informative data."

In these directories, rarely accessible to the lay public (because they are expensive and usually sit only on the shelves of law libraries or larger public libraries), the lawyer may list a variety of biographical data, including schools attended, public offices held, military service (why military service?), legal authorships (why can't Louis Auchincloss note the novels he has written?), bar memberships and positions, foreign language ability, references, and, with consent, names of clients. Some of the directories, like *Martindale-Hubbell,* the most well-known and comprehensive nationwide directory of lawyers, rate lawyers according to proficiency and reputation, and the ABA blesses this practice.†

One of the peculiar compromises that the code allows the directory

---

*Most states carry over verbatim this sentence from the CPR: "A law list is conclusively established to be reputable if it is certified by the American Bar Association as being in compliance with its rules and standards."[24]

†According to Monroe H. Freedman, "Not every attorney is permitted to advertise his or her professional autobiography, prestigious associations, and important clients in *Martindale-Hubbell.* One must await an invitation from the publisher to apply for an 'a' rating, which can be achieved only upon submission of favorable references from 16 judges and attorneys who have themselves already received an 'a' rating. For all other members of the profession, *Martindale-Hubbell* is a closed book." Freedman points out also that *The Attorneys' Register,* another list holding a certificate of acceptability from the ABA, states explicitly that its purpose is to enable the listed attorney to secure "SUBSTANTIAL" legal business. The *Register* states that it is distributed free to "a careful selection of banks and trust companies, important industrial corporations, insurance companies, financing institutions, and the like, who are believed to be prolific forwarders of SUBSTANTIAL legal matters."[25]

to make is in the area of specialization. It is a closely guarded non-secret that lawyers specialize. Even "general practitioner" connotes a limitation of practice to certain substantive areas. No lawyer can know or practice well more than a fraction of the law. Except for patent, trademark, and admiralty lawyers, however, attorneys are not permitted to state on their letterheads or elsewhere what they actually feel competent to do. (Why these three and not others? Because historically practitioners of these branches of the law had so listed themselves before the code came along to prohibit it; the custom lingered.) So it happens all the time that troubled people ring up a lawyer's office (having picked the name at random from the telephone book) and say they wish to make an appointment, only to be told that Mr. So-and-So handles oil and gas interests exclusively.

Putting this nuisance on the general public is not regarded as a great curse, but it would obviously foul up the engines of business were the corporate client to have to call around blindly to find an antitrust lawyer rather than an automobile accident litigator. So the ABA code, while still forbidding the blunt announcement of specialization, allows the lawyer to state in lists like Martindale-Hubbell "one or more fields of law in which the lawyer or law firm concentrates [and] a statement that practice is limited to one or more fields of law." Roughly, this means that the lawyer should say "practice limited to labor law," rather than "I specialize in labor law." On such metaphysical subtleties do right and wrong hang.

There is still another way by which some lawyers can legitimately advertise and others cannot. That is by holding office in bar associations (especially in bar association committees dealing with various branches of the law). Frequently lawyers have told me that they would talk to me in their capacity as a bar official but not as a mere lawyer. In either capacity, their names and pictures look the same in print. But one way is sanctioned and the other is not. It should not need much emphasis that lawyers with institutional practices have far more time and resources to give to bar associations; hence they are disproportionately represented among those who "advertise" in this bar-approved manner.

In 1974, Consumers Union decided to compile a directory of lawyers in Arlington County, Virginia, just across the river from Washington. The idea was to publish for general consumer use as complete
a directory as possible of how the lawyers in that county conduct their
practices. Consumers Union is not interested in rating the lawyers; it
supposes that publication of answers to a select list of questions by a
nonprofit organization in a pamphlet which lawyers have not subsi-
dized will make the information less biased than current lawyer directories.

Among the questions Consumers Union asked were these:

> Do you regularly participate in continuing legal education ac-
> tivities?
>
> Estimate the percentage of time you spend, and your firm
> spends, handling matters for the following types of clients. [The
> questionnaire set forth the following categories: individuals,
> small businesses, large businesses, institutions such as schools
> and unions.]
>
> Is it your policy to discuss fees with the potential client at the
> initial interview?
>
> Do you customarily charge a fee for an initial consultation
> when no further services are rendered to the client on the mat-
> ter?
>
> What is the hourly billing charge for your services?
>
> Do you itemize your bills?
>
> How do you handle client complaints about billing?[26]

The questionnaire also called for a listing of average fees for a
variety of common types of legal problems, including uncontested
adoptions, change of name, incorporating a small business, individual
bankruptcy, closing and settlement on single-family homes, simple
wills, and others.

The Virginia bar was unhappy about these questions, the answers
to none of which will be found in an ABA-approved directory. Some
lawyers at first inclined to answer the survey soon discovered that the
Virginia state bar would not look kindly on their cooperation with

Consumers Union. (Virginia has no procedure to certify legal lists as reputable; the state defers to the ABA, which made clear that it would reject the list if presented.)

So Consumers Union together with the Virginia Citizens Consumer Council filed a federal suit against the ABA, the Virginia state bar, and the Virginia Supreme Court (which has the final word in the state on such matters). In December 1976, the court ruled that, with the possible exception of the questions concerning fees, the Virginia ethics code is unconstitutional in forbidding lawyers to cooperate with the CU survey.[27] (The court had previously dismissed the ABA as party since it had no official role in Virginia.)

The state agencies had argued that the bar's ethical rules were a permissible means of regulating the free speech rights of lawyers. This argument was premised on the belief that advertising would lead to deception and that the state had constitutional authority to regulate false, misleading, and fraudulent advertising. But the state could not show that the rule of overkill is the only way to regulate deception. The Virginia authorities said that to permit advertising subject only to rules against fraud would be "prohibitively expensive and time-consuming." (The court responded: "Speculation and hyperbole are the imaginative foundations of any such contention.")[28]

The same reasoning, of course, applies to all types of advertising. A case could be made for the proposition that most advertising is to some degree misleading. But we don't *therefore* ban advertising. We can say that children who get up and go out of the house during the day are bound to come to mischief. So we can order them to lie abed. This is a risk-free procedure, but it also transforms children into vegetables. Lawyers' rules against advertising, whether directly or through directories and other lists, smack of the same logic. In their attempt to create an antiseptic environment, they foreclose to lawyers and potential clients a large realm of freedom to do much good.

That this is so is evident from the question that went unasked in both Arizona's case against Bates and O'Steen and Virginia's case against lawyers wishing to cooperate with CU; namely, what actual harm did or might occur as the result of the publication of the advertisement or the circulation of the directory in controversy? When you operate under an overkill rule, you don't have to worry about the facts. That is why the argument over lawyer advertising so frequently has an unreal quality to it.

But an honest answer to the question would reveal that there is very little danger, if any, in these two cases. It is beyond dispute that the "reasonable fees" Bates & O'Steen advertised are in fact reasonable, in view of the prevailing rates in Phoenix. Moreover, no one has suggested that Bates & O'Steen indulges in "bait and switch" (advertising one rate but telling clients who actually walk in the door that for one reason or another the fee will be different). And the protestations of some that the fee quotations are misleading because the categories (like uncontested adoptions and divorces) are fuzzy don't stand up. The categories that Bates & O'Steen listed are precisely those that occur in prepaid legal insurance policies—and, more pertinently perhaps, in the now discarded "minimum fee schedules" (see Chapter 5) that lawyers long looked to.

Still, the fee question is vexed. As many rightly point out, the bald declaration that the attorney charges, say, fifty dollars an hour may be misleading. "Fee information on services, as opposed to products or goods, may encompass so many variables as to make accurate comparison between fee statements on specified services literally impossible. . . . Attempts to publish a set cost, or even an average cost would prove to be meaningless and misleading."[29] But this argument is hardly dispositive of the question. That certain types of fee ads may be misleading says nothing about those that are not, and a look at the Consumers Union list of fee questions shows none whose answers could not be structured to avoid deception.

To argue against advertising of legal services is to exalt those services into mysteries as complex as any that a medieval theologian ever had to wrestle with. It presumes that the nature of a lawyer's work is so arcane that the public is better served by believing that all lawyers are virtually the same in competence, patience, eagerness to help, and professionalism. For in the absence of advertising, the public has little else to believe, given the enormous difficulty of finding out anything concrete about lawyers. But this presumption is erroneous. Though they may not be able to solve their own problems, people know only too well what ails them. The public is not so divorced from reality, nor is the law so complex. Moreover, what is deceptive in public advertising is not likely to be much less deceptive in private consultations. (How many people have ever heard a lawyer say, "Oh, that's easy. I can write that will [or fix that problem] with no trouble at all"?)

In the final analysis, such arguments are the equivalent of President Nixon's celebrated statement just before his second inaugural that the American people are like children who have to be led by the hand and told what to do. This attitude is the very antithesis of self-government, presuming as it does an ignorance and a helplessness so vast as to belie the traditions on which this nation was founded. Since lawyers are often heard to celebrate these verities, the argument is especially unconvincing when it comes from their mouths.

The only meaningful way to understand the bar's traditional prohibition against advertising, I submit, is as a complex and heretofore successful conspiracy in restraint of trade, a manipulation of law in the naked self-interest of lawyers as a collective entity. By transforming an otherwise mundane agreement not to compete through advertising into an article of faith that professionalism excludes all forms of promotion, no matter how well-intentioned and informative, the bar has managed for decades to avert the public gaze from what has really been going on: higher prices, a comfortable existence for many lawyers, and a consequent diminution in the delivery of legal services. That this is the purpose of the rule is made all the clearer by the forms of self-promotion that the bar allows.

When in 1975 the Supreme Court finally ruled squarely that the legal profession is subject to the antitrust laws, the deep crack in the ethic of advertising finally reached the surface. Almost immediately the bar leadership reacted. It was quite clear by then to those with high office in the national organization that the bar would have to make some effort to reform itself, if not for legal reasons then for public relations purposes. That is why the ethics committee busied itself rewriting the rules of canon 2 to let lawyers do all sorts of promotion, like placing fee information in the Yellow Pages. But the flip-flop was too sudden and drastic for the leaders of the local bar, who constitute a large proportion of the voting members of the ABA's policy-making body. In February 1976, the ABA voted down all but a few relaxations of the rules.* And even these changes have won little acceptance since then at the state level, where the rules of ethics count.

A few months later, therefore, in June 1976, after several years of prosecuting other professional groups for similar restraints of trade, the Justice Department finally stepped in to test the question directly. As we saw, it sued the ABA for its role in the promulgation of the various bans against advertising, naming more than 200,000 members as co-conspirators. The suit itself is peculiar, however, because it presumes that the mere writing of a "model code" by a private association with no enforcement powers amounts to both an agreement to restrain trade and to some evidence of its power to do so. (Though I may have agreed to abide by its code when I joined the ABA, the real source of any legal obligation I have derives from the rules of the courts to which I have been admitted to practice, and since these are not the rules of a private association, the antitrust conspiracy is a little hard to detect.) The ABA has announced its intention to fight the case tooth and claw, and it will doubtless drag on for some time beyond the publication of this book.

Another ground of attack seems more promising, and that is the ground taken by Bates and O'Steen, to whom we must now return.

*Among the new items of information that lawyers may list: whether credit cards are accepted; office hours; statement of initial consultation fees; statement of availability on request of a written schedule of fees. But these are qualified by the requirement that each new item be listed according to a rigid form to be specified in each state; ethically, says the ABA, there can be no individuality in the manner of stating these interesting bits of information. If the state does not choose to set forth such a form, then presumably the lawyer may not list these items.

We left the two Arizona lawyers appealing to the Supreme Court, having been advised that their simple advertisement was unethical and hence a violation of Arizona law, for which a censure was to be the penalty. Their suit parallels that of Consumers Union: in each case the argument is that the state may not constitutionally enforce a rule abridging anyone's right to publish a non-deceptive advertisement (or other form of self-promotion), or cooperate in such a publication.

A closely divided Supreme Court agreed in late 1977.[30] For a bare majority of five, Justice Harry A. Blackmun declared that the First Amendment protects advertising of routine legal services and the prices of those services. The decision is thus relatively narrow; Justice Blackmun explicitly declined to consider whether advertisements are permissible that boast of the quality of service to be performed, nor did he spell out precisely what divides a routine from a non-routine service. The Court also declined to pass on the constitutional propriety of a ban on broadcast advertising.

To the argument that "advertising does not provide a complete foundation on which to select an attorney," Justice Blackmun responded that "it seems peculiar to deny the consumer, on the ground that the information is incomplete, at least some of the relevant information needed to reach an informed decision. The alternative—the prohibition of advertising—serves only to restrict the information that flows to consumers. . . . [W]e view as dubious any justification that is based on the benefits of public ignorance."

He also rejected the argument that advertising would adversely affect the quality of service by forcing the lawyer indiscriminately to use the "standard package" of services advertised, even if a particular client would not benefit from it. "An attorney who is inclined to cut quality will do so regardless of the rule on advertising."

Finally, Justice Blackmun dismissed the supposition that advertising will create mammoth "enforcement" problems. The argument is that "because the public lacks sophistication in legal matters, it may be particularly susceptible to misleading or deceptive advertising by lawyers," hence a regulatory agency will be necessary to monitor lawyers' ads. And because ads will be numerous, the argument goes, the regulatory burden may be too great. This is a curious argument on its face: it could just as easily be advanced as justification for outlawing all advertising. How many people, after all, know enough about biochemistry to judge whether or not advertisements for pain-killers are misleading? Justice Blackmun noted that "it is at least somewhat incongruous for the opponents of advertising to extol the virtues and altruism of the legal profession at one point, and, at another, to assert that its members will seize the opportunity to mislead and distort."

Left unspoken was the bar's real worry: that the current regulatory mechanism, the "grievance committees" operated by the bar itself, would be wholly unable to function if presented with any sizable number of questionable ads. (Such inability is likely true, as we will note in some detail in Chapter 8.) If the bar's enforcement mechanism cannot function, therefore, the duty of disciplining lawyers for violating the code of ethics will be removed from the private hands of the bar and placed in those of a public body. This troubles lawyers mightily: if they lose the power to discipline, the centerpiece of their power to control competition through self-regulation would vanish.

For that very reason, the bar's reaction to *Bates* v. *State Bar of Arizona* has been predictable. With a few exceptions, the leadership of the bar, especially at the national level, has pressed for as narrow a liberalization of the rules as possible. Because *Bates* is itself narrow and opaque, the bar has ample opportunity to continue to exert authority over the manner and content of advertising.

Thus, the ABA Task Force on Lawyer Advertising, appointed immediately after the Court's ruling, wrote two alternative redrafts of the ethical rules relating to advertising. One, the so-called "regulatory" approach, was highly restrictive; it forbade all advertising except for a narrow category of acceptable statements. The other appeared less parsimonious; it permitted the advertising of any information not "false, fraudulent, misleading or deceptive." But the Task Force defined these terms in a generously broad way—so broad, in fact, that the executive committee of the Association of the Bar in New York concluded that the original Bates & O'Steen ad would violate the rule (the very ad, that is, that the Supreme Court said could not constitutionally be prohibited). This recalls the bar's technique in its fight against prepaid legal services.

In any event, the governing body of the ABA accepted the more restrictive draft, after modifying it slightly to permit a modest kind of radio, but not television, advertising.

Because changes to the code of ethics have legal force only when adopted in each state, the ABA voted to circulate both sets of proposals to the various state committees, so the prospect is that there will be no uniform bar rules in the near future. That means that the fight over legal advertising has only just begun. Another long struggle, no more edifying than the battle against prepaid legal services, may thus be in the offing.

A Note on Soliciting

In the folklore of the bar, a lawyer sins most grievously when he solicits the business of a particular individual. The reports of bar committees in the first decades of the century are full of investigations and denunciations of lawyers who employed "runners" at the scenes of accidents. The runner advised injured persons that their employers could bring in a nice verdict against the wrongdoer. This was the ultimate degradation because it was the ultimate commercialization —and because it was a course of conduct on which well-heeled and well-connected lawyers need never embark. The practice has never died completely. A New York court censured a lawyer in 1974 for sending Spanish-speaking runners to the courthouses to suggest to any confused-looking potential plaintiff or defendant that he knew a lawyer who could help.[31]

Like advertising, solicitation, it has been variously claimed, "would lead to the assertion of fraudulent claims, the corruption of public officials, the stirring up of litigation, attacks on marital stability, and the unnecessary invalidation of transactions due to the discovery of lawyers' mistakes, . . . overreaching, overcharging, underrepresentation, and misrepresentation."[32] Quite a heady list.

A rather large irony stalks all these arguments, however. Advertising is condemned because of its alleged tendency to deceive people who cannot be expected to evaluate lawyers' claims. If that is true, this very ignorance will prevent them from undertaking to vindicate their legal rights. Law is complex, the number of statutes creating rights is by now truly staggering, and the circumstances under which these statutes can be used, as interpreted by the courts, defies neat summary. The lay public can no more be expected to understand all this than it can to evaluate the competence of a lawyer. To hold that lawyers cannot broadcast to the public the nature of their rights and a suggestion as to the means to vindicate them is to misread entirely the nature of an open society. We all depend on the initiative of those who know to tell us how we can benefit from what they know.

Will such a position, if implemented, stir up litigation? Of course —if it is possible to stir up any more litigation in this suit-drenched land. But what of it? As with the issue of competence and advertising, there are other rules that forbid the filing of frivolous suits. And if a suit is not frivolous, is it conscionable that a class of people with no ready access to lawyers should be deprived of the opportunity to assert their rights?

As before, the rules against solicitation are written in such a way as to permit the very evil to go on at one level removed from popular notice. Thus lawyers are permitted to solicit friends, relatives, clients, and former clients.

Lawyers with corporate clients have ways to solicit that are denied to the class of personal lawyers who can best serve the most ignorant. The institutional lawyer at a cocktail party overhears a conversation between the head of a company and a social friend concerning some problem the company is having. The lawyer insinuates himself into the conversation and, affecting a casual manner, says, "Gee, Fred, if that's what's going on, you really ought to talk to my partner, Bob, who is one of the country's leading experts on exactly that problem. He saved one of our clients a million dollars last year just on that point alone." These remarks violate the code in half a dozen ways, and yet they are all too typical. (Statistics are impossible to come by, but during 1976 I asked various lawyer friends to keep their ears open at cocktail parties and like gatherings, and such remarks, of which the above is an amalgam, were reported on a handful of occasions. They involved partners of some of the most glittering of blue-chip firms.)

But solicitation is valuable not only as a way of lining a lawyer's pocket. It also serves—or can serve—to further the legal interests of the public. A bar that proclaims as fundamental the duty to ensure that all people have access to legal counsel ought to acknowledge that it is no less fundamental for people to have access to legal *knowledge* about what a lawyer's time would be worth to them. If it is legitimate for a group like the United Mine Workers or the National Association for the Advancement of Colored People* to engage in acts of solicitation to inform a select group of people of their rights, it ought to be no less permissible for individual lawyers to do likewise.

*In 1963, the Supreme Court ruled that Virginia could not prohibit NAACP lawyers from soliciting plaintiffs in school desegregation cases. Local chapters of the NAACP had invited members of the legal staff to address meetings of parents, at which time printed forms were circulated for parents to sign up as litigants authorizing the staff to represent them and their children. Under a hastily enacted amendment to the Virginia lawyers' code, the procedure was declared a criminal solicitation. The Virginia Court of Appeals ruled that the NAACP and its affiliates were "fomenting and soliciting legal business in which they were not parties and have no pecuniary right or liability, and which they channel to the enrichment of certain lawyers employed by them [the NAACP lawyers made less than the prevailing rate], at no cost to the litigants and over which the litigants have no control." In voiding the law, the U.S. Supreme Court ruled that litigation "is a means for achieving the lawful objectives of equality of treatment. . . . It is thus a form of political expression. . . . [Under the anti-solicitation law] a person who advises another that his legal rights have been infringed and refers him to a particular attorney . . . for assistance has committed a crime. . . . There thus inheres in the statute the greatest danger of smothering all discussion looking to the eventual institution of litigation on behalf of the rights of members of an unpopular minority."[33] The NAACP case served as precedent for the Mine Workers case four years later.

For some years the District of Columbia has been more tolerant than most states in acknowledging these heretical views. In 1971, it pioneered the first use of solicitation in civil matters unconnected with basic constitutional rights. The Stern Community Law Firm, a private, nonprofit, foundation-funded organization, placed an advertisement in 1970 in the Washington newspapers commenting on the overcrowded conditions of the community's orphanages and other public institutions for unwanted children. "One solution to this tragic problem is adoption," the ad continued, noting that "many people who would like to adopt a child have been wrongly discouraged" and had been given a host of reasons that were not in fact legal impediments to adoption. The advertisement listed five commonly stated but erroneous discouragements (e.g., the prospective parent is over forty-five). The Stern Firm offered free legal services to any parent who wished to adopt a child or to any prospective parent who wished to give his child up for adoption.

The local grievance committee "began with an attitude hostile to the idea of advertising," according to Monroe Freedman, then the Stern Firm's director, but in time the bar was persuaded that the advertisement was essentially proper (it made Freedman take his name off the ad, in which he was identified as director of the firm).[34] This was apparently the first time any bar association had sanctioned commercial advertising by a group of lawyers to make the public aware of their services and to invite the public to stop by.

Of course, the novelty of the District bar's opinion is tempered by the realization that its approval was extended only to nonprofit organizations. Nevertheless, the bar ought not prevent attorneys in private practice from soliciting in a like manner. Marna S. Tucker, a member of the District of Columbia's ethics committee, suggests one situation in which such solicitation might make its first appearance. She represented a federal employee whom the Civil Service Commission had unlawfully deprived of a considerable sum of money. Tucker took the case to court and won an increase in his salary. But government agencies that lose such cases don't immediately apply the logic of the rule to all other comparable situations. "There are many other people who are making less than they should under the same circumstances," Tucker notes. "Why shouldn't I be permitted to circulate to them a notice to the effect that there is a payable claim? Why shouldn't I be able to put an ad in the *Washington Post?*"[35]

It is difficult to see what harm could ensue. The solicitation or advertisement would pressure the Civil Service Commission to abide by court rulings; it would alert people to their rights. But it would not unjustly enrich anyone. It would, however, bring the expertise of the lawyer to bear on the problems of the public. It would magnify the people's access to legal services by creating in them an awareness of the usefulness of such services, not as an abstract proposition but as a concrete and personal concern. If a new breed of lawyers grew comfortably wealthy because they could more efficiently litigate common concerns, there is nothing the present leadership could say that would not be more embarrassing than effective.

Is it possible to look with equanimity on the spread of lawyer advertising and solicitation? Can it ever be professional? I believe so. I believe the cases just discussed demonstrate the possibilities. Those who suppose it will inevitably demean the profession in the eyes of the public believe so largely because they identify professionalism with the willingness to forgo advertising. To a lawyer steeped in this tradition, there is little solace to be offered. But there is another way to view the changes that are coming. Professionalism consists in doing right though the sanctions of law are absent. Permitting advertising and solicitation—insofar as neither is deceptive or misleading—finally gives each lawyer the freedom to demonstrate a true professionalism. Some lawyers will doubtless transgress the ethic of honor and service and will attempt to mislead and deceive, but at least it will be reasonably clear who they are, and we need no longer mistake them for the leadership of the bar.

CHAPTER 5

The Ethics of Fees:
The Bar vs. Its Clients

Preliminary Double-Talk

We have seen that lawyers have drawn strict rules designed to avoid commercialization of the bar. One would suppose, therefore, that when it comes to the core of commercialization—the receipt of money for services—the bar would be at its strictest. One would be wrong. In the area of fees almost anything goes.

In *The Superlawyers,* Joseph C. Goulden tells the story of the fee that Clark Clifford (adviser to presidents, Secretary of Defense in 1968) charged Charles Revson, head of Revlon Corporation, in 1959. Revlon was under investigation as the sponsor of the discredited "$64,000 Question" television show. Max Kampelman, another politically connected Washington lawyer, after considerable work, persuaded a Senate subcommittee that Revson had no knowledge of the show's rigging and that the subcommittee had no need to call Revson to testify. Kampelman was glad to have the decision, but Revson was talked into demanding time to "clear his name." Kampelman decided that "it couldn't help but be a disaster," and turned the matter over to Clifford. "I took Revson to Clifford's office, and we went through the papers and laid it out, the whole background," Kampelman said. "Clark couldn't have spent more than a handful of hours on the case, him and his whole firm . . . and that includes the hearings." Clifford's bill? $25,000.[1]

The ABA's code of ethics does not openly advocate human vanity and greed, or even the desire to be more comfortable than others, as an excuse for a large income. An Ethical Consideration under canon 2 says that "a lawyer should not charge more than a reasonable fee."[2] That is something, but not much, rather like a canon that would read: "A lawyer should act rightly in all things." Strangely, this sentence is the sole remark in the Ethical Considerations about the propriety of fees.

The corresponding Disciplinary Rule[3] is no more help. Part A says: "A lawyer shall not enter into an agreement for, charge, or collect an illegal or clearly excessive fee." Notice that it says "clearly excessive." "Just a little bit excessive" or "perhaps excessive but then again maybe not" are permissible under this wording. One looks to Part B, the definition of "clearly excessive," for guidance. Part B says: "A fee is clearly excessive when, after a review of the facts, a lawyer of ordinary prudence would be left with a definite and firm conviction that the fee is in excess of a reasonable fee."

A fee will thus be deemed excessive only when an ordinary lawyer reviews the situation and, try though he may, cannot avoid the conclusion that the fee is excessive! Note that he must have a "definite and firm conviction" of the excessiveness. If he has any doubts, the fee must be within the bounds of professionalism. And why must the reviewing attorney be one of "ordinary prudence"? Why not expect the bar to raise itself to a height of moral excellence by reflecting on fees through the eyes of one above the norm of ordinary virtue? About all that can be safely concluded is that a *grossly* inflated fee is unethical. This is hardly the stuff of overkill.

Was Clifford's $25,000 fee "clearly excessive" for working a "handful of hours"? Clifford achieved no particular result for Revson; according to Kampelman, "the Committee clobbered Revson. They knocked his brains out." Clifford did not have his time pre-empted, nor were the time and labor involved anything other than minimal. Dealing with Revson may have been novel, but many other Washington lawyers who understood Congress could have done the job. There had been no prior relationship with the client. The fee was more than would be customarily charged; at least it was considerably more than Kampelman would have charged.

What, then, can account for the fee? Only Clifford's reputation. Under the circumstances, of what use was that reputation? Very little, it seems, except for Clifford's reasoning (again, according to Kampelman): "When Revson gets the bill, he'll cuss and call me a son of a bitch and the whole business. But he'll pay it. And next year, when he's down in Miami Beach playing gin rummy with his buddies, he'll talk about his 'friend Clark Clifford' and his 'lawyer Clark Clifford,' and how much the so-and-so charged him —and it'll be worth $25,000 to him." This is an interesting argument. It amounts to saying that under the circumstances no fee however large would have been "clearly excessive" because the value of the fee lay in its very size. And if Revson did boast of it, then the fee took on another character. It became, in a way, an indirect advertisement and solicitation, for other businessmen would be impressed by fees that size: obviously a lawyer must know what he is doing to charge like that.

But ethics committees seldom raise an eyebrow over inflated fees.* Why should they? A fee of the Clifford variety is a comfortable umbrella for lesser lawyers to sit beneath. If their own clients object, they can always say, with truth, that their own fee is "less than other lawyers charge around here."

The point is this: While the rules of ethics talk about excessive fees, the bar rarely detects excesses in actual cases. A West Virginia ethics committee in 1962 went so far as to say that even when a court found a lawyer's fee to be unreasonable, the committee would not call it

---

*Because of inflation, $25,000 in 1959 is the equivalent of more than $51,000 in 1977.

unethical.*[4] Lawyers talk about excessive fees in the abstract, but their
real concern is rather with fees that are too low. At the nether reaches
of the fee question, lawyers take action.

The Minimum Fee: How Lawyers Broke the Law

In 1971, Lewis and Ruth Goldfarb purchased a home in Fairfax
County, Virginia. To secure a mortgage, they were required to take
out a title insurance policy. To do that they needed the services of a
Virginia lawyer. Although Lewis Goldfarb is an attorney himself (he
worked across the river in Washington at the Federal Trade Commission), he was not a member of the Virginia bar, and in any event a
person cannot certify his own title. The first lawyer Goldfarb talked
to said the fee would be 1 percent of the value of the property, exactly
the charge called for in the Fairfax County Bar Association fee schedule, which was a printed list that indicated a tariff for a variety of
transactions (divorces, wills, property closings, and the like). The
Goldfarbs thought 1 percent of the property value was a steep price
for title insurance, so they shopped around. Of the nineteen replies
they received to thirty-six letters sent to attorneys in the county, all
said the charge would be 1 percent of the property value. Some of these
lawyers indicated that they knew of no lawyers who would deviate
from the minimum fee schedule.

About eight hundred local and county bar associations had established fee schedules, which they periodically updated. Lawyers were
not the only class of entrepreneurs to publish such a list, but they were
among the few to get away with adhering to it. Others who had tried
it, like manufacturers, were sued for violating the antitrust laws,
which forbid competitors to make agreements in restraint of trade.

---

*Courts frequently are called on to decide the reasonableness of fees under various
statutory provisions allowing one party in a suit to collect attorney's fees from the other
side. But most clients still must bear their own attorney's fees, and the courts rarely
hear arguments about whether these fees are excessive.

From the earliest days of antitrust, the courts have held that agreements to fix prices and devices that have that tendency—like printed lists of suggested prices—are unlawful. Lawyers said that as professionals they were exempt from the antitrust laws, a position that was for a long time not seriously challenged.

Minimum fees were mentioned in the old (1908) canons, and the 1970 revision said that "suggested fee schedules . . . provide some guidance on the subject of reasonable fees."[5] The canons did not say that minimum fees were obligatory, however. Indeed, in 1930, when one local bar association announced that it was considering disciplining any members who failed to adhere to a proposed schedule, the ABA ethics committee stated that "any obligatory fee schedule must necessarily conflict with that independence of thought and action which is necessary to professional existence."[6] Of course, obligating an attorney to charge a fixed fee would preclude his charging *more* than the bar thought reasonable. Ever mindful of the public interest, the bar has been wary of the dangers in setting maximum fees.

On the other hand, to *undercut* the fee schedule has always been thought unprofessional. The ABA ethics committee codified this belief in 1961, when it wrote that "the habitual charging of fees less than those established in suggested or recommended minimum fee schedules, or the charging of such fees without proper justification may be evidence of unethical conduct."[7] This opinion had wide influence. "Consult, and be bound by, minimum fee schedules," said the *Michigan Basic Practice Workbook,* a set of guidelines for the practicing lawyer, in a discussion of ethics and fees.*

If lawyers had been free to disregard the minimum fee schedules,

---

*1964 edition. The Michigan booklet also, unconsciously, summed up the pervasive influence of fees on the profession, while suggesting that the minimum fees were not as reduced as they might be: "One of the most difficult aspects of the practice of law [the guide said], particularly to the new lawyer, is deciding the amount to charge for his services. Frequently, he is hesitant to comply with the minimum fees set forth in minimum fee schedules of the local bar association since he is fearful of alienating what few clients have been attracted to him at an early state of his practice. *What should be one of the most enjoyable and rewarding facets of the practice of law, the charging and receiving of fees,* frequently is the most perplexing."[8]

the tariffs might have made little impact on the general level of legal fees. But in many states, such as Virginia, lawyers were virtually forced to adhere to them. The Virginia state bar is an official arm of the state supreme court (as are the state bars in more than half the states; New York is the notable exception). Thus, when the state bar adopts a code of ethics it is backed by the force of law. In 1962, the Virginia state bar published a report listing a series of minimum fees; shortly thereafter the Fairfax County bar adopted a fee schedule. Although neither bar bound their lawyers to the tariffs listed, the state bar Committee on Legal Ethics said that if a lawyer "purely for his own advancement, intentionally and regularly bills less than the customary charges of the bar for similar services . . . [in order to] increase his business with resulting personal gain, it becomes a form of solicitation contrary to Canon 27 and also a violation of Canon 7, which forbids the efforts of one lawyer to encroach upon the employment of another."

In 1969, the minimum fees were scaled upward. The county bar said that lawyers should not feel guilty about charging fees higher than the minimums; in fact, it said, "to . . . publicly criticize lawyers who charge more than the suggested fees herein might in itself be evidence of solicitation." And in 1971 the state bar reiterated its position: "Evidence that an attorney habitually charges less than the suggested minimum fee schedule adopted by his local bar association, raises a presumption that such lawyer is guilty of misconduct." According to the opinion, this presumption would arise whether or not the discounting lawyer belonged to the county bar, which was a purely voluntary organization. In other words, a lawyer who decided to undercut the fee schedule on a regular basis could be suspended or even disbarred for violating the tariff of an organization to which he did not belong and to whose opinions he did not subscribe. Against such authority few lawyers were willing to rebel.

In January 1973, the federal district court in Virginia upheld the Goldfarbs' contention that the county bar association had violated the federal antitrust laws. Fee schedules around the country began to be withdrawn. In October of that year, the ABA Board of Governors recommended "that state and local bar associations that have not already done so give serious consideration to withdrawal or cancellation of all schedules of fees, whether or not designated as 'minimum' or 'suggested' fee schedules."[9] The ABA itself did so in February 1974, deleting all mention of fee schedules from the CPR. It is obvious that this precipitate change of heart was due not to the prickings of conscience but to the realities of a lawsuit. Although a federal court of appeals reversed the Goldfarbs' victory the following May, the Department of Justice, signaling its intention not to be outdone by private litigants, sued the Oregon state bar the day after the reversal was announced. It was the first time that the Department of Justice had ever gone after a bar association.

A year later, a unanimous Supreme Court dissolved the system of controlled fees that had prevailed throughout the century. In upholding the Goldfarbs and reversing the court of appeals, the High Court declared that fee schedules and ethical opinions "coalesced to create a pricing system that consumers could not realistically escape. [The bar's] activities constitute a classic illustration of price fixing."[10]

Thus the minimum fee schedule, a seemingly permanent feature of the legal profession throughout the twentieth century, is now a thing of the past.* But bar leaders have yet to confess that the profession had made a serious error of ethics. At most, they are willing to concede that they erred in failing to perceive the "technical" violations of the nation's laws.

---

*In theory, that is. In the fall of 1976, a sophisticated non-lawyer purchased a home in Connecticut. Knowing of the *Goldfarb* case, he assumed that his lawyer would bill him on an hourly basis for the routine closing. The lawyer sent a bill for 1 percent of the value of the house. The buyer called his lawyer in some dismay. "How much time did you spend on this?" he asked. "Oh, very little," said the lawyer. "Then why this bill?" the buyer wondered. "Listen," said the lawyer, "you won't find any lawyer around here who will charge you less."

Supplemental Income: The Strange Custom of Kickbacks

To go a step beyond the Goldfarbs, let us suppose you are about to purchase a house and you have negotiated with a lawyer on his fee. What will he do for you? Although the answer varies from state to state (in some states lawyers are rarely used), in general the lawyer will act as follows. He will review the contract that the seller's lawyer prepares. He may help arrange financing with a bank or savings and loan association. And he will examine the abstract of title.

Let us pause.

In no other personal transaction do we as consumers consult lawyers; we buy and sell automobiles and appliances, and contract for all sorts of services, and never dream of asking for legal assistance. But a home is different because the law governing real property is bizarre. When you sell a car, you sell it outright; you don't retain for yourself the right to drive it, say, on alternate Tuesday nights. You wouldn't dream of telling the new owner that he can have it as long as he doesn't paint the top yellow. And when you buy a car, you scarcely expect to be told that if you insist on keeping it outside at night, the original dealer will repossess it. But owners of homes frequently place restrictions on their land, and the law recognizes the right of a prior owner to burden the property for all subsequent purchasers—by granting an easement, for example. The law also gives spouses and children of owners certain rights in the property, rights that go with the land unless signed away or otherwise recompensed. And there are all sorts of sub-rights that can be created in land and vested in a person temporarily occupying it; leases, for example.

These restrictions and conditions are recorded in the courthouses of every county in the United States. When buying a piece of land, it is crucial to check these records before taking title or else you may discover that the seller sold you something he had no right to sell.

During the nineteenth century, checking title to real property was a staple of the lawyer's work. He would pull heavy volumes off the shelves of the county registrar, look through the records, ascertain which encumbrances lay on the property, and advise his client what they were. If the lawyer was sloppy and missed an entry or forgot to search far enough back (usually they looked back about seventy-five years), the buyer's only recourse would be to sue his lawyer. Sometimes it could even happen that the buyer would lose his land through no fault of the lawyer. The facts might have been improperly recorded or forged or not recorded at all; the rightful claimants to the property could then cause havoc. The buyer would have no recourse, except perhaps against the seller, if the seller could be found. The new homeowner might just lose all.

Beginning in 1876 in Pennsylvania, a new form of protection arose: title insurance. The idea is to insure title to your property just as you insure your car in case of accident. If something goes wrong, regardless of fault, you can at least recover the property's value. For a one-time premium, the title insurance company will check the records and insure the property against loss due to defects in title.

Today title insurance is a business grossing hundreds of millions of dollars a year. So strong has been its growth, in fact, that in many Western states, lawyers have completely dropped out of the transaction. The title company routinely processes the papers instead.

But in many states both lawyers and title companies are used. A title company clerk, rarely a lawyer, checks through the records, noting previous transactions affecting the property. In most areas, title company clerks don't need to make a trip to the county land offices, because they maintain complete records of their own.

The lawyer's role in all this is pretty thin. He will examine the title abstract that the insurance company has prepared and will advise his client what exceptions, if any, the company has put in the policy. (An exception is a condition that the company will not insure against. If, for example, it turns out that an electrician has put a lien on the property for unpaid electrical work, the title company will not be liable in the event the electrician tries to foreclose to collect his bill.)

As a legal matter, title insurance is not required. (In thirty-four states, title insurance is purchased in less than half of all land transactions.) You may gamble on your attorney's opinion being accurate. Most of the time it will be. But, as in the Goldfarbs' case, the odds are that you will take out title insurance because the bank loaning you the mortgage money will demand that you do so.

In the early years, when title insurance companies were struggling to make inroads into the lawyers' professional territory, they began to pay a "commission" to the lawyer who persuaded his client to buy a policy from the title company: the lawyer would examine the title abstract that the clerk had prepared. If he thought the title sound, the lawyer would then write out ("issue") the policy on forms provided him by the company. In effect, the lawyer acted—and in many states still acts—as agent for the company at the same time that he was acting as your lawyer. The commission was and has remained a percentage of the total premium.

The practice spread quickly, forcing all title insurance companies to offer commissions to all lawyers at the peril of losing much of their business. In most states where the practice exists today, the lawyer's commission is 15 percent of the premium, as it was, for example, in New York until 1975, and as it is in Pennsylvania and New Jersey today. In the Chicago area the rate is 10 percent; in Florida the commission can go as high as 20 percent.[11]

When a buyer goes to a closing in a state where the lawyer and the title company are both participating, here's what happens. You write out a check for the bank's title policy. You may write out a separate check for your own policy. You will then write out a check for the bank's lawyer. (Your own lawyer usually has the decency to bill you later.) What you may not know, because your lawyer may not have told you, is that in addition to his fee (which you have earlier negotiated with him) he is going to get a check from the title insurance company. This is his commission. What you certainly will not know is that the bank's lawyer, whom you will just have paid a large fee, will also receive a check from the title company, representing his commission. In gross, this is not a small amount of money. The New

York State Insurance Department estimated in 1974 that in that state lawyers were collecting between $4 and $6 million annually in title commissions alone.

These lawyers are collecting fees from people or institutions who are not their clients—a practice, you will recall, that the bar condemned when lawyers sought salaries from such "lay intermediaries" as union legal aid plans. Is this an oversight on the part of the bar? Or has it closed its eyes because it does not want to see the evidence of unethical behavior all around it? Neither. The bar's response is that these kickbacks are not unethical as long as the lawyer makes full disclosure to the client or clients and obtains their consent to collect the commissions.

Here is still another cause for astonishment. The lawyer salaried by a union legal assistance plan was said to be drawing pay from an interest that is potentially adverse to his client, the union member. But in collecting fees from the title company, the real estate lawyer is likewise being paid by an interest that is potentially adverse to his client. The conflict is blatant whenever title insurance is not actually required or one company offers a policy for less than another. The temptation is strong for the lawyer to induce the buyer to take it, and to take the higher-priced policy where available.

What possible purpose can the commission serve? The lawyer can set his fee in advance. Why should a lawyer ever put himself in so tenuous a position as to appear to be on the take, corrupted by a non-client? It is difficult to see how it could ever be considered ethical to accept these payments.

Yet the bar expressly allows the lawyer to do so. The ABA's formal opinions are devoid of analysis, simply reiterating that the lawyer must obtain his client's consent after full disclosure. Yet it is widely known throughout the bar that a substantial number of practitioners keep the kickbacks—for that is what they are—and never tell their clients. In some areas, title companies delay paying the rebate for as much as a year, so that the lawyer can pretend the kickback has no relation to a client. In New Jersey, title companies have been known to prepare separate "gross" and "net" bills. The lawyer submits the gross bill to the client, who pays the title insurance premium to the lawyer. The lawyer then remits the premium (minus his "commission") together with the "net" bill to the company. What purpose can there be for this subterfuge but to let lawyers avoid telling their clients how the system works?

Interestingly, in 1972 when the ABA's ethics committee wrote its last opinion on the subject, it ignored a resolution of the ABA's Board of Governors six months earlier.[12] The resolution said that kickbacks are reprehensible and ought to be abolished.[13] The committee took the position that it was not bound by the Board of Governors. It conveniently neglected to mention the Board of Governors' condemnation. Thus, the committee avoided a certain awkwardness.

As for the title insurance kickback to the bank's attorney, the scheme can only be described as unconscionable. The bank lawyers never advise the buyers about the kickbacks and never (except for perhaps a few scrupulous attorneys occasionally) pass the discount on to the buyer.

Despite repeated opportunities, the committees of the ABA and of the various state bars have almost uniformly refused to scrutinize the actual practice and to adopt tough rules. In 1973, I invited the New York State Bar Association to consider declaring these kickbacks unethical. Ellsworth van Graafeiland, then president of the state bar association (and now a federal district judge), replied that his association's ethics committee "has never been asked to issue an opinion on the specific question of title company discounts."

This is interesting for two reasons. When ethics committees are upset about something, they need no invitation to issue an opinion, and the situation in New York State concerning title insurance kickbacks had been notorious for years. Moreover, a member of the state association's real estate section told me that his group was well aware of the problems and specifically knew that many lawyers were taking the "commissions" (a word he insisted on using) without ever informing their clients. But, he said, it was a "touchy" matter, and for "political reasons" his section could not move to end the practice.*

Prompted by my query, the ethics committee in December 1973 issued Opinion No. 320, simply reiterating the position of the ABA: with the "consent of the client after full disclosure" acceptance of the commission is proper. Finally, in 1975, after several previous attempts had failed, the New York State Legislature passed a law making it illegal for title insurance companies to give or for lawyers to accept their customary percentages. That the bar did not (and in many states still cannot) declare an end to a rule that begs to be flouted remains a testament to how unprofessional the bar can be in the face of pressures to decommercialize the practice of law.

To clinch the argument, consider the case of a seemingly maverick bar in Connecticut. There the association has made it clear that the attorney's acceptance of a commission from a commercial title insurance company is unethical, whether or not he tells his client and gets his consent. Does this suggest that enlightenment is possible? Sadly, no. For Connecticut lawyers have their own title insurance company.

Beginning in the 1950s in Florida, lawyers in a dozen states have formed their own insurance companies (called title guaranty funds) in order to counter the title companies' encroachment on their business. The lawyer makes a capital contribution to the fund and receives

---

*The ABA showed similar reluctance to face up to the realities. In its 1974 report, the Special Committee on Residential Real Estate Transactions sought to ascertain "appropriate methods of compensating the lawyer for his services," and came up with the following: "We understand that in some areas the title insurance company will give the attorney a commission for bringing it the business. If and to the extent that this unearned compensation influences the advice he gives his client as to the company that will best protect the client at the lowest cost, that is, of course, clearly improper and contrary to the recorded position of the Association, and has justifiably created the present indignation over 'kickbacks.' The solution currently being advocated is an abolition of 'kickbacks,' but *the Committee considers that the real offense is not the acceptance of the commission or rebate, but the failure to account for it to the client.* "[14] The problem, to the contrary, is that the existence of a rebate system always gives rise to the improper influences that the committee decries.

shares in return. When he examines title for a client, he issues a policy on the guaranty fund, which acts exactly as a commercial title insurance company would. In the event of a defect, the fund will pay the loss. But because the funds are nonprofit, or so the lawyers claim, the premiums tend to be considerably lower than in states where commercial title companies and lawyers work hand in hand.

In Connecticut, the Connecticut Attorneys Title Guaranty Fund, Inc., offers premiums between 15 and 25 percent less than the competing commercial companies. But this supposedly nonprofit company has provisions for paying dividends, though they are not paid out immediately. To make the operation sound, and, perhaps not so incidentally, to disguise the meaning of the payments, the company imposed an initial fifteen-year payout moratorium, which expires in 1982. At that time, judging by the Florida experience, lawyers will begin to get rebates on the fees they charged their clients for insurance coverage. In Florida, these dividends are paid by the lawyer-owned title company every year, but the dividends represent the earnings of the company seven years earlier. Thus a 1970 surplus would not be handed out until 1977.

This effectively insulates the lawyer from any qualms about whether to consult his client either in 1970 or in 1977—because in 1970 it was not yet clear whether there would be a surplus and in 1977 it is not clear where the clients are. By ruling that Connecticut lawyers may not accept commissions from commercial companies, the state bar is thus engaging in an antitrust conspiracy to promote its own business and dry up that of its competitors. The lawyer will ultimately receive his commission. The subtlety is true Yankee ingenuity.

The Ethics of Inconspicuous Production

The reasonableness of a fee does not depend only on its size. It depends also on what the lawyer actually did to earn it. No matter how small the amount, if the work for which the bill was rendered was unnecessary, the bill is too large. Unfortunately, useless work is a commonplace in legal practice.

In December 1975 in Chicago, the ABA leadership staged a one-day meeting to sell state and local bars on the necessity of easing the rules against advertising. A delegate from the Massachusetts bar claimed the floor in the middle of the morning. "You know," he said, "people think that if legal services are advertised then they will become more available and they will not cost so much. But I think we have to go behind this and face up to the fact that a lot of what we lawyers do is absolutely useless and only exists because the laws are written to provide us with work. If we really wanted to talk about doing a public service, we should try to find ways to simplify the law and get us out of all this inessential work." After he sat down, there was a minute of embarrassed silence; other lawyers seemed to be looking around wondering whether anyone would be so foolish as to start a discussion. Better to let a subject like that just drop. Which is what happened: the chairman of the meeting announced a new topic and the others, relieved, turned to it.

But the Massachusetts speaker was correct. The problem of artificially high fees has another dimension, and that is the problem that I have previously termed *inconspicuous production:* the problem of artificial work.[15] This is a growing disease of the industrial world, and many professionals other than lawyers engage in it. They do so because they wish to belong to the leisure class.

Inconspicuous production is the principal method by which the techniques of the old-fashioned absentee landlord can be transferred to the person who has no sizable capital holdings. The trick is to assign to high-priced specialists work requiring low-grade skills. If the work is simple enough, the actual mechanics can be transferred to clerks or secretaries (or paraprofessionals). In law inconspicuous production has a second form: work that is intrinsically unnecessary but that must be paid for because the law requires it or seems to require it.

Inconspicuous production operates at every level of the legal profession, from the one-lawyer office to the largest Wall Street firms. But the clearest examples—and probably the most socially significant—are those that occur in the practice of the personal lawyer. They are most prevalent in the areas of probate, bankruptcy, real estate, divorce. Let's consider divorce.

A substantial number of divorce cases are uncontested. Husband and wife want out; the amount of property is small; there are no children (or, where there are children, both parents agree on custody arrangements). So husband and wife separate and live apart for the year or eighteen months that an increasing number of states have made sufficient grounds for divorce. The actual granting of the divorce remains within the province of a court, however, and until very recently this has seemed to necessitate hiring lawyers.

According to a report in the *New York Times,* Mrs. Marion Strong, of Dobbs Ferry, New York, earned $5,000 a year as a secretary when her one-year wait following a legal separation ended in 1975. She looked for a lawyer but, with four children to support, the fees quoted were beyond her means. The Lawyer Referral Service, operated by the Westchester County Bar Association as a lame substitute for a prepaid plan, told her that she could not be serviced for less than $750. So Mrs. Strong decided to do it herself.

First she bought an inexpensive paperback called *How to Get a New York Divorce for under $100.* Next she purchased the forms from a local stationer for $4 (though she bought several, it later turned out she needed only two). Service of summons on her husband (by a college friend of her son) cost $5. A notary public friend notarized the documents for free. The court filing fee was $25. For advice in filling out the forms she found a sympathetic clerk in the county courthouse in White Plains, New York. Several weeks later, following a four-minute hearing before a judge, her divorce was granted. To obtain a copy of the final judgment she paid the court another $25. Total cost for the divorce, not counting her paperback book: $59.[16]

This is a typical case, not an aberration. In an empirical study of the economics of uncontested divorce cases, the *Yale Law Journal* sampled somewhat more than 25 percent of all such cases filed in New Haven and Bridgeport, Connecticut, between April 1 and September 30, 1975. One finding was that the lawyers' fees were high relative to the work. In 77.8 percent of the cases in which neither child support nor property was a factor, the litigants paid $500 or more for their divorces, and the lawyers who were paid these sums could fill out the forms in less than one hour. Nine people "had been quoted prices averaging $750 for divorces they ultimately obtained themselves with the aid of the four-dollar *Pro Se Dissolution Kit.*"[17]

The *pro se*—or do-it-yourself—divorce is burgeoning. Dozens of books, kits, and other non-legal services are springing up to guide the would-be litigant. The bar's reaction, predictably, has been nasty. Lawyers fear movements such as these more acutely than the advertising issue or other heterodoxies that have infected their brethren. To combat the threat, the bar brings out its heaviest artillery, prosecutions for *unauthorized practice of law.*

Unauthorized practice of law committees operate under a franchise from the state courts. They sue to enjoin laymen and lawyers alike from "practicing" law in an unapproved manner. Though one of the nine basic canons deals with it, unauthorized practice is a violation of law, not merely a breach of ethics.

The first such committees were formed during the Depression. They soon spawned a vast number of lawsuits and judicial decisions. I have already mentioned one aspect of their work: to stop lawyers themselves from practicing in ways that the bar finds intolerable. Thus lawyers paid by associations and civic organizations to assert rights on behalf of members were consistently told that they were aiding and abetting the unauthorized practice of law (by the associations). No less significant, though clearly less bizarre in conception, has been the fight of these committees against non-lawyer "practitioners."

The premise is reasonable. If law is to be a licensed profession, then there must be some mechanism to prevent those who are unlicensed from practicing it. A person without any training, who decides that he can make a good living by hanging out the proverbial "honest lawyer" sign, ought to be stopped—though not necessarily by the bar. But for obvious reasons, the pretender does not often set up shop.

Most of the energy of the unauthorized practice committees is devoted, instead, to prosecuting other professionals who, the bar fears, are encroaching on lawyers' territory. That is why Norman F. Dacey's best-selling *How to Avoid Probate,* a large-format paperback containing 55 pages of advice on wills and trusts and 310 pages of do-it-yourself forms, was attacked in New York State. Dacey, the bar charged, was practicing law, though the only act of which he was accused was authorship of his book; he did not give personal advice to particular individuals. The highest state court ultimately vindicated the book and Dacey (as well as the publishers and a bookstore, whom the bar had also sued) but not before all were put to the expense of a long lawsuit.

Many other sorts of professionals do things in the course of their work that overlap things that lawyers do. We live in a commercial society and commerce is interwoven with law. These facts of life have led to equally concerted attacks by the bar on the business of these other professionals. The most celebrated case was the fight in Arizona over the right of real estate brokers to prepare contracts for the sale of homes.

In 1960, growing apprehensive about the title companies' and realtors' penetration of the business of drafting documents and transferring title, the Arizona bar sued to enjoin them from doing so. The state supreme court agreed and issued a sweeping injunction against practices that were by then decades old. All "those acts, whether performed in court or in the law office, which lawyers customarily have carried on from day to day through the centuries" were forbidden to any but lawyers, the court ruled.[18] Never mind that others had been doing these things as well.

Especially pointed was the court's declaration that its decree was issued under the court's constitutional authority to regulate the bar. In other words, this was not a mere interpretation of a statute spelling out who may or may not practice law. No matter the public sentiment, the legislature could not change the court's decision. A matter this important, said the court, must *inherently* be left to the courts.

To reverse the court's decision would therefore require a constitutional amendment, and this is exactly what happened. After a bitter campaign, the realtors and title companies succeeded in pushing through an amendment to the state constitution in 1962 expressly permitting a licensed realtor "to draft or fill out and complete, without charge," purchase agreements, deeds, mortgages, leases, bills of sale, and the like.

But the court did not give up. A few weeks after the voters approved the amendment, the Chief Justice of the Arizona Supreme Court made a speech in which he said that realtors would now be judged by the ethical standards of the bar to the extent that they now practiced law. "You may find that the rope leading up to the hayloft is a tiger's tail," he said.[19] Lawyers never call it quits.

With the explosive growth of the do-it-yourself movement, the bar associations' committees are active once again in quashing the threat to the public well-being. Divorce kits, bankruptcy kits, and others are under attack.* In California, the founder of the Wave Project, a counseling group for couples about to be divorced, was disciplined even though he is himself a lawyer; as a consequence, he has ceased practicing. His successor, Phyllis Eliasberg, also a lawyer, has been charged, like Jacoby and Meyers, with moral turpitude, dishonesty, and corruption—and, for good measure, with soliciting clients and aiding and abetting the unauthorized practice of law.[21] Yet the bar feels no need to prove that advice proffered by the Wave Project is incompetent.

Perhaps more novel are the troubles of the American Bankruptcy

---

*Divorce kits, says Frederick Buesser, Jr., a former chairman of the ABA's Unauthorized Practice of Law Committee, "are like a knocked-down outboard-motor kit. Without help, it's useless. Most of the people selling kits sit down with the people, show them how to fill out the forms, tell them what to say and generally give the kind of counsel a lawyer would, but they don't know what they're doing. I think the bar has a duty to see to it that people are protected from charlatans."[20]

Council, another private self-help counseling group in California. The Council's difficulties and the bar's attitude toward it sum up all that is wrong with the lawyers' attitudes about the work they do. The state bar's counsel, T. Andy Richey, has been quoted as saying that "bankruptcy is the most dangerous" form of do-it-yourself law. In fact, Richey says, "a lot of lawyers won't handle it [bankruptcy]" because the law is so complex.[22] In 1974, the Bankruptcy Council began advertising its kits. Since that time, personal bankruptcy filings have risen steeply in California. As a result, the Council has been in constant friction with the bar and the courts.

One incident is illuminating. Judge Robert Hughes of Oakland, a federal bankruptcy judge, has ordered the Council's founder, John Slavicek, to make partial refunds to his customers on the ground that his services were not worth the price. Slavicek was charging $40 for his kits; Judge Hughes said the materials were worth only $10. Since many people used the kits successfully, this says something about the value of a lawyer's service in this connection: in California the standard charge is roughly $300.

On what ground does Judge Hughes interfere with Slavicek's sacred American right to charge whatever he wants? A court rule permits judges to pass on the reasonableness of a *lawyer's* charge to his client, and Judge Hughes reasoned that Slavicek was acting like an attorney (though he is not one). But Judge Hughes agreed to let Slavicek continue selling the bankruptcy kits, which means that no one believes he is actually practicing law. The bar (judges included), in other words, cannot conceive that there are other ways to help people than through lawyers.

In the Bates & O'Steen case, an Arizona Supreme Court justice unconsciously revealed the absurdity of the bar's inconspicuous production. Objecting to the clinic's advertisement, the justice said: "I am able to foresee instances in which the $175 fee quoted for this [uncontested adoption] service would be unreasonably high. Is it deceptive to advertise [these] legal services . . . when . . . the county attorney, upon application, is required to perform similar services without expense to the petitioner?"[23] Here in a nutshell is an admission of the failure of unauthorized practice and legal ethics. For how much more unreasonable is the general practitioner's higher fee for the same low-grade service? And if the county attorney is allowed to do the paperwork for adoptions for free, why does the bar itself not advertise that he will, to rid itself of a time-consuming chore?*

In April 1977, federal district judge Robert R. Merhige, Jr., delivered a serious blow to the concept of unauthorized practice committees, at least as they now operate (like Houdini, the bar is adept at escaping from seemingly rigid restraints). The case arose in Virginia. Surety Title Insurance Agency, Inc., decided it could save money for consumers and make money for itself if it could hire non-lawyers to search real estate titles and then issue title insurance policies directly to home buyers. It would not first submit the policy to a lawyer for examination. On a $30,000 home, the estimated savings to purchasers was $211; on a $60,000 home, $491. Moreover, Surety Title said, it would provide additional services, such as surveying the land, at no additional charge (services that home buyers must now pay for separately).

Standing in its way were opinions of the council of the Virginia state bar. These opinions said in effect that rendering a title policy to consumer without using a lawyer as a middleman is unauthorized practice of law and, hence, unlawful. Surety Title's response was that it was not giving out legal opinions; it was simply backing up its own conclusions about the soundness of title with an insurance policy naming the risks that it would cover. The lender could tell from the policy whether the insurance coverage was enough.

---

*The belief that lawyers may legitimately perform services that others can more cheaply undertake is, however, deeply ingrained. Even Bates and O'Steen are infected with its germs. Asked at their hearing before the Arizona state bar why they advertised a service that someone else would do for free, one responded: "[I]t's not my job to inform a prospective client that he needn't employ a lawyer to handle his work." Strange sentiment for one who wishes to advertise to the public. Why should that not be his job? Why should not all lawyers be so obligated? Law, lawyers like to remind, is not just any service but a professional service. The true professional ought always to give advice about alternative means of accomplishing the client's goal.

Under Virginia law, the power to define "unauthorized practice" lies in the state supreme court. That body adopted broadly defined rules drawn by a committee of lawyers. The court delegated to the council of the state bar the power to give advisory opinions concerning professional conduct of lawyers in the state. The council, in turn, has delegated its power to advise on matters of unauthorized practice to a five-member committee appointed by the president of the state bar.

The opinions on unauthorized practice announced by this committee have never been approved by the state supreme court. Nevertheless, as we have seen, Virginia lawyers do not lightly disregard pronouncements by the state bar. Only ten of between 200 and 300 lawyers who were contacted were willing to prepare deeds for home buyers in transactions where Surety Title proposed to issue an insurance policy with only lay help in searching the title. (Without the deed, of course, there can be no sale.) The lawyers' timidity was due to another rule that it is unethical to cooperate with someone who engages in unauthorized practice of law.

Unable to introduce its low-cost service, Surety Title sued, charging a violation of the antitrust laws. The state bar defended, as in *Goldfarb*, by claiming that it was not a private body but one charged with public duties by the supreme court and hence exempt from the antitrust laws.

Judge Merhige disagreed. In his decision enjoining the state bar from issuing any further such advisory opinions, he wrote: "The Unauthorized Practice of Law process places attorneys in the unique position of being able to define the extent of their own monopoly. It belabors the obvious to point out that lawyers in general would financially benefit from an expansive definition of the practice of law. The danger is crystallized under the facts [of the Surety Title case]. An attorney engaged in a real estate oriented practice stands to lose substantial fees should the issuance of title insurance be held to lie outside the parameters of the Virginia Supreme Court's definition of the practice of law. . . . The absence of judicial participation aggravates the anti-competitiveness of the Unauthorized Practice of Law opinion process. The State Bar rules make no provision for court review of such opinions."[24] In short, the lawyers of Virginia had found what, until they met Judge Merhige, was a foolproof method of privately outlawing competition. The case is on appeal.

But the bar ought not to await the outcome. The bars of other states ought to relinquish such responsibilities voluntarily. Instead, the bar ought to create "*unnecessary* practice of law" committees to *prevent* lawyers from doing what others can do for the public for much less cost. Then and only then might the unauthorized practice committees be remitted to their proper function: to prevent others from practicing real law where three years of training might make a difference.

A Curious Rule against Contingency Fees

In recent years, doctors and others have condemned the legal profession for its continued acceptance of the contingent fee. This is the fee the client pays only when the lawyer wins the case. Critics charge that the contingent fee stirs up lawsuits. In England, the critics point out, the bar is not allowed to work on contingency and there are virtually no malpractice suits.

But the contingency or lack of it does not account for the whole of this difference. There may be a difference in the style of American and British physicians; there is obviously a difference in the willingness of American and British citizens to litigate. And in England winning plaintiffs can recover the cost of their lawyers from their adversaries. In America this is not generally possible.

Primarily because the American client must foot his own legal bills, win or lose, the contingent fee has always been accepted here as necessary. Otherwise the hundreds of hours of expensive time required for trial preparation would deter most potential plaintiffs from pressing a claim in this increasingly damage-causing society.

But for all that, the contingent fee has been accepted only uneasily.

Unlike most other lawyers' bills, the contingent fee may be questioned in court. (When Joseph Weintraub, the late chief justice of the New Jersey Supreme Court, announced his court's decision to place ceilings on the contingency percentage that the state's lawyers can keep, he was booed by the several hundred lawyers in the audience—further evidence of the bar's delicate sense of ethics and public relations.)*[25]

The reason for the uneasiness is the similarity of the arrangement to an ancient evil, "champerty," whereby a lawyer or someone else would purchase the claim in question at discount and then at his own cost chance the recovery of the full amount through litigation. This was—and still is—thought to stir up non-meritorious lawsuits. The contingent fee is a variety of champerty, because the lawyer in effect owns a percentage of the claim once he begins the action. But until lawyers' services are made generally available, the contingent fee will necessarily continue to be tolerated, for an overkill rule designed to foreclose such fees would choke a huge variety of legitimate claims.

But the bar *has* fashioned an overkill rule against an interesting variant of the contingent fee. That is the rule against contingent expert witness fees.[26] Here the bar for years has succeeded in using lawyers' ethics as a lever to control non-lawyers and their clients.

Consider this case. A small, innovative automobile dealer decides to take on his established competitors. His idea is to buy automobiles either directly from General Motors or on a fleet basis (at a considerable discount for bulk purchases) from GM dealers. He will then resell the cars to regular retail customers at prices lower than dealers normally charge. He soon discovers that neither GM itself nor GM dealers will sell to him. He contacts a lawyer, who agrees to file an antitrust case on his behalf. The lawyer will be paid only if he wins. Under the antitrust laws, the losing defendant will pay the winning plaintiff's attorney's fees, as well as triple damages.

---

*The scale established was this: no more than one-third of the first $50,000 recovered; 20 percent of the next $50,000, and 10 percent of any amount collected in excess of $100,000. Thus, out of an award of $75,000, a New Jersey lawyer can keep no more than $21,666.67.

The lawyer sets out to prove that GM, through its dealers, has structured the market in an anti-competitive (and unlawful) manner. But he runs into trouble. In order to learn how the automobile industry works and whether or not its practices are reasonable under the circumstances, he needs to consult various experts. But they will not devote hours of their time for free. Some agree to help provided that the client promises to pay them for their time out of his damage award, should he win the suit.

The code of ethics unequivocally condemns this arrangement, however. Lawyers who pay, offer to pay, or even acquiesce in the payment of fees to a *witness* contingent on winning the case are declared to be acting unethically. The rule seeks to guard against an incentive to give false testimony; knowing that his fee depends on winning, the expert, it is assumed, will shade his statements in court to conform to the client's position. Under this rule, the lawyer is severely handicapped in representing clients who cannot afford to pay for extensive pretrial litigation, and the client is therefore doomed before he has started.

If the code forbade paying experts any fees, whether or not contingent, then you might suppose the bar was seriously concerned about the ethical proprieties. But the code is not evenhanded. It permits a lawyer to "advance, guarantee, or acquiesce in the payment of" an expert's reasonable expenses in connection with his appearance in court. It also permits payment of reasonable fees for his time and "professional services." This means that a wealthy client who can afford to employ on salary or otherwise retain an expert can enjoy a decided advantage in a wide variety of lawsuits—especially those involving personal injury (automobile accidents, product liability, and medical malpractice cases) and financial and business cases (including patent, antitrust, securities, and accounting). Frequently, the expert witness will make the difference not only between winning or losing, but between filing and not filing the lawsuit.

Now, experts are not naïve. It is not to be supposed that they are unmindful of who pays for their services and what their patron expects for his money. There is no less incentive for the paid than for the contingent expert to shade his testimony. The expert who testifies against his paymaster's interest is not likely to remain on the payroll for long. So the net of the rule is to provide an incentive to experts who wish to shade their testimony in favor of wealthy litigants and a disincentive to experts who might wish to shade their testimony in favor of non-wealthy claimants.

This rule has been in effect for several decades. It was not challenged formally until 1975, when the automobile dealer's lawyer, Carl E. Person of New York, filed suit against the Association of the Bar of the City of New York and the Appellate Division of the state supreme court to block both from enforcing the rule against him. In May 1977, the federal appeals court reversed a Brooklyn federal district court's ruling in his favor,[27] and the Supreme Court refused to hear an appeal, so the rule will stand.

Fees for Those Who Can Afford Them

A word should be said about the fee practices of the large metropolitan law firms. For the most part, they are above petty pilferage of the client's pocketbook, though every now and then there is a firm that tries to make money in peculiar ways. For example, some firms apply a "double billing" rule when their lawyers travel. The client for whom the lawyer is traveling pays expenses and the lawyer's time while en route (an important enough lawyer can earn $500 to $1,000 just flying from New York to San Francisco). If the lawyer takes work related to another client, the same hours aloft will be billed also to that other client. A lawyer can't do this on the ground, so airborne offices can be lucrative.

Then there are law firms that make a profit on every piece of paper that pops out of the Xerox machine. According to Joseph C. Goulden, "A firm such as Steptoe & Johnson [a well-known Washington firm] bills clients 15 cents per Xerox page, although the direct cost is two cents. S & J routinely makes eight copies of most pleadings—some as extras required by Court rules, others for the client and its own files. The 240 copies required for a 30-page petition hence translate into a gross profit of $31.20. In the Alaska pipeline case, one submission alone contained an estimated 10,000 pages. Firms justify high duplication charges as being an offset against general office expenses."[28]

The larger overcharge of clients goes unremarked because of its pervasiveness. That is the practice of Grandly Inconspicuous Production (GIP). No corner of the client's case is overlooked; associates in the big firms are assigned to spend as much time as necessary to check every conceivable byway, track down every last citation, polish every sentence.

I once spent an entire day debating with several colleagues the wording of a twenty-page draft statement that a client was going to present in Congress. The client's impact on the legislative process was foredoomed to be about nil. The speech would be duly placed in the hearing record, but few, if any, would consult it. Yet four of us sat in a stuffy conference room for more than eight hours haggling over such niggling matters as the use of transitive verbs. Even the substantive (i.e., legal) parts of the discussion were silly in view of the low probability that any of it would make a difference (it did not). Our time could not have been worth less than $1,500 for the day (though whether the firm billed that much I cannot say). But what we did was consistent with the highest ethics of the profession. Besides, the client was not complaining; it could afford our bills.

The incentive to question the propriety of the practices that lead to these bills is low. Rich corporations do not quibble over a few thousand dollars here or there—or even over a few hundred thousand dollars. For the very largest corporations, the total annual legal bill will be far less than 1 percent of gross revenues, not a particularly significant cost. (IBM, with billions of dollars in cash and liquid assets, can be excused for not screening a million or two or even more.)

I once interviewed the general counsel of a corporation based in

New York with annual sales of more than $1 billion. He had spent the first years of his professional life with a major New York law firm, whom he then retained as his company's outside litigation counsel. We were discussing a trial then under way in Los Angeles. I asked him how carefully he scrutinized the bill, and what he would do if he found that the firm was sending, say, four young lawyers to the West Coast when two would do. (The expense under such circumstances is large, especially during protracted proceedings, because the lawyers are boarded at the best hotels and drink French wines at dinner and incur who knows what other expenses, all of which will be billed to the corporation.) "Well," he said, "it doesn't happen very often and when it does I can't complain, because these young lawyers have to get some experience, which I will wind up paying for one way or another."

This answer is disingenuous. The lawyer has a duty not to enrich his former employers at the expense of his current ones. But the unruffled response is symptomatic of an insensitivity to the effect of high costs on the system as a whole. If it becomes widely accepted that a large number of lawyers are necessary on a particular kind of case or that long memoranda or briefs are prerequisite to high-quality work, it will be difficult for anyone to complain that these services are unnecessary. The level of legal fees for institutional clients will soar. This will be reflected in insurance costs of business and price legal services beyond the reach of many smaller companies. The institutional lawyer will not be troubled; plenty of companies will pay him well for his own brand of "work." The difference between him and his colleague in the "lower" ranks of personal lawyering is that his inconspicuous production will be done with a flourish and heralded by trumpets.

We end where we began, questioning the legitimacy of lawyers' fees. An adequate level of fees is doubtless necessary to guarantee quality performance, but "adequacy" is a word without built-in limits. What many lawyers over the years have termed adequate is in fact excessive. High fees may thus function less as a guarantor of competence than as a bribe to the lawyer to overlook the ethical position of the client himself.* To this topic we now turn.

*One writer, comparing the bars of Germany and the United States, notes that German lawyers may more easily quit the client, and there may therefore be less need than in America to screen the client's cause in advance.[29] If so, a high fee proffered to (or demanded by) the American lawyer at the outset may help quell doubts about the propriety of representing a particular client (or may buy the lawyer's later silence and continuing cooperation).

CHAPTER 6

The Ethics of Doing Harm:
Clients vs. the Public

The Bad Client

A basic tenet of the lawyer's creed is that it is ethical to aid those bent on acting unethically. Summing up the bar's attitude, Sharswood wrote that the lawyer "is not morally responsible for the act of the party in maintaining an unjust cause." Lawyers may legitimately take on corrupt clients and often do. Lawyers help the guilty go free. They cover up their clients' misdeeds. They prepare legal instruments that are disadvantageous to the weak and the poor. They help industrialists pollute the air and the water. They aid many in blunting the force of bills pending in Congress and the statehouses that would protect the public against these and other evils. And the bar is in trouble collectively because collectively it appears to help a few injure the many; people perceive individual lawyers as agents for malefactors.

Lawyers justify this seeming perversity by noting that a free society makes a sharp distinction between legally and morally permissible action. Professor Richard Wasserstrom has given three down-to-earth examples:

Suppose that a client desires to make a will disinheriting her children because they opposed the war in Vietnam. Should the lawyer refuse to draft the will because the lawyer thinks this is a bad reason to disinherit one's children? Suppose a client can avoid the payment of taxes through a loophole only available to a few wealthy taxpayers. Should the lawyer refuse to tell the client of a loophole because the lawyer thinks it an unfair advantage for the rich? Suppose a client wants to start a corporation that will manufacture, distribute and promote a harmful but not illegal substance, e.g., cigarettes. Should the lawyer refuse to prepare the articles of incorporation for the corporation?[1]

On this view, the lawyer's task is to provide professional help to those who wish to accomplish some lawful objective. Since a halfhearted effort may be worse than no effort at all, the lawyer must steel himself to go all out for his client. This duty is summed up in canon 7: "A lawyer should represent a client zealously within the bounds of the law."

This rule is as important for the lawyer as it is for the client. If the lawyer were judged according to how well he struck a balance between law and morality, he would ever stand in jeopardy of being condemned (by client or society) as public sentiment changed. Moreover, virtually any piece of advice given to even the most virtuous client could be called into question according to some moral principle. Zealous representation is therefore a standard for judging whether the lawyer has met his fiduciary duty to client.

Nevertheless, this response is unsettling. The law is at best an imperfect means of controlling human behavior. Many evils may be perpetrated in the law's name. Moreover, it is a commonplace that laws are made or blocked by those with power to influence legislation; many harmful activities are lawful only because those with a vested interest in continuing them have the money and power to forestall legislation.

The bar's apprehension over these defects in the system are mirrored in exceptions to the zealous representation rules. Thus a lawyer need not continue representing a client whose objective is morally repugnant to him. These limits on the requisite zeal are often unclear and contradictory, however, and it is the confusion over how far a lawyer may go in representing a client that we will now explore.*

Guilty Secrets

In July 1973, Robert Garrow, a thirty-eight-year-old mechanic from Syracuse, New York, killed, apparently randomly, four persons. Three were camping in the Adirondack Mountains. In early August, following a vigorous manhunt, he was captured by state police and indicted for the murder of Philip Domblewski, an eighteen-year-old student from Schenectady. At the time of the arrest, there was no evidence connecting Garrow to the other deaths. In fact, two of the others were not even then known to be dead. One was a twenty-one-year-old Illinois woman; the other a sixteen-year-old Syracuse high-school girl listed as a runaway. The third, a camping companion of the Illinois woman, was a twenty-two-year-old Harvard student, whose body was found on July 20, before Garrow's capture. The court appointed two Syracuse lawyers, Francis R. Belge and Frank H. Armani, to defend Garrow at his forthcoming trial.

Some weeks later, during discussions with his two lawyers, Garrow told them that he had raped and killed a woman in a mine shaft. Belge

---

*Justice Potter Stewart put the confusion nicely in a speech on "Professional Ethics for the Business Lawyer" in 1975. Said Justice Stewart: "Every lawyer should keep his word and deal honorably in all his association. . . . But beyond these and a few other self-evident precepts of decency and common sense, a good case can be made, I think, for the proposition that the ethics of the business lawyer are indeed, and perhaps should be, no more than the morals of the marketplace."[2] What can this mean? The "morals of the marketplace" are usually condemned for dispensing with a fair degree of honorable dealings; that, indeed, is the implication of the phrase. What then can Justice Stewart have intended by his remarks? I believe that he is mirroring the deeply felt desire of the bar to have its cake and eat it too. But this can never be done, and particularly not today.

and Armani investigated, locating the mine shaft and the body of the Illinois woman. "Frank lowered me into the shaft by my feet and I took pictures," Belge later reported. Neither lawyer took their discovery to the police at that time, however. The body was finally discovered four months later by two children playing in the mine. In late September, the lawyers found the second body in a Syracuse cemetery, following Garrow's directions. This discovery, too, went unreported; the girl's body was uncovered by a university student in December.

The Illinois woman's father read that Belge and Armani were defending a man accused of killing a camper in the Adirondacks. Knowing that his daughter's companion had also been found dead there, he journeyed from Chicago to Syracuse to talk to the lawyers. He asked them whether they knew anything about his daughter. Denying any knowledge, they said they could not help him. Belge and Armani maintained their silence until the following June. Then, at trial, Garrow, to try to show he was insane, made statements from the witness stand that implicated him in the other three murders. At a press conference the next day, Belge and Armani outlined for the first time the sequence of events just detailed.*

Predictably, the local community was outraged. "Justice shamed," read the editorial headline in the *Albany Times Union.*[4] "I can't imagine anyone living with such a thing; it must be illegal," said the mother of the Illinois woman. The district attorney immediately announced an investigation (which later led to the prosecution of Belge).

The lawyers did not apologize. To the contrary, they made it clear they believed they had honored the letter and spirit of their professional duty in a tough case. "We both, knowing how the parents must feel, wanted to advise them where the bodies were," Belge said. "But since it was a privileged communication, we could not reveal any information that was given to us in confidence."

---

*According to some newspaper accounts, the lawyers had offered to plea-bargain the previous September with the district attorney. In exchange for a promise to commit Garrow to a mental institution rather than to stand trial, Belge and Armani were said to have offered to help the police find the missing bodies, an offer the D.A. rejected.[3]

Their silence was predicated on canon 4, which admonishes the lawyer to "preserve the confidence and secrets of a client." The lawyer-client "privilege" (against disclosure of confidences) is one of the oldest and most ironclad in the law. It is also one of the most sensible rules of ethics. The lawyer is often the possessor of guilty secrets. The client has done something wrong; he bares his soul to the attorney (or the attorney drags the facts out). If the lawyer were duty bound to reveal statements his client has communicated to him in private, the lawyer would be incapable of zealous representation.

This answer frequently seems unconvincing. It certainly did not convince the people of Syracuse and environs. Suppose a man is guilty of a heinous crime and tells his lawyer so. Why shouldn't the lawyer come forward with the news as a non-lawyer would have to, if summoned to testify? Standing alone, the counterargument has force. But the matter does not stand alone; it is part and parcel of a larger constitutional setting. Under the Fifth and Fourteenth amendments, no suspect or defendant can be compelled to be a witness against himself. The privilege against self-incrimination means that the accused has no legal duty himself to come forward. The burden of proving the crime is the state's. (This is not the place for a discussion of the policies underlying this privilege. For purposes of our discussion, we will accept it as principled and sound, as I personally believe it to be.)*

If the defendant has no duty to confess his guilt or complicity in a crime, it can make no sense to assert that his lawyer has such a duty. Otherwise the accused will tell his lawyer nothing or a deficient version of the facts—or else render his lawyer dangerous to him and hence useless.

---

*The controversy of recent years concerning the privilege against self-incrimination —the *Miranda* case and its progeny—centers not on whether the privilege is proper but on what constitutes police compulsion. Although they are connected, the propriety of the privilege is not the same issue as determining when the privilege is violated. There are no critics I know of who suggest that in Garrow's situation, when the police were unaware of the other crimes, the *defendant* has a legal obligation to come forward to confess.

In the ordinary criminal case, nothing beyond the conviction or acquittal of the accused hinges on the lawyer's silence. But sometimes something much more portentous may hang on what the lawyer does or does not do. Suppose, for example, that a client tells his lawyer that he has committed a murder for which another person has been convicted. Convinced of his client's guilt, the lawyer is unable to persuade his client to confess publicly. Is the duty to respect his client's confidences inviolable?

Just this situation arose following the Leo Frank trial in Atlanta in 1914. Frank was the wealthy Jewish manager of a pencil factory. An employee, Mary Phagan, was found dead; on shaky evidence, Frank was convicted of a sex murder and sentenced to death. There was a tremendous outcry from, among others, the Atlanta clergy and the Northern press; the governor of Georgia commuted Frank's sentence to life imprisonment. But xenophobia stirred up by a professional Jew-baiter, Tom Watson, led a mob to pull Frank from his cell and lynch him. Shortly after Frank's conviction had been affirmed on appeal, an Atlanta lawyer named Arthur Powell received a visit from a client who persuaded Powell that he had killed Mary Phagan and that Frank was completely innocent. Powell decided to keep this communication confidential. In an autobiography thirty years later, Powell, then a judge, noted that his conscience was relieved somewhat when Frank's sentence was commuted.[5] (Was it eased still further when Frank was lynched?)

The possibility that a lawyer with knowledge of a client's wrong might be able to prevent harm to another troubles those most devoted to the ideal of professional ethics. Professor Freedman, probably the most unyielding proponent of a lawyer's strict fidelity to client, confesses that he would break the confidence of a client if in so doing he could spare the life of a person wrongly sentenced to death, but not if sentenced to life imprisonment.[6] Henry S. Drinker, in his 1953 treatise, would make an exception if disclosure were necessary for the public safety (as, for example, if one were representing an enemy agent in time of war).[7] And Francis Belge, who opted against disclosing the fact and location of two dead bodies, said: "You have your duty to your state, to your law and order, but my primary duty is to my client —so long as I don't jeopardize anybody's life or property. If the girl had been alive, then we would have had the duty to save her life because life is primary. A body is a sacred thing but I couldn't give it life and I figured somebody is going to find it."[8]

What a muddle! Could "property" really be a consideration that would lead this fearless man to disclose a confidence? Suppose his client confessed that he had stolen a hundred dollars and intended to buy his wife a watch for her birthday. Is the return of the victim's money more important than the continuing anxieties of bereaved parents that Belge's silence helped to foster?

Some suggested that Belge and Armani ought to have telephoned the police anonymously to let them know where the bodies were. Though it may seem a sensible compromise at first glance, it does not solve the ethical dilemma. If there is a duty to the client, an anonymous tip serves only to mask the lawyer's violation of that duty. If there is no duty, the disclosure need not be anonymous.

Unable to get a bar association to take action against the lawyers, and apparently stung by the charge that state prosecutors and police might have been aware of the bodies all along, Onondaga County District Attorney Jon K. Holcombe obtained an indictment against Belge on the only remaining ground: covering up a "continuing crime." Specifically, Belge was charged with two counts of "violating and interfering with the rights of burial." The Public Health Law of New York State requires anyone who knows that someone has died without medical attendance to report the fact to the health authorities so that a proper burial can be arranged.[9]

More sensibly, the D.A. should have been concerned with obstruction of justice (itself a crime). In this case, the obstruction consisted of the concealment of the bodies, thus hampering the bringing of Garrow to trial for the other murders. But the Fifth Amendment would bar a charge of obstruction on this ground, for the reason discussed above. The murderer has no legal duty to confess, and his lawyer's knowledge of the crime cannot become a means for subverting the privilege against self-incrimination. The burial charge thus became a convenient, though transparent, substitute for a charge that the defendant and his attorney were engaged in the continuing crime of obstructing justice. (Armani avoided indictment, inconsistently, on his proof to the grand jury that he had sought the opinion of an unnamed senior state judge who instructed him not to divulge Garrow's gruesome secret.) But the subterfuge was too obvious, and the courts dismissed Belge's indictment before he came to trial.

Through it all, the bar associations maintained a discreet silence. Though the consensus seems to be that what Belge and Armani did was ethically correct, if not exemplary, the bar made no attempt to use a splendid opportunity to educate the profession or the public in this murky area.

In view of its reluctance to commit itself in a less ambiguous situation in which lawyers serve as partners in crime, the bar's hesitation is not surprising. I refer to the raging controversy over the conduct of securities lawyers who must deal daily with their own type of guilty secrets. Here the code is a maze of contradictions, providing the lawyer with ammunition to defend almost any course of action he chooses.

The corporate president calls his lawyer in. He has discovered that his predecessor, recently retired, had approved secret payments to the Albanian Communist party for five years in the hopes of establishing trade relations. The amount would not damage the company in the slightest but, at $5 million, was too large to be irrelevant, even to a multibillion-dollar corporation. No one had found out because the former president and his personable treasurer had skillfully laundered the funds through phony invoices issued by a Liechtenstein subsidiary. Unfortunately, this means that for five years the company has probably violated the federal securities laws in releasing false financial reports and doubtless has violated the tax laws. But that's so much water over the dam. The important question is whether the company must now bring any of this to light. This is not an idle question, either, because the company is about to make another of its periodic stock offerings. The final version of the prospectus is at the printer. Should it be pulled back to include this new information?

The lawyer clears his throat.

"While you're thinking about that," the president continues, "we have another problem.[10] Just this morning one of our house lawyers discovered that the main factory has been sitting on someone else's property. Somehow the title search was botched a few years back. In fact, nineteen years and six months ago. In another six months," he continues, "we could gain complete title just by virtue of our having sat there for twenty years ('adverse possession,' the house counsel called it). But now, since we don't own it free and clear yet, do we have to disclose this, too? If we do, you know that means the true owner will sue us to recover his land and our operations will be disrupted; we'll lose millions."

"Well," the lawyer begins.

And as if that weren't enough, says the president, he has just learned from the marketing director that his company has had an agreement for seventeen years with the chief competitor to raise prices jointly every eighteen months. The marketing director claimed he didn't know that was illegal. "My God," says the president, "if that has to be disclosed, the company will be wiped out." The president opens up a yellow-backed folder. "I have the calculation here," he says. "Let's see, seventeen years of excess profits, trebled, amounts to $3 billion. Who could ever pay that? What do you think?"

The lawyer, an ethical fellow, pales. He could retire now, at fifty-two, but he has three more children to put through college, two mortgages, expensive tastes in vacations, and an obligation to continue his status as a Rufus Wheeler Peckham Donor to his law school's scholarship fund. So he forthrightly faces his client and says: "There aren't any answers, Charles."

Of course I have saddled our lawyer with the toughest questions. There are no answers, though nearly daily headlines from 1975 on have testified to the many companies that thought it prudent to confess to political payoffs in previous years.

The problem is that, unlike Garrow, corporate clients in such situations have a clear legal duty to disclose information of material value to their public stockholders. Failure to disclose (or partial disclosures that are misleading) can lead corporate executives to the federal penitentiary.

Let us suppose that the corporate counsel, who always used to lose at poker in college, advises his client to disclose everything. "My rule," he explains, "is if you have to ask me, you have to disclose." Since the corporate president would sooner become an ax murderer than be the agent of his company's demise, he tells his lawyer that, having heard counsel's advice, he rejects it.

The ethical trap has been sprung. The corporate lawyer cannot avail himself of Belge's and Armani's rationale for preserving their client's guilty secrets because the president has just announced his intention to continue on a course of unlawful conduct (at least so the lawyer believes). At this point, the code of ethics appears to carve a large hole in the sanctity of the confidentiality of the lawyer-client relationship.

There are four pertinent rules.[11] The first says that a lawyer *may* reveal "the intention of his client to commit a crime and the information necessary to prevent the crime." (This is a little odd: the code permits but does not require the disclosure, yet it gives no guidance whatsoever as to the circumstances under which he ought to disclose. One might expect a "disciplinary rule" to state a rule; this one offers no discipline, states nothing.) The second rule says: "A lawyer should never encourage or aid his client to commit criminal acts or counsel his client on how to violate the law and avoid punishment therefor." The third says: "In his representation of a client, a lawyer shall not . . . counsel or assist his client in conduct that the lawyer knows to be illegal or fraudulent." And the fourth says that "a lawyer who receives information clearly establishing that his client has, in the course of the representation, perpetrated a fraud upon a person or tribunal shall promptly call upon his client to rectify the same, and if his client refuses or is unable to do so, he shall reveal the fraud to the affected person or tribunal, except when the information is protected as a privileged communication."

Together, these rules circle around an obvious limitation of zealous representation: representation must always be within the law. It would be unseemly to contemplate lawyers who advised clients on the technical aspects of breaking and entering in order to help them plan a robbery.*

In the quasi-hypothetical situation I have outlined above, the lawyer has been told that his client, the corporation, intends to commit a crime, one taking the form of a fraud on the investing public. The four rules just quoted seem to require the lawyer to quit the client and possibly to disclose the facts that the company preferred to keep secret. But by now we know that what seems obvious in the code at first glance is often the reverse on succeeding inspections. The two principal problems are how to define "fraud" and what it means to "know" the client intends to commit it.

The securities laws are like mushrooms after a spring rain. They might pop up anywhere in a company's affairs. That is because their broad phrases, requiring disclosure of "material" facts, are far from precise clues as to what must be publicly revealed and what need not be. Hence anything might be.

"Clearly a lawyer does not 'know' that his client's conduct is 'illegal' or 'fraudulent' simply because there is a possibility that the law

---

*These things do happen. As a Navy lawyer, I was once asked by a Chief Petty Officer in all seriousness whether it would be permissible for him to kill a man who was dating his estranged wife. After I recovered from the question, I tried to elicit the man's story and he tried to elicit the best way of doing the job. He was persuaded, I happily report, that in addition to being unlawful, his intended course was imprudent. But I have no doubt that had he stalked out of my office with the announced intention of killing the man, I would have been obligated to tell him that I would have to report his intentions to the proper authorities and would then have had to do so. (Suppose he had then told me he was only kidding?)

might be interpreted by the SEC or the courts to prohibit it," Chicago lawyer Justin A. Stanley, 1976–1977 president of the ABA, argues.[12] There is force in the argument; it seems plain that lawyers ought not to be compelled to cease giving advice to a client the moment a particularly tricky or obscure section of the securities law comes into play. Since the law "progresses" case by case, the lawyer must give the benefit of the doubt to the client who in good faith wishes to test the law. Otherwise, lawyers, fearful of their own vulnerability to lawsuit, will simply advise their clients to disclose everything, which is not what the law requires.

But that does not dispose of the problem. Colossal stock frauds in the past few years are reminders that in addition to fine questions of judgment there are also gross conspiracies within some very large companies. Sometimes corporate officials and lawyers are conscious partners in the carrying out of the fraud. But true fraud is more likely to be withheld from a company's lawyers. This raises problems of knowledge. When does a lawyer "know" that his client is engaging in fraudulent activities?

The code does not say. The nearest rule says that only if the information "clearly establishes" the fraud must the lawyer reveal it to the affected person.* But that is a slippery concept. Almost never will the information *clearly* establish the intent of corporate officials to defraud. The lawyer is not an auditor; information that comes to him is carefully prepared, not raw. At most, the lawyers will detect from hints and clues that something is wrong.

In 1972, the SEC stunned the securities bar when it filed suit against two of the nation's most prestigious law firms, White & Case in New

*The rule has a loophole: "privileged" information, such as that gained *from the client* in the course of representation, cannot be disclosed, even if fraudulent. This provision was added to the code in 1974, when enough securities frauds had come to light to make it clear that without it hundreds of lawyers had acted unethically in failing to come forward with evidence they had heard from their clients' own lips. But the loophole is not all that large. If the information did not come from the client, then there is no privilege to begin with. More important, if the fraud consists of the continuing failure to disclose corporate information, then a continuing crime is being committed and the privilege no longer applies.

York and Lord, Bissell & Brook in Chicago, in connection with the collapse of the National Student Marketing Corporation (NSMC). Through this civil suit, still pending in part as this is written, the SEC is asserting a novel proposition: that the lawyer has a definite legal obligation to pick up on the hints and clues and probe for possible fraud—and, if any is found, to report it to the SEC itself, unless the client can be persuaded to adopt an honest course.

The case itself is complex. In broadest outline, it concerns NSMC's 1969 acquisition of Interstate National Corporation, a Chicago insurance holding company with lots of cash. National Student Marketing was a Wall Street phenomenon of the late 1960s. Its premise was that a burgeoning youth market with billions of dollars to spend could be exploited by a company that knew how to retail to the "now generation." NSMC went public in 1968, four years after its founding, offering its first shares of stock around $6. By then it had some seven hundred campus representatives who marketed everything from beer mugs to inflatable furniture to computerized horoscopes. In 1969, NSMC expanded aggressively, acquiring some twenty-five companies along the way. Its stock shot up to $144 (before stock splits) at its peak, shortly after the Interstate merger.

To consummate the merger, NSMC had to prepare a variety of documents, including proxy statements. Circulated to stockholders of both companies, these documents detailed financial consequences to the stockholders if the merger were to take place. Among the matters listed in the proxies was an unaudited statement concerning the earnings of NSMC as of May 31, 1969. Under the terms of the "merger plan," NSMC's auditors, Peat Marwick & Mitchell (one of the "Big 8" accounting firms), had to supply a "comfort letter" prior to the closing. The comfort letter would have to state that the financial condition of the company conformed to the earlier unaudited projections. Otherwise, Interstate could call the deal off.

On October 31, 1969, the date of the closing, the principals met in the offices of Marion Jay Epley III, the White & Case partner who served as NSMC's outside counsel. On that day, in a series of telephone calls (the exact timing and content of which will forever remain in dispute), Epley learned that PMM's comfort letter would contain a surprise. What was expected to be a $700,000 profit as of May 31 was instead an $80,000 loss. The contents of the comfort letter were dictated from Washington by Anthony M. Natelli, the PMM man on the NSMC account. (He later went to jail for knowingly accepting false figures from NSMC.)

This was apparently the first that any of the outside lawyers had heard of difficulties. According to the SEC, a sentence in a supplementary paragraph to the comfort letter was relayed by telephone to Epley before the closing documents were signed. It said that, based on the now audited May 31 figures, the company's nine-month figures would show that NSMC would just break even. Epley has denied that such a sentence came to him before the merger took place. In any event, the merger was consummated that afternoon. The unsigned comfort letter was shown to Interstate's lawyers and principals (though how much was shown is still in dispute); they caucused privately and agreed to go forward.

The following January, NSMC's bubble burst. The auditors by now had turned up enough discrepancies to make it clear that NSMC's growth was built more on fraud and financial manipulation than on sales. The stock slid to under $3 per share when trading was suspended. The president and general counsel later went to jail.

In the case against the outside lawyers, the SEC charged that they should have insisted that the last-minute information be transmitted to the stockholders (Interstate had some 1,200) before any merger was allowed to take place. To ensure that this was done, the SEC says, the lawyers should have refused to issue an opinion that all legal prerequisites had been met. Moreover, asserts the SEC, because the closing did take place, Epley and the other lawyers should have come to the SEC itself and given the government attorneys the disquieting news that the proxy statements contained materially inaccurate information.

Epley and White & Case flatly disagreed. As they put it in their trial brief: "After ensuring that the proposed adjustments were fully disclosed [to Interstate's representatives], Epley had neither the right nor the duty to substitute his judgment concerning the effect of the proposed adjustments for the business judgment of the principals." Moreover, asserted Epley and his firm, they had no knowledge at the time of the closing or until long afterward that the principal officers of NSMC were engaged in fraudulent activities. Indeed, the government itself maintained at the criminal trial of NSMC's general counsel that he "intentionally concealed . . . from outside attorneys . . . what was really going on." The law does not require a comfort letter to be issued, they noted; "Interstate had the right to waive any noncompliance of the comfort letter with the merger agreement and to close the transaction as a matter of business judgement." Epley's job, he said, was to advise "NSMC's management of the risks which would arise either from disclosure or nondisclosure under the circumstances," not to demand that NSMC "issue an immediate public announcement concerning the adjustments proposed by PMM in the comfort letter."[13]

Because the facts are sharply disputed (and intricate: the full story is more complicated than the brief picture painted here), it would be rash to condemn Epley or the SEC. But one aspect of this case is worth looking at closely. That is the claim of the defendants that "neither White & Case nor Mr. Epley had an 'intent to deceive, manipulate or defraud.' "

The claim is important because of a 1976 Supreme Court decision involving accountants.[14] A group of investors in a bankrupt company sued the company's accountants for damages, claiming that the accountants were negligent in failing to detect corporate fraud that led to the bankruptcy. The Supreme Court ruled that the accountants could not be held liable to the investors unless there was evidence that the accountants had intended to deceive, manipulate, or defraud; mere negligence was not sufficient.

When the Supreme Court announced this decision, a sigh of relief was almost audible throughout the bar. For the first time since the NSMC suit was filed in 1972, securities lawyers were encouraged to believe that they might avoid being made guarantors of their clients' virtue. Lawyers have repeatedly cited the 1976 decision as a basis for limiting their duty to the public. Unless a lawyer *knows in fact* that his client is engaging in fraud, the bar is now saying, the lawyer cannot be legally liable for what happens, regardless of whether the client accepts or rejects the lawyer's advice. What he *knows in fact* means just that: inferences from suspicious circumstances are not facts. And failure to take the lawyer's advice is not enough, legally, even to give rise to suspicions warranting a closer look. So, it seemed, White & Case was arguing. In its trial brief, the law firm pleaded that "the adjustments proposed by PMM in its comfort letter were not *clearly* material as a matter of law so that Mr. Epley was required to attempt to stop the Interstate merger."

But these arguments, on which the bar appears to be placing so much faith, are perverse and ultimately unconvincing. That there is no legal liability is not dispositive of ethical considerations. Ethics is not the art of forgoing what it is unlawful to do.

More concretely, the facts in the *Student Marketing* case, looked at in a different way than the lawyers see them, are revealing of a dense attitude about what the lawyer is actually doing. Consider that on the very day of the closing, for the very first time, everyone suddenly learned that the accountants are erasing a large profit; now, for the first time, when the accountants' own necks are on the block, they are unwilling to produce a clean bill of health. Instead, they say that a hot company whose earnings are supposed to be booming—hence the appreciation in stock value, the critical centerpiece of the merger—may in fact be in trouble. According to Epley, this set off no warning bells. More astoundingly, this dramatic vanishing of profits is somehow not "clearly material."*

Must the lawyer stick silently by the client unless the stink is sharp

---

*All the lawyer defendants have claimed that the evaporation of nine-month profits was not legally material because the NSMC principals explained the changes as mere auditing adjustments and that the year-end profit, ultimately the only significant figure, would come in on target—which, in fact, it did (though it did so because NSMC rigged the books).

enough to detect outside his office? The bar appears still to believe that he must. I believe that he must not, that the bar must change its perception of what the lawyer is actually doing.

"I would suggest," said then SEC commissioner A. A. Sommer, Jr., in a 1974 speech that drew wide attention within the corporate bar, "that the security bar's *conception* of its role too sharply contrasts with the *reality* of its role in the securities process to escape notice and attention—and in such situations the reality eventually prevails. Lawyers are not paid in the amounts they are to put the representations of their clients in good English, or give opinions which assume a pure state of facts upon which any third-year law student could confidently express an opinion."[15]

Sommer declared that the "professional judgment of the attorney is often the 'passkey' to securities transactions." Without the lawyer, the registration statement, the proxy, the opinion that the prerequisites to a merger have been satisfied could not be made. The lawyer is not a mere adviser; in many ways he is a principal in securities transactions. As a principal, he should not be permitted to hide behind the client; the client's guilty secrets are his, because his efforts contribute significantly to the harm that the bad client causes.

"A lawyer preparing a registration statement has an obligation to do more than simply act as the blind scrivener of the thoughts of his client," Sommer noted in his 1974 address. The new conception "means he will have to adopt the healthy skepticism toward the representations of management which a good auditor must adopt." But skepticism implies something more; in the final analysis the securities lawyer cannot discharge his professional responsibility unless he acts, at least to some degree, as an auditor. That is not to say that he must become an accountant, or hire his own accountant to recheck the corporate auditor's calculations. But it does mean that he must become far more independent of the client than he has been in the past. He must treat the corporation as a potential adversary. He must seek to assure himself that the client is not merely using him. He cannot ignore warning signals or avert his gaze. Hints and clues of malfeasance must be followed up. Negligent failure to do so might not be unlawful, but it should certainly be branded irresponsible and unprofessional.*

The Lawyer as Advocate

The question of how far a lawyer may go in furthering his client's interests is at the heart of a number of ethical dilemmas. In this and the next three sections, we will consider some of them by examining the different roles the lawyer plays—as advocate, counselor, negotiator, and lobbyist. In each situation, the central factor to observe is the lawyer's confusion between his client's right to legal services and his (asserted) "right to win."

In his role as a courtroom advocate, the lawyer frequently encounters three specific problems:

May a lawyer put a witness on the stand who he knows intends to commit perjury?

May a lawyer discredit a witness he knows to be telling the truth?

May a lawyer accept any case, regardless of how flimsy, and fight it to the last?

The perjury question is age-old. The code seems to answer in the negative, and certainly most lawyers will tell you that it is improper to do so. But Monroe Freedman, the iconoclastic law professor, makes an interesting argument. He claims the lawyer has three con-

*Just before the trial in May 1977, the SEC and White & Case suddenly settled the *Student Marketing* case on ambiguous terms. Neither Epley nor the firm admitted or denied the SEC's allegations. Epley agreed to a six-month suspension from practice before the SEC; also, he was enjoined from future violations of certain securities laws and from issuing certain types of legal opinions. No injunction was issued against White & Case, but it did agree to adhere to internal procedures designed to scrutinize the securities activities of its clients. Many supporters of both the firm and the government were angered because the settlement precluded any test of the SEC's theory of the lawyers' responsibilities.[16] But the SEC's case is still pending against Lord, Bissell & Brook, the Chicago firm that was counsel to Interstate National, and a judicial pronouncement is still possible.

flicting duties in the representation of a client in a criminal case. First, the lawyer must ascertain "all relevant facts known to the accused." To avoid potentially incriminating facts disserves the client because the lawyer cannot adequately prepare a case when an element of it is missing. Second, the lawyer is bidden to respect the confidences of his client. Third, the lawyer has a duty not to deceive the court or to participate with others in doing so. These three duties pose a "trilemma": "The lawyer is required to know everything, to keep it in confidence, and to reveal it* to the court."[17]

Freedman poses the following ingenious situation:

> Your client has been falsely accused of a robbery committed at 16th and P Streets at 11:00 P.M. He tells you at first that at no time on the evening of the crime was he within six blocks of that location. However, you are able to persuade him that he must tell you the truth and that doing so will in no way prejudice him. He then reveals to you that he was at 15th and P Streets at 10:55 that evening, but that he was walking east, away from the scene of the crime, and that, by 11:00 P.M., he was six blocks away. At the trial, there are two prosecution witnesses. The first mistakenly, but with some degree of persuasiveness, identifies your client as the criminal. At that point the prosecution's case depends upon that single witness, who might or might not be believed. The second prosecution witness is an elderly woman who is somewhat nervous and who wears glasses. She testifies truthfully and accurately that she saw your client at 15th and P Streets at 10:55 P.M. She has corroborated the erroneous testimony of the first witness and made conviction extremely likely. However, on cross-examination her reliability is thrown into doubt through demonstration that she is easily confused and has poor eyesight. Thus, the corroboration has been eliminated, and

---

*By "it," Freedman appears to be referring to the "everything" a lawyer must know about his client's case. But no one supposes the duty to disclose literally everything. Freedman means to say, I take it, that the third horn of the trilemma requires the lawyer to reveal fraud or deceit on the court.

doubt has been established in the minds of the jurors as to the prosecution's entire case.

The client then insists upon taking the stand in his own defense, not only to deny the erroneous evidence identifying him as the criminal, but also to deny the truthful, but highly damaging, testimony of the corroborating witness who placed him one block away from the intersection five minutes prior to the crime.[18]

Freedman insists that under these circumstances the lawyer has a duty to help his client lie on the stand, or at least not prevent him from doing so. Freedman reasons that to refuse to participate when the client takes the stand or to withdraw from the case is a violation of the lawyer's duty to respect the client's confidences and to ascertain all the facts. Why? Because refusal to participate or withdrawal is a clear giveaway that the client is up to no good. But to give this away will harm the client—the one thing the lawyer promised he would not do if his client told him the whole truth in confidence.

The flaw in Freedman's argument is its equating the duty to keep a secret with a "duty" to see to it that nothing untoward happens to the client. The privileged communication translates into the right to win by lying. But there is no such duty and there is no such right. The client does himself in by deciding to lie. If the client decides to forgo his right to remain silent, then he himself incurs a duty—the duty to tell the truth. In short, the client does not have to lie, and if he does lie, he ought to bear the consequences.

Nor is Freedman's too pat example convincing. Freedman "knows" his client is innocent only because as creator of the hypothesis he can posit it. In the real courtroom, the lawyer is not God and cannot know with any assurance. We may feel for the truly innocent client caught in such a bind, but it is not clear why the lawyer must help a client violate the law simply because the circumstances of the world can be unfair.

The bar officially has condemned the notion that Freedman advances. The 1971 ABA "Standards Relating to the Defense Function" excoriated Freedman's position with a stentorian blast: The "mere advocacy" of his concept "demeans the profession and tends to drag it to the level of gangsters and their 'mouthpiece' lawyers in the public eye." It is a "transparently spurious thesis" that is "universally repudiated by ethical lawyers."[19] The purple rhetoric is directed at Freedman himself, who has engaged in a running debate on the subject since he first raised the "trilemma" in 1966.

But the official rebuke seems not to be translated into compliance. Freedman points to a 1972 survey of District of Columbia lawyers in which 90 percent said that they would call the perjurious defendant to the stand and treat him as though he were telling the truth.[20] Doing so is wrong, but there can be little doubt that "ethical lawyers" do it and that Freedman has given the rationale that most of them follow.

The second of the three questions concerning the lawyer as advocate is whether the lawyer may discredit the truthful witness. Lawyers do it all the time. In a damning indictment of the adversary system, Anne Strick in her book *Injustice for All* presents a comic catalogue of tactics that the most well-read legal writers have recommended to the bar to "destroy," "demolish," and "annihilate" witnesses on cross-examination.[21] Thus, says Lake in his *How to Cross-Examine Witnesses Successfully:* "No matter how clear, how logical, how concise, or how honest a witness may be or make his testimony appear, there is always some way, if you are ingenious enough, to cast suspicion on it, to weaken its effect."

Destruction of truthful witnesses is popular in rape cases.[22] The usual technique is to suggest that the victim encouraged the rapist or that she was a woman of loose character. Cross-examination can be exceedingly rough. The good cross-examiner does not see a human being sitting on the stand across from him; he sees an animal ready for sacrifice. He will be disappointed if he fails to slaughter it by ancient formula.

At a Federal Bar Association symposium in 1966, the following

hypothetical case was presented. I set it out in full as it was presented
to the participants:

> The accused is a drifter who sometimes works as a filling station
> attendant. He is charged with rape, a capital crime. You are his
> court-appointed defense counsel. The alleged victim is the
> twenty-two-year-old daughter of a local bank president. She is
> engaged to a promising young minister in town. The alleged rape
> occurred in the early morning hours at a service station some
> distance from town, where the accused was employed as an
> attendant. This is all you know about the case when you have
> your first interview with your client.
>
> At first the accused will not talk at all. You assure him that
> you cannot help him unless you know the truth and that he can
> trust you to treat what he says as confidential. He then says that
> he had intercourse with the young woman, but that she "con-
> sented in every way." He says that he had seen her two or three
> times before when he was working the day shift at the station,
> and that she had seemed "very friendly" and had talked with
> him in a "flirting way." He says that on the night in question she
> came in for gas; they talked; and she invited him into the car.
> One thing led to another and, finally, to sexual intercourse. They
> were interrupted by the lights of an approaching vehicle which
> pulled into the station. The accused relates that he hurriedly got
> out of the young woman's car and waited on the customer—an
> old man about sixty-five or seventy years old. The young woman
> hurriedly drove off.
>
> The accused tells you he was tried for rape in California in
> 1962 and acquitted. He has no previous convictions.
>
> The young woman refuses to talk with you because, she says,
> "The district attorney says there is no way in the world you can
> make me say anything. He said to call the police if anybody
> tampered with me."
>
> At the grand jury proceedings the victim testifies that she was

returning to her father's house in town from the church camp, where her fiance was a counselor, when she noticed that her fuel gauge registered empty. She stopped at the first station along the road that was open. The attendant, who seemed to be in sole charge of the station, forced his way into her car, terrified her with threats and forcefully had sexual intercourse with her. She says he was forced to stop when an approaching car turned into the station. As he got out of the car he is alleged to have told her, "If you yell on me, lady, I'll kill you. I'm warning you. I know where to find you." The alleged victim's father testified as to fresh complaint. No other testimony is presented. The grand jury returns a true bill.

The prosecutor declines to say whether he has knowledge of any witnesses other than the victim. The accused tells you, at a second interview, that he now remembers that as he was hurriedly getting out of the woman's car he agreed to meet her again and said, "I know how to find you, don't worry." He also says that the old man who drove up to the station had picked him out of a police line-up.

You are able to locate the old man despite the prosecutor's recalcitrance. He wears a hearing aid and is very nervous and feeble. He willingly tells about the line-up and that the prosecutor apparently plans to call him. He tells you that he drove up to the gas station at about one o'clock A.M.; he then saw the attendant, who later serviced his car, getting out of a car meeting the description of the victim's car, parked by the gas pumps. As the attendant got out of the car the old man heard him say to the driver of the car parked by the pumps, whom he could not see, "Don't worry, lady, I know where to find you," or something to that effect. The other car then drove away at a fast rate of speed. He says that the attendant spoke in an angry or excited voice but was not shouting. He says, furthermore, that the attendant seemed anxious about something as he filled his car with gas, and kept looking down the dark road towards town.

You learn that the victim has had affairs with two local men from good families. Smith, one of these young men, admits that the victim and he went together for some time, but refuses to say whether he had sexual intercourse with her and indicates he has a low opinion of you for asking. The other, Jones, apparently a bitterly disappointed and jealous suitor, readily states that he frequently had intercourse with the victim, and describes her behavior toward strange men as scandalous. He once took her to a fraternity dance, he says, and, having noticed she was gone for some time, discovered her upstairs with Smith, a fraternity brother, on a bed in a state of semi-undress. He appears anxious to testify and he states that the girl got what she'd always been asking for.

You have serious doubts about the accused's truthfulness. You believe Jones, but are somewhat repelled by the disappointed suitor's apparent willingness to smear the young woman's reputation.[23]

The symposium participants were asked whether it would be proper to call the witness Jones on behalf of the defendant. Those who spoke to the issue said that it would be. Chief Justice Warren E. Burger (then a circuit court judge) said that even if the lawyer knows his client is lying and is guilty, "the testimony of bad repute of [the victim], being recent and not remote in point of time, is relevant to her credibility."[24] David G. Bress, then U.S. Attorney for Washington, said simply: "Jones should certainly be called by the defense, notwithstanding that he was a disappointed suitor."[25] Addison M. Bowman, then deputy director of the Legal Aid Society for the District of Columbia, agreed, adding: "The fact that the young lady's reputation suffers is one of the unfortunate consequences of the law."[26] The excuse is that it is always proper to "test the truth of the prosecution's case," but the effect is to destroy the woman's reputation in order to suggest, falsely, that she is lying.

Freedman is among those who agree that such cross-examination is proper. But he poses a harder case, that of the innocent defendant at 16th and P:

> The defendant has been wrongly identified as the criminal, but correctly identified by the nervous, elderly woman who wears eyeglasses, as having been only a block away five minutes before the crime took place. If the woman is not cross-examined vigorously and her testimony shaken, it will serve to corroborate the erroneous evidence of guilt. . . . However, if you destroy her reliability through cross-examination designed to show that she is easily confused and has poor eyesight, you may not only eliminate the corroboration, but also cast doubt in the jury's mind on the prosecution's entire case. On the other hand, if you should refuse to cross-examine her because she is telling the truth, your client may well feel betrayed, since you knew of the witness's veracity only because your client confided in you, under your assurance that his truthfulness would not prejudice him.[27]

Freedman's conclusion that it is ethically proper to discredit the witness again flows from an identification of a legitimate right of representation with a spurious right to win. Failure to cross-examine would not violate a confidence because nothing would be disclosed, Freedman admits. But, he says, "the same policy that supports the obligation of confidentiality precludes the attorney from prejudicing his client's interest in any other way because of knowledge gained in his professional character."[28]

The adversary system practically screams out for the lawyer to destroy the veracity of the elderly lady, but it is an unreasoning cry. What is the client's interest? Acquittal, obviously. But he is not entitled to acquittal at any cost. That the client is in an unenviable position does not excuse the harm that the lawyer's forensic brilliance can cause the witness. Freedman's justification is a little like supposing you are hired as a bodyguard for an important person and find him in a situation where you can save him only by throwing someone else in front to catch the bullet. Is this permissible? I think not.

A bad drubbing on the stand can seriously hurt a person unprepared for the scorn and abuse that is part of many lawyers' theatrical repertoire. The code of ethics says that "needless harm" is not to be inflicted on witnesses. But if what is needful is what helps the client, then anything a lawyer wishes to subject a witness to can be rationalized as proper. Unfortunately, that is the lawyers' daily perception. The rule of the code is empty, when it ought not to be.

The third problem for the advocate, that of fighting a flimsy case to the last, is more difficult. The code says that the client is entitled to the benefit of every doubt about the lawfulness of his objective. The lawyer may assert any position that "is supported by the law or is supportable by a good faith argument for an extension, modification, or reversal of the law" and "without regard to his professional opinion as to the likelihood that the construction will ultimately prevail." But the lawyer may not make a "frivolous" argument in litigation, nor may he "file a suit, assert a position, conduct a defense, delay a trial, or take other actions on behalf of his client when he knows or when it is obvious that such action would serve merely to harass or maliciously injure another."[29]

Because Americans believe so deeply in the unexamined maxim "Every person is entitled to his day in court," the prohibition against provoking or prolonging baseless claims is frequently violated. Most lawyers see their jobs as picking nits on behalf of clients. The lawyer's training is to debate.

"There's no such thing as a frivolous position," says Monroe Freedman, speaking in hyperbole to make a point. "You give me a case and I will find a way to distinguish it from my client's," he claims.[30] That is why the prohibition against frivolous actions is an ethical, not a legal, one. Each case depends upon nuances too numerous to be controlled by definable law. One must have a sense of propriety about how far to bend in accommodating a client.

Many lawyers do have such a sense. A Savannah, Georgia, lawyer who handles employment discrimination cases on behalf of poor and black workers throughout the South says his definition of what is a legitimate suit is "pretty loose." As he explains it: "For the most part, no other lawyers will touch these cases [despite a law providing for payment of the attorney's fee by the corporate defendant if the suit is successful], so I have to be liberal if they are to be represented at all." But the equal employment laws have an unfortunate side effect: they provide incentives to extortion. (Libel laws are another example: newspapers, magazines, and broadcasting stations are often hit with suits whose merits are too small to be seen by the naked eye.) In "nuisance suits" such as these, the plaintiff's idea is to exact a settlement to save the defendant the greater sum of money it would take him to win.

"I had a client once," the Savannah lawyer says, "a black man who claimed he had been fired because he was black. I couldn't find any evidence of it. He was let go along with hundreds of other workers during the middle of the recession, whites as well as blacks. In two months he even found another job, and it paid him more than he had been making at the company he wanted to sue. They offered him $5,000 to settle the case, but he didn't want it. He wanted to sue them for much more. What did I do? I removed myself from the case and slapped a lien on any judgment he might get, so before his next lawyer could get paid I would have to be reimbursed for my time. He is not likely to find a lawyer under those circumstances."[31] The judgments that a lawyer must make in this area are sensitive, and it is not surprising therefore that the canon against frivolous actions remains more platitude than doctrine.

But there are times when lawyers violate this ethic deliberately, vigorously, and collectively. The most spectacular example in our history was the battle that lawyers fought in the South after the Supreme Court's 1954 desegregation decision. Ensuing legislation and court decrees made it clear that segregation had no place in America. But the Southern bar resisted. When suits were filed to enforce the rights of blacks, lawyers fought them on patently frivolous grounds.

The most absurd contention, raised repeatedly, was that the Supreme Court's decisions are not the "law of the land." Instead, they were said to be the "law of the case."[32] The theory was that when one school lost a desegregation case, other schools in identical circumstances had no obligation to abide by the decision.

The theory is nonsense. Stripped to essentials, it would obliterate the meaning of civil liberties in the United States. A policeman who decided to search the home of a youth without a warrant "on suspicion of having long hair" could reply with a smile to protests: "Oh, that thing in the Constitution about needing a warrant doesn't apply to me. At least I don't think it does. It only applies if some court tells me it does. So why don't you and I fight this out in court, and if I lose I may apologize. Of course, the judge's decision will only apply to your case, so it won't stop me from poking around in someone else's house." That is not a good faith argument, to be sure, and by the code of ethics anyone who asserts the proposition is surely acting unethically. Yet, during a decade and a half while all this was going on, the bar did not condemn it.

The problem of frivolous claims and defenses remains serious. The bar has negligently failed to devise ways to keep lawyers from participating in socially harmful conspiracies. As Professor Murray Schwartz has asked, "How can we enforce a demand that the school board lawyer not help the board obstruct the implementation of desegregation decrees?"[33]

So far the bar has assumed the problem away. Their argument: Since lawyers are in general respectable people, their arguments should be taken as being made in good faith. Consequently, when any large segment of the bar advances for a class of clients arguments for the modification or reversal of existing law, they cannot be thought in the nature of things to be making frivolous demands. Perhaps frivolousness, like pornography, cannot be defined, but you and I frequently know it when we see it. Expressing the intuitive feeling in an articulate manner is urgently needed.

Because it often depends on frivolous motions and tactics, *delay* in judicial and administrative proceedings is a closely related problem. Usually delay is a defendant's tactic. The plaintiff, after all, is seeking a court judgment. That means we must look to the defendant's bar, generally institutional lawyers, for the most splendid illustrations of the delaying tactic. To note only one, Covington & Burling, the premier Washington law firm, managed to stall a Food and Drug Administration proceeding over the proper labeling of peanut butter jars for twelve years. During that time, an enormous record was compiled. "Perhaps one [strategy] was to browbeat the government into submission," said one C & B attorney who spent time on the case, "but I can't say that with confidence. Certainly there is something suspicious about a 24,000-page hearing transcript and close to 75,000 pages of documents on a case involving peanut butter."*[34]

Because delay for its own sake is unlawful, few lawyers can be counted on to admit that they (or their brethren) regularly engage in it. So I will have to rely on Bruce D. Bromley's well-known confession at Stanford Law School in 1958. Bromley is one of the last colorful characters at the corporate bar (he has been at Cravath, Swaine & Moore for nearly sixty years and served briefly on the New York Court of Appeals). To judge by his talk, he is not easily embarrassed, blushing neither for himself nor for the bar. Addressing a group of federal judges, Bromley enlightened them on how he had managed during his career to drag out antitrust cases and how certain judges had managed to stop him.

> I was born, I think, to be a protractor [he began]. I quickly realized in my early days at the bar that I could take the simplest case that [the Justice Department] could think of and protract it for the defense almost to infinity. [Of one antitrust case he

*In an angry speech in 1973, James T. Halverson, director of the FTC's Bureau of Competition, told how these tactics work:

"While not intending to exhaust the means available for intentional delay of investigations, I would point to the following types of conduct which may be evidence of bad faith on the part of counsel: Promises voluntarily to comply with document demands, in lieu of compliance with subpoenas, which are not promptly kept and were not intended to be kept; motions to quash subpoenas, the bases of which are boilerplate objections which have already been repeatedly rejected by the Commission; request after request to extend the deadline date for compliance with the subpoena, while no reasonable effort has been made in the document search. Litigation is also fraught with opportunities for inexcusable delay, e.g., making unnecessary motions to extend deadlines or to change pretrial conference dates; and asking for subpoenas to be issued to third parties, knowing full well that enforcement of them will probably be tied up in federal court, while little valuable evidence is expected to be forthcoming."[35]

crowed:] [It] lasted fourteen years. The record was nearly 50,000
pages and there were thousands of exhibits. I was on the road
for four years almost without interruption, sitting in sixty-two
cities. . . . If any of you gentlemen had been in control of that
proceeding, at the very outset you would have developed [what
the company's policy was]. Despite the 50,000 pages of testimony, there really wasn't any dispute about the facts at all.
. . . We won that case and, as you know, my firm's meter was
running all the time—every month for fourteen years. The president of that company was a good friend of mine and the company was very prosperous. He was accustomed to road-show
productions of the most lavish nature and feature pictures that
cost a million dollars or more. He saw nothing at all untoward
in this young lawyer of his making a road show production out
of his lawsuit.[36]

Bromley also defended United States Gypsum Company, which the
government was prosecuting along with the rest of the industry for
antitrust violations.

I will never forget the day in 1940 [Bromley reminisced] when
[Thurman Arnold, the government's antitrust chief] said, "I'll
fix your kite, my friend. I'm going to file an expediting certificate
in this case and convene a three-judge court. This will get rid of
the case fast and secure the prompt judgment to which the
Government is plainly entitled." That was in 1940. The case
came to an end three weeks ago [1958]. . . . We had discovery
of hundreds of documents. . . . But it is perfectly apparent, now
in retrospect, that if we had been called on the carpet and asked
to admit [the crucial facts] we would have done so. The motion
for summary judgment could have been made at the outset, and
all these years of proof could have been avoided. The case would
certainly not have lasted eighteen years. However, I think I
ought to confess that during the last part of this period I stirred
up a fight among the co-defendants just to keep the case going
a little longer, and all of it was not the Government's fault.

Bromley concluded by showing how stern judicial control of attorneys could effectively blunt the "Bromley protractor touch"—his phrase. In the current IBM case, however, which Bromley is fighting in his characteristically flamboyant style (at one point he asked Judge David N. Edelstein to hold him in contempt in order to litigate a point on which he later gave in), he and his colleagues have participated in discovering (i.e., searching government files for) millions of documents (much of it initiated by the government, to be sure). The case was filed in 1969 and is still at trial as this is written in 1977. It is likely to last well into the 1980s.

The usual justification for the inordinate number of memos, replies, interrogatories, depositions, questions, objections, motions, and all the rest is that in adversary proceedings no quarter need be given. The other side is represented too; let them make their own objections and countermotions if they don't like what's going on. But that, of course, is precisely the problem. The adversary system is prone to abuse; that is why we desire lawyers to behave ethically toward it. We may shrug and wink when IBM and the United States government slug it out for ten years at a time (though the drain on an already pinched antitrust enforcement budget is severe). But smaller parties can be cowed into submission, bankrupted, or, forewarned, suffer in silence. Once in a great while, a judge will refuse a lawyer's motion because it is oppressive or frivolous, but for the most part judges let lawyers have their way, and bar associations sit mute. When the object of the delay is to keep a dangerous drug or chemical on the market or to continue monopolistic practices for as long as possible, the harm is palpable.

The Lawyer as Counselor

A lawyer is not supposed to "do anything furthering the creation or preservation of false evidence."[37] Clients frequently call on lawyers for such assistance, although they may not know when they enter his office the reasons for doing so. A couple wants a divorce; what do they have to do? The lawyer begins to recite the various grounds for divorce in the state: cruel and abusive treatment by one spouse, adultery, and so forth. Unfortunately, incompatibility is not a ground. What constitutes cruel and abusive treatment? the wife asks. Physical abuse, for example, or in one case a court held that chronic nagging was enough. The husband and wife look at each other. Can we just say that or do we have to prove it? the husband wonders. Well, replies the lawyer genially, you will need some proof. Perhaps there is a witness other than yourselves. Or you could each testify to acts of cruelty. If you have been keeping a record of difficult times, that would be helpful.

Without ever saying so, the lawyer can thus coach the clients on exactly what kind of evidence they can manufacture to secure the divorce. Devising evidence solely for the purpose of maintaining a legal action is fraud on the state. Is it ethical for the lawyer to give such advice? One answer might be that the law is irrational when it refuses to sanction "no fault" divorce; states with stringent requirements are practically begging spouses to break the law. But that is not a sufficient answer for a system of ethics. For individuals to violate seemingly irrational laws—of which there are many—is to invite anarchy.

If, however, such questioning is unethical, a lawyer gives advice at great peril. The difference between lawful and unlawful use of legal knowledge often turns on the intent of the user. If the husband had beaten the wife, and if the wife had written letters about the beatings, the advice would be wholly proper. But the lawyer doesn't know this at the outset. He could say: "I understand you want to see me about a divorce. Before we begin, I must ask you whether you have been beating your wife." When the husband asks, "Why do you want to know?" the lawyer's explanation will tell the clients everything they need to know to fake the evidence if they are so inclined. But if the lawyer refuses to tell the clients about the law, he is prevented from carrying out his primary function—counseling

—and the client is barred from obtaining legitimate information.

Is the lawyer simply the repository of knowledge—a "lawbook," as one professor put it,[38] or a library, which anyone may open or enter on payment of a fee? Many lawyers think so. A survey of New York City lawyers during the 1960s revealed that most came right out and told their clients how to develop evidence to rig tax cases.[39] (The question had to be dropped from a survey of legal ethics because lawyers so uniformly approved the practice that it was thought no one surveyed would condemn it.) But "the lawyer in the tax case is, purely and simply, the active instrument in establishing—and ultimately, presenting—a fraudulent case." As in the securities practice, lawyers might become partners in crime, for without their assistance the unlawful acts could not take place.

I wish, however, to challenge the related notion that a lawyer can never counsel a client to break the law. Consider this example from a legal aid attorney. Her client has been charged with some minor crime. He is out on bail pending trial. On the day of trial, he oversleeps and arrives at the courthouse an hour late. The frantic attorney has been unable to keep the presiding judge from issuing a bench warrant for the client's arrest. The presiding judge is mean-spirited; many lawyers consider him unfit to sit on the bench. He is well known for dealing harshly with defendants against whom he has had to issue arrest warrants. There is always the chance that the lawyer can persuade the judge that the client is well-intentioned; that the delay was due to oversleeping rather than, say, to a broken subway will count heavily against him, however. So the lawyer counsels the client to stay away from the court. The likelihood that the police will look for him is as near zero as anything can be. They are otherwise occupied. The lawyer is confident tomorrow's judge will pay no attention to the warrant, since his fellow judge's foibles are well known.

In advising the client to ignore the warrant, the lawyer is obviously counseling "conduct that the lawyer knows to be illegal," a violation of the disciplinary rules.[40] But it is not apparent that the lawyer's conduct is harmful. The world is full of small things, like judges of mean temper, little compassion, and no tolerance for human error. Whether they intersect with a defendant's life is a purely random event that can nevertheless have sizable consequences for the individual. To aid a client in avoiding these consequences is surely an essential function of the lawyer who understands the court or administrative system.

Whether the lawyer acts rightly or wrongly depends on his own motives and the manner in which he gives his advice. Telling the client the odds are low that the police will find him if he moves west permanently would be unethical because it cheats the legal system altogether. Telling a client he will be much better off going to the movies for a day in order to face a more humane judge in twenty-four hours is not cheating the system; it is only cheating the judge who would make sport of a missing defendant.

This case, and others like it, present difficulties to anyone seriously entertaining questions of ethical behavior. But the answer is not to be found in outright condemnation of all such advice. A lawyer may on balance need to be more sensitive to the needs of his client than to the needs of the system.

The Lawyer as Negotiator

Negotiation is a task that lawyers constantly perform, but its ethical perplexities are not covered in the code. The older canons exhorted lawyers to deal fairly and candidly with each other; this sensible statement has vanished from the new code.

On a personal level, lawyers generally do behave honorably toward one another. In smaller towns it would be suicidal not to; even in large cities a lawyer who acquires a reputation for double dealing will quickly find himself handicapped by the refusal of other lawyers to deal informally. Sometimes, indeed, lawyers carry their chumminess too far. Most lawyers in practice for any length of time can tell of some opposing attorney who asked that the first lawyer give up his client's case ("You really have to help me out on this one; I know the settlement offer is too low, but if you take it, I'll give you whatever you want the next time").

Good faith often disappears, however, when the negotiations between lawyers are for something of financial value (rather than when confined to incidental matters of trial procedure). The rules against deceit that are so starkly proclaimed in the code are ignored when lawyers tell each other how to go about bargaining. Thus, books written for students during the 1970s recommend (or at least discuss in great detail) many disreputable tactics. Among the suggestions in a 1972 book: "Make false demands, bluffs, threats; even use irrationality."[41] A 1974 text includes these ploys: "Claim that you do not have authority to compromise," and "after agreement has been reached, have your client reject it and raise his demands."[42]

The usual excuse is that in negotiating situations everyone is expected to act in a deceitful manner. Any lawyer who naïvely puts all his cards on the table expecting the others to do likewise is not acting in the best interests of his client. This objection goes more to the difficulty of changing behavior, however, than to the rightness or wrongness of negotiating tactics. Where such tactics are employed, we can at least point to the adversary system and say that both sides are equally culpable and equally capable of bluffing.

Yet even within the adversarial system, there are times when such amorality can cause serious damage. Consider this case.[43] There has been an automobile accident. Apparently the brakes failed. A mechanic had just recently finished extensive repairs at the driver's request. The driver sues the garage. But the driver's lawyer is worried. First, the law of negligence in his state is well known: if the victim is even a little bit at fault, he cannot recover for his damages. The victims were not wearing seat belts; had they worn belts, their injuries would have been minimal. Second, at pretrial depositions the mechanic swore emphatically that the brakes were adjusted and tightened and said that he would describe in detail how he performed the work to demonstrate that he was not negligent in the shop.

The lawyer advises his client that the chances for a large recovery are not high and that it would be more prudent to seek a reasonable settlement, even though it might not reimburse the driver and his passenger for all their expenses and suffering. Knowing these facts also, the lawyer for the garage offers to discuss a settlement.

Unbeknownst to the driver's lawyer, however, but well known to the garage lawyer, the state supreme court has just changed the old rule of negligence. Under the new rule the plaintiff will no longer be thrown out of court if he was a little negligent. Instead, if he was 10 percent responsible for the accident, his recovery will be limited to 90 percent of the damages. Moreover, the garage lawyer knows, and the driver's lawyer does not, that the day before the settlement meeting the mechanic changed his story. Worried that his lie will be found out, the mechanic has confessed privately to the garage lawyer that he knew the brakes were defective but forgot to repair them. He also says that if asked this in court, he will own up to his error.

Must the garage lawyer remind the driver's lawyer that the law has changed? Must he tell him that the facts of the case have rather significantly changed as well?

If the situation had arisen at trial, the code says the lawyer has an obligation to inform the court about the law. Since the mechanic will testify as to the facts, the repair shop's responsibility would not then be hidden.

The code is silent, however, about the lawyer's responsibility around the negotiating table. The garage lawyer will not likely confess the shortcomings of his case to his adversaries. His client's interest is in a quick settlement, not simply to avoid the expense of trial but to avoid the liability that is sure to be imposed at its end. Unwary, the driver's lawyer will grab at what he thinks is a reasonable offer. And injustice will have been done, because the facts will never come out. If the driver's lawyer later discovers his error, he will not likely raise his own ignorance as a reason for upsetting the settlement.

The bar's ethical blindness has been condemned from time to time.

In a trenchant analysis, Judge Alvin B. Rubin of the New Orleans federal district court concluded that "another lawyer, or a layman, who deals with a lawyer should not need to exercise the same degree of caution that he would if trading for reputedly antique copper jugs in an oriental bazaar. It is inherent in the concept of an ethic, as a principle of good conduct, that it is morally binding on the conscience of the professional and not merely a rule of the game adopted because other players observe (or fail to adopt) the same rule."[44] But lawyers, like antique dealers, make a good living by the same strategies: recall that the chairman of the ABA's ethics committee himself believes that the lawyer's shading of truth in negotiations is merely tactical (page 32). As long as that attitude prevails, no wonder the public sees the lawyer as a "hired gun" rather than as the professional he aspires to be.

The Lawyer as Lobbyist

When the lawyer goes to Washington to represent a client before a congressional committee, whether in the committee room itself or in the bar of the Cosmos Club, he has departed as sharply as possible from the traditional model of what lawyers do. In fact, Washington lawyers (and those who do essentially the same work in the state capitals) comprise an emerging profession—that of, let us say, "industrial diplomat." The industrial diplomat must have a thorough knowledge of the legislative and political processes and an understanding of public opinion and its formation. He must know something of public and private bureaucratic organization, its strengths and its limits. And he must know law; that is to say, he must be able to intuit how the laws that Congress enacts will affect both the corporations they are meant to control and the courts and regulatory agencies that are meant to be the controllers.

This assignment is not for the faint of heart. Perhaps only lawyers as a class have the nerve to assert that they possess so much knowledge. But they do know the law, and that is why law, rather than, say, public administration, has served as the fundamental training for this new professional.

The work of the industrial diplomat is difficult to categorize. He is on perpetual retainer to block, dilute, or subvert proposed legislation that his client perceives as harmful to its interests. He may draft legislation or the language of agency regulations. He may be called in to push a favorable tax law through Congress. He may present testimony on the Hill or intercede with the president. He may lobby intensively or make a phone call now and then. He may direct his client's case before a regulatory agency all the while, or he may have to fight in court simultaneously with his legislative battle. He will probably pass in and out of government two or three times during his career. In short, he holds all licenses and is prepared for anything.

But whatever he does, he works in a domain that lacks the two prerequisites of the traditional (legal) professional model. First, his work is not part of any conventional adversary system. Second, his work lacks "law-boundedness."

The first point is easily enough understood. The well-paid representative of a corporate interest is most successful in his role as industrial diplomat when there are no other contending parties. That does not mean there are not natural adversaries. A company seeking a particular trade regulation may hope to word it in such a way that it favors only the company and not its competitors. Tax legislation may be of doubtful benefit to the public at large but of considerable benefit to a restricted clientele. But even when the industrial diplomat confronts an adverse bill—which means that someone is fighting for opposing interests—the public is not often represented by counsel (or, when it is, not by counsel who musters the resources at the command of private corporations).

The second point is a bit more subtle. In the typical courtroom fight, two parties through their lawyers contend for their interpretation of already established law. If, faithful to the law, the outcome is in some sense unfair or even arguably harmful, the fault lies in the law itself. A contrary view would undermine the democratic system of lawmaking. A change in the law is for the legislature, not for partisans in a courtroom. One is entitled, therefore, to use laws that are in one's favor, and the lawyer who aids the cause is not acting improperly.

In the legislative setting, however, the very question is what the law should be. We must distinguish sharply between representing some-one (or some institution), no matter how odious, whose civil liberties are being threatened and helping someone in the exercise of his civil liberties to achieve an odious goal. Of course, every person (including corporations) must be free to assert any position—no matter how irresponsible—to the legislative body. The job of the industrial diplo-mat is to assist the presentation of the client's position, whatever it is, no matter how foolish, dangerous, or immoral. But in so doing, the lawyer is helping to make law, not to apply it.

Taken together, these features—lack of representation and of law-boundedness—sharply differentiate the role of the lobbyist and legis-lative representative from that of the court-bound lawyer. When the lawyer-lobbyist suspends his moral judgments, he becomes a partner in attempts to do harm to often sizable segments of the public. The lawyers' ethic that permits this inside the courtroom is irrelevant outside.

Those who disagree say that such a judgment is highly idiosyn-cratic. To say that a lawyer must temper his client's conduct in the legislative arena, these critics argue, is to assume that one can know what is or is not harmful. But such knowledge is not vouchsafed to any of us with any certainty, they conclude.

Reformers can retort that some harm is palpable. Pollution *is* harmful. Lobbying that defeats or dilutes laws or regulations aimed at reducing industrial pollution will surely contribute to the continu-ing injury that the pollutants cause.

The traditionalist may agree with the reformer about the harm. Yet he can still lodge an important objection against the almost evangeli-cal rhetoric of some modern reformers who argue that lawyers ought to temper or forgo altogether their representation of odious clients (or clients who do odious things) in the legislative arena. The objection is this: the client may have legitimate reasons for causing or trying to cause the harm. This sounds peculiar only because the word "harm" is so heavily freighted with evil connotations. But it is impossible to argue for the abolition of all harm or all risk of harm. Laws against pollution impose costs on industry; these costs tend to drive smaller competitors out of business, cause prices to rise, and may lead to a loss of jobs. These are also harms. Flammable children's sleepwear is harmful, so lawyers who opposed for their clients FTC rules requiring fire-resistant coatings may be thought to be arguing for harm, but suppose the chemical coatings are carcinogenic?

There is risk in any action; it is the job of the policy maker to weigh the risks and strike a proper balance. Lawyers who argue for pollution or fire-prone materials may thus be supporting other values. Certainly they cannot be prevented from making the arguments, for in a democracy policy makers are publicly elected legislators and public regulators, not the private bar.

So the objection to the lawyer-lobbyist's role lies not in what he supports or opposes but in *how he does it.* He may meet privately with members of regulatory bodies or Congress. He may ask for provisions "in the interests of fairness" that he has devised solely as a means to stall regulatory proceedings indefinitely (for example, by giving private interests the right to cross-examine witnesses at a regulatory hearing or the right to appeal in the courts interim rulings during a proceeding). Or he may suggest provisions that would render the proposed legislation impotent (as lawyers have done for themselves in some states with ineffective no-fault automobile accident laws). Perhaps worst of all, the lawyer can aid the client in fundamental distortion by suppressing facts known only to the client, facts that could change the outcome of votes in committee or in Congress as a whole.

All these things may be in the best interests of the client. But if they are, it will be necessary to find a broader obligation of the lawyer than service as a general in the client's war. In short, representation of the bad client in a legislative setting may entail a duty to the client's adversary, that is, to the public.

CHAPTER 7

In the Best Interest of the Client: The Problem of Conflicts

The Revolving Door

Dean Burch, deputy director of Barry Goldwater's 1964 presidential campaign, became chairman of the Federal Communications Commission in 1969. More than four years later, in desperate trouble, President Nixon brought him to the White House staff as counselor. In 1975, lawyer Burch was out of a job. So he took the path well trod by sensible former government lawyers without previous ties to the legal establishment; he joined a prominent law firm. Burch became a partner in Pierson, Ball & Dowd, a well-known Washington firm that frequently appears before regulatory agencies.

When Burch arrived, one of the firm's clients happened to be RKO General, Inc., then involved in a battle over television Channel 7 in Boston. Like all broadcast proceedings, this fight had been going on for a while; in fact, it had come before the FCC when Burch was chairman.[1] In that capacity, he had been "personally" and "substantially" involved in the case. Burch could not represent RKO General as a private attorney. Besides being a violation of the federal criminal code, the code of ethics unequivocally condemns it. A disciplinary rule declares that "a lawyer shall not accept private employment in a matter in which he had substantial responsibility while he was a public employee."[2]

Unfortunately for his new colleagues, the code seemed to tar them as well—guilt by association. "If a lawyer is required to decline employment or to withdraw from employment under a Disciplinary Rule, no partner, or associate, or any other lawyer affiliated with him or in his firm, may accept or continue such employment."[3] So reads the rule. But if you think that this required Pierson, Ball & Dowd to resign its client, you are not thinking like a lawyer.

Alarms were sounded. Important lawyers in government would be practically banned from becoming partners in important law firms, it was said. After heavy lobbying in big Washington firms in the summer and fall of 1975, the ABA's ethics committee announced a slight circumscription of the plain language of the code.

This is explained as follows. Under the rule, the former government employee is barred from work on a case only where his prior involvement was "substantial." A broader ban would unnecessarily "inhibit government recruitment" and deny "the opportunity for all litigants to obtain competent counsel of their own choosing, particularly in specialized areas."

To disqualify everyone in the firm "would thwart those purposes." They would be served "so long as the individual lawyer is held to be disqualified and is *screened from any direct or indirect participation in the matter.*"

Therefore, said the committee, the disciplinary rule that flatly prohibits the firm from continuing with representation whenever one of its members is barred from doing so doesn't really mean what it says and must be reinterpreted. It only applies "to the firm and partners and associates of a disqualified lawyer who has not been screened, to the satisfaction of the government agency concerned, from participation in the work and compensation of the firm on any matter over which as a public employee he had substantial responsibility."[4]

This is extraordinary. The basis for the disciplinary rule is canon 9: "A lawyer should avoid even the appearance of professional impropriety." Here the appearance of impropriety is the so-called revolving door: the tradition of lawyers going from high places in government to positions in important firms. To minimize actual impropriety, the former government employee is not permitted to work on his former cases. To minimize the appearance of impropriety, his partners and associates are also forbidden to do so. But the rule is immediately swallowed by its exceptions. Let the government waive the firm's disqualification and let the firm "screen" and "isolate" its new partner, and all's suddenly well.

How has the appearance of impropriety been eliminated? In my judgment, it simply looms larger. Self-interested government lawyers, who themselves will want to move to private firms someday, routinely grant the waivers on the assurance of the law firm, which wants the business, that the partner is screened. What could be more dubious? What reflection must the agency give to the request for waiver? How can the firm screen its partner from both conversation and fees? Is it not conceivable that an attorney's foreknowledge that he could be offered a prestigious partnership might influence his judgment in a given case, to make it easier for the clients of his future firm?

In Burch's case, a group called Community Broadcasting of Boston, Inc., which was challenging RKO's right to the television license, petitioned the FCC to disqualify Pierson, Ball & Dowd. The FCC rejected the petition.

About this time, the ethics committee of the District of Columbia bar, which Monroe Freedman then chaired, proposed to adopt a tough interpretation on its own. It would have obliterated the ABA's exception to the general rule. The activists on the committee believed that the revolving door was redolent of improprieties and proposed to lock it. In July 1976, the committee voted unanimously to adopt the tough interpretation but, whether because of summer vacations or caution, too few members were present to give an absolute majority, necessary for adoption. The proponents lacked three votes.

The Washington establishment was aghast at how close the reformers came.[5] Senior partners talked darkly of being unable to hire Supreme Court clerks, the cream of the previous year's law school graduates. Government lawyers became practically hysterical, fearing they would be shunned as "Typhoid Marys" and "pariahs." Said Werner K. Hartenberger, the FCC's general counsel, "For all practical purposes [an FCC attorney] would be asked to accept a lifelong career in government." (For impractical purposes, of course, the lawyer could always strike out on his own; nothing compels a lawyer to join a big firm except the practicalities of money.) Others spotted the dangers in an overkill rule. Harvey Pitt, general counsel of the SEC, complained that the "opinion responds to hypothetical and exaggerated problems and imposes restrictions substantially in excess of those actually required." (The same objection, as we saw, can be made to the rules against lay intermediaries, a subject on which the bar remained quiet for years.)

When the committee reassembled in November to vote again, the membership had changed. Freedman had stepped down as chairman and William Allen, a partner in Covington & Burling, which was leading the fight against the rule, had succeeded him. Of nine new members (out of nineteen all together), seven came from large firms. The proposed interpretation was defeated.

The status quo was not necessarily restored, however. The committee sent the matter to another bar committee with jurisdiction to rewrite the District's formal code of ethics. (Freedman's proposal was to have been an "interpretation," and thus less weighty than an amendment to the code itself.) The committee's instructions were to develop a concrete mechanism for isolating the disqualified partner.

A few weeks earlier, the Association of the Bar in New York, through its Committee on Professional and Judicial Ethics, rushed its own opinion into print, rejecting the Freedman approach, apparently to give wavering members of the Washington committee something to lean on.[6] But, prodded by the controversy, the New York committee took a forward step. It suggested that a law firm should file an affidavit with the court or agency, listing the methods it will use to isolate the partner from any discussions about the client's problems and from all fees generated by the firm's representation of the client. The firm's mere say-so, said the committee, is not enough. (Sample question that the firm might address: "What was the firm's competence in the area involved prior to the arrival of the disqualified lawyer?")[7] The committee suggests no answers and provides no guidelines on how the disqualified partner's annual earnings are to be kept pure of the tainted money. However, this much can be said: the questions are sharply etched, and if firms live up to their spirit, a new ethic may eventually emerge.

But if it does not emerge from within, it may be forced from without. President Carter has put the regulators and the bar on notice that the revolving door is inimical to public policy.[8] Whether he can bolt it shut or merely slow it down remains to be seen, but with Congress voting a tough code of ethics for its own members, the previous reluctance to legislate in this area may vanish.

In the Boardroom

Lawyers frequently serve as members of corporate boards of directors. This is supposed to be a mutually beneficial arrangement. The company gets a person of legal sophistication, business acumen, reputation in the community, and sound judgment. The lawyer gets business: a large number of lawyer-directors serve through their law firms as counsel to the corporations. Between 1974 and 1976, partners in 1,100 law firms served on the boards of more than 1,800 public corporations in the United States.[9] Some of these lawyers took in spectacular fees. Mayer, Brown & Platt of Chicago got $2,100,000 in 1975 from Continental Illinois Corporation—the single largest fee during that period.* Partners of Baker & Botts, the large Houston firm, sat on

---

*Single largest, that is, from public corporations that paid a fee to a director's law firm. By law, such fees must be reported to the SEC. Fees to lawyers not on the board or from privately held corporations are excluded from the reporting requirements.

twelve boards and reaped more than $6 million in fees in 1975 from the connections.

The lawyer on the board runs serious risks of conflict and loss of independence. Here the conflict is internal—not a conflict between clients but a conflict between roles. "Serving on a client's board impairs a lawyer's freedom to give disinterested advice," says one thoughtful student of the problem, Stanley J. Friedman, whose New York firm Shereff, Friedman, Hoffman & Goodman prohibits any of its lawyers from accepting directorships.[10]

Corporate counsel will often have occasion to give advice that directors are not beholden to follow. One or the other position will have to be compromised; but independence of thought is the highest duty in each role. Also, the lawyer in a sense comes to work for himself; his advice as a lawyer may be tempered by how it will reflect on him as a director. Too, he may be more careless of the corporation's funds by billing high, since it is hardly likely that the other board members will repudiate, or even question, actions taken by their fellow director-counsel. Moreover, the lawyer can never be sure whether for purposes of confidentiality he is speaking to management as a director (in which event his conversations are not privileged) or as counsel (in which event they are). Finally, service as director makes it likely that (whether or not acting as counsel) he will be seen as a principal, forcing him to worry about his own liability as well as that of the company. Such worries could hamper him in giving his most considered judgment.

For all these reasons, many members of the corporate bar have become wary of this dual role. More and more firms are prohibiting their lawyers from serving as a director of a corporate client. There is some evidence that the number of lawyers withdrawing from boards is increasing,[11] and lawyers in prominent firms have told me that while they do not want to publicize the fact or wish to withdraw from boards on which they are currently serving, new policies have been established to prevent members from accepting new invitations.

Despite the heated debate, the official organs of the bar still recognize the practice—witness the high number of the "best" firms that indulge in it. Simon H. Rifkind argues that the code of ethics ought to contain a flat ban against director-lawyers.[12] But he is a member of two corporate boards (Sterling National Bank & Trust, and Revlon), and, despite his beliefs about the proprieties, apparently intends to stay on rather than resign, as he is free to do.

Likewise, the ABA's ethics committee, which could do something, has never confronted the problem. Notwithstanding the controversy, the committee remains silent; and not surprisingly, since committee members themselves belonged to firms whose partners have sat as directors of clients. The latest figures show that the committee chairman, Lewis Van Dusen, has sat on two boards himself—the Girard Company, a bank holding corporation (1975 fee to his firm: $214,676, not including fees paid by bank customers); and IU International Corporation (1974 fee: $76,600).[13] A change in the code thus seems unlikely.

What Is the Client's Interest?—And for That Matter, Who Is the Client?

James Neal, the Watergate prosecutor who obtained the convictions of Haldeman, Ehrlichman, and Mitchell, is a practicing lawyer in Nashville. He has a retainer from the *Nashville Banner,* the city's afternoon newspaper. In June 1976, E. Bronson Ingram, president of Ingram Brothers, a billion-dollar energy conglomerate with principal offices in Nashville and New Orleans, and several other individuals were indicted by a federal grand jury in Chicago for allegedly offering a $1.2 million bribe to land a sewage contract with that city.[14] Neal became Ingram's attorney. The *Banner* picked up some news about operations of the brothers Ingram, and a colleague of mine who had once worked for the *Banner* telephoned the reporter covering the story. The information was interesting enough for my colleague to talk to Wayne Sargent, the *Banner*'s publisher, about the possibility of using some of it in *Business Week.* Sargent seemed receptive, but he said he had to consult with Neal about potential problems. A few days later, Neal himself phoned to say that the *Banner* had decided against cooperating; then, speaking as Ingram's attorney, Neal also cautioned against using the story. How much less intensively the *Banner* poked into the story than it otherwise might have had Neal not been Ingram's attorney is impossible to know.

Did Neal do wrong? I do not know, and I am not sure a good answer is possible. The code says: "The professional judgment of a lawyer should be exercised . . . solely for the benefit of his client and free of compromising influences and loyalties. . . . The interests of other clients . . . should not be permitted to dilute his loyalty to his client."[15] And in another place it says that ". . . a lawyer should always act in a manner consistent with the best interests of his client."[16] But nowhere does the code define or attempt to discuss "interests," "loyalty," or "best interests."

What was the *Banner*'s best interest? Was it fearlessly to publish stories about possible corruption, prepared to defend itself against charges of libel? Was it to give every benefit of the doubt to someone who would prefer not to see his name in the newspaper? Was it to avoid libel actions at any cost? The code gives no guidance.

That several answers are possible points to a grave difficulty for the lawyer in Neal's position. If the best interest (or even a strong interest) of the newspaper was to print the story, then Neal's representation of Ingram posed a conflict. On the other hand, a newspaper may potentially report on any client a lawyer may conceivably represent. A strict reading of the canons (which counsel against the appearance of impropriety as well as the conflict itself) would require a newspaper's lawyer to forgo all other clients. Few would carry the argument so far. The lack of standards is troublesome.

Similar situations arise all the time. In the criminal courts, legal aid attorneys are faced with agonizing dilemmas that the code, and the legal literature generally, simply ignore. For example, many petty crimes carry relatively small sentences. In the large metropolitan

D.A.'s offices, any experienced public defender can, through plea bargaining, get the prosecutor to reduce the severity of the charges in the indictment. Felonious assault becomes simple assault, grand larceny becomes breaking and entering, and so on. These lesser charges often carry short sentences—thirty or sixty days, perhaps, rather than a year or more. People are also brought to court for minor disturbances that should not be a police matter to begin with. These offenses also carry trivial sentences.

Now, most of those who come through the "criminal justice system" are not innocent; they have done something to warrant being brought before a magistrate. But many of these people are also profoundly disturbed. Chronic alcoholics and mildly deranged (or "antisocial") people without family, funds, or purpose are frequent visitors to the criminal courts. They can legitimately plead mental incapacity. Doing so in most jurisdictions, however, will result in their being sent to psychiatric wards for observation. Because hospitals are underfinanced and often insensitive to the needs of the unbalanced, the wait in the ward can be longer than the sentence. Moreover, the hospital will not treat the patient; doctors will merely make observations. There are not sufficient funds to permit hospitalization of all those who need it, and too many of these defendants are, though antisocial, not mentally ill (the latter condition, however defined, is necessary for civil commitment).

What is the lawyer to do for these people? Should she plead the client guilty or send him for observation? Many clients do not understand their own predicament; to say "let the client choose" is not a meaningful answer. To opt, as many lawyers do, for the guilty plea, thus ensuring that the maximum incarceration will be less than the time spent in the hospital for observation, runs the risk that a client in genuine need of medical help will fail to get it. The client may be sicker than the lawyer knows, and a psychiatrically untrained lawyer plunked down in the maelstrom of an urban criminal court can scarcely make these judgments accurately all the time. To send a sick person through the criminal process routinely, without judging the probability that the same person will be back several weeks later, solves nothing.

The course that most lawyers take in this predicament is to explain the options to the client, hope that he understands, and let the client dictate the choice. That the choice is probably uninformed is not an ethical fault of the attorney, who must labor as best she can in a system that itself is cruel and reprehensible.

Still, in many cases, responsibility toward the client may entail disregarding the client's own choice. "Just make some deal and get me out of here" may well be in his short-run interest, but if he is likely to wind up in jail a few months later, his long-term interests will not have been served. The real answer is a complete overhaul of the criminal justice system. To effect such change calls for political action. The code does not discuss the lawyer's obligation to work for political change in the interest of a class of clients whom she sees most regularly. But this is just one more place where the code has been outdated by events.

For the institutional bar, the difficulty of reckoning the client's best interests has led to a curious rationalization. Typically, large law firms will not represent clients with causes that are broadly antagonistic to those of their regular clientele, even though there may be no connection whatsoever between the two. This reluctance is most marked in cases that public interest groups wish to bring. Then, according to F. Raymond Marks, who conducted a pioneering study of the bar's response to public interest groups, the firms suddenly discover that they represent "interests," not clients. This discovery allows them to avoid their duty to make legal counsel available. The excuse is that to accept a client with an "interest" contrary to the general interest of the corporate clients would be a conflict.

That is a play on words, however, not a reasoned conclusion. Say that a regular client has an interest in industrial production and hence is generally opposed to air pollution controls. A citizens' group asks the firm to represent it in a fight against a water polluter who has no connection with the first client. This is not a conflict of interests; it is at most a conflict of orientations—about which the code is silent, as it should be. As Marks says:

> When a firm decides whether or not to accept employment from a paying client, only narrow and immediate conflict of interest is considered. . . . True, in this process it does review the clients it currently represents in order to avoid possible future conflict. Speculation about conflict, however, rarely ranges far afield. That way lies madness, for the large law firm represents many large clients, each of which has diverse operations and interests. Potential conflict between clients lies everywhere. The prevalent view is that the classic conflict can be dealt with as it arises. Meanwhile there is the salient point: The interests of regular clients are all substantially the same except when they are in strict or classic conflict. Law firms may think they represent clients, but they really represent *interests* after all. That is, they represent clients who have similar interests. Few clients of large law firms have system grievances. Few seek major changes in the distributive system. The similarity of basic interests is understood, as is the possibility that these interests will occasionally come into conflict with each other. The law firms scrutinize the public interest client in a more searching manner. Threats are seen; conflicts are imagined or manufactured.[17]

Sometimes the excuses are positively bizarre. In 1971, just after President Nixon froze wages and prices, he announced that he was suspending a pay raise scheduled to go into effect on October 1 for all military personnel. A friend, a Coast Guard officer, insisted that the suspension was unlawful because a specific enactment of Congress, signed by President Nixon *after* the wage and price freeze, mandated the raise. Nixon, he said, was simply ignoring the law. He asked me to file a class action on behalf of all persons in the armed forces to recover unlawfully withheld salaries. I asked the partner for whom I worked whether the firm would take the case on as part of our *pro bono publico* program. I also noted that we might get a sizable fee for our troubles, since the claims totaled tens and possibly hundreds of millions of dollars. The firm turned the case down. Quite aside from its merits, my senior informed me, "We don't like to sue the people we work for." I puzzled over this statement for years afterward, because as a private law firm in Washington we did not work *for* the government. But our representation entailed negotiation with government from time to time, and the fear of antagonizing someone—the President?—may have been real. Since a lawyer is under no ethical compulsion to accept any particular client, we were not, I suppose, derelict in refusing the case, but the conflict of interest was (and remains) hard to detect.

It is evident how far lawyers (or a class of them) have moved from the model of conduct which they still profess. Abraham Lincoln, the epitome of that traditional model, represented clients, not interests. Thus he took cases on both sides of the fugitive slave issue.[18] In so doing, he maintained his status as an *independent* practitioner, a status the institutional bar has nearly forfeited. Today there are bankruptcy specialists who will represent only creditors, labor specialists who will represent only management or only unions. The excuse is conflict of interest. The reality is fear of offending clients.

In 1970, the editors of the *American Bar Association Journal* took exception to the statements of radical lawyer William Kunstler. What irked them was his assertion at an interview recorded in the *New York Times* that "I only defend those whose goal I share. I'm not a lawyer for hire. I only defend those I love."[19] Said the editors: "All lawyers who can afford it do a certain amount of selection of their clients and causes undertaken. . . . But with respect to representing unpopular persons, to be a 'lawyer for hire' is a badge of honor. To hold otherwise is to take a reactionary direction and cast aside centuries of human experience and striving. A lawyer for hire is available to the bad and the ugly, the scorned and the outcast. We know from long collective experience that many will go without legal defense or representation if they must depend upon finding a lawyer who 'loves' them."[20]

The editors seemed blithely unaware that the rules against conflicts of interest were rationalized to confine the practice of the institutional bar to those they love, a narrow class of those scorned—the corporation, which can scarcely be considered outcast. The *Journal* editors missed the irony that not until lawyers came along who "loved" their dissident clients were they able to find competent counsel. "But I don't love my corporate clients," protests the lawyer; "the biggest cruds in Florida," Chesterfield Smith said. But is there virtue in representing only those you hate?

This sophistical approach to conflicts of interest instills a habit of wearing blinders that hurts both lawyer and client. Constant repetition of the same arguments on behalf of the same clients mists the eyes and dulls the intellect. Representation of disparate clients brings the lawyer into contact with the hurly-burly; it teaches him what he too easily forgets when commuting between boardrooms. The lawyer made narrow by excessive fidelity to the interests of similar clients often cannot render—even to those clients—desperately needed advice because the lawyer is not equipped to see the broader outlines of the client's interests. A narrow view of the world leads to a narrow conception of an institution's place in it. Such narrowness is, in short, a violation of the lawyer's ethical duty to serve his client competently.

Accepting, then, the lawyer's obligation to help his client find his interest, the lawyer must become something of an adversary. "A lawyer may inadvertently mislead a client by being subservient to the client's perceptions of the problem and tailoring advice to what he thinks the client wants to hear," Joseph A. Califano has written. And, he continues, "a lawyer has an obligation to argue with his client when not to do so would jeopardize the client's interest or put the client in significant conflict with the public interest."[21]

Califano gives this example of disservice through narrowness. "When the Traffic Safety Act of 1966 was being drafted, any decent [i.e., competent] Washington lawyer knew that strong legislation would sail through the Congress. Instead of recognizing that their interest lay in acceding to the public clamor for legislation, the auto industry resisted vociferously to the bitter end. Those lawyers who advised a fight to the death merely contributed to serving up the auto industry as one of Washington's favorite whipping boys for at least a decade—a course of events that could hardly be thought of as furthering the client's interests."[22]

In advising the private client to consider the public interest seriously, the lawyer, let it be underscored, is not involving himself in a conflict of interest. Conflicts arise only when two interests are known and opposing. But by hypothesis, the client does not know what his interest is. The lawyer's task is to help him define it. The lawyer can do so effectively only by practicing the independence he preaches.

Figuring out *who* the client is often is no less difficult than deciding *what* the client's interests are. Under the conventional model of practice, there were few difficulties: the client was the person who came to your law office. But during the gestation of professional ethics in this century, two institutions, the corporation and the government, made hash of the conventional model. The canons touch on these institutions, but obliquely; "watch out for quicksand" is more or less the way it is put.

For example, the corporation lawyer "owes his allegiance to the entity and not to a stockholder, director, officer, employee, representative, or other person connected with the entity."[23] Apparently his loyalty is to the pencils and coffeepots in the offices, files in the cabinets, and buildings on the corporation's land: hard to interrogate, to be sure, but then they won't talk back either. This example of legal metaphysics obscures the real problems. The lawyer does not go to the office of the entity; he goes to the office of the president or the chairman or some other person who has a voice in the collective concerns of the people who comprise the corporation. Every such person is potentially in conflict with the entity. More often than we acknowledge, they are in actual conflict with it.

Let us say, for the sake of argument, that the long-run interest of the corporation is in survival and growth. Its short-run interest might be a large profit this year, but various strategies for achieving this will be at the expense of the corporation in the long run, as the stockholders of plenty of bankrupt companies have discovered. Now, it is difficult to fix one's eye steadily on the long-run interest of a corporation. Whoever is so devoted to the long-term prosperity of an entity ought to feel comfortable toiling in a Russian factory, where everyone supposedly works for the greater glory of the state. Whatever else they may be, American managers are not likely to be comfortable doing that. To the contrary, American managers are capitalists; top managers have risen to the top by watching out for themselves. As a group, top managers are also closer to retirement than others in the corporation. No doubt their long-run interests coincide with the corporation's short-run interests—that is, they wish to make lots of money for the company and for themselves and retire quietly with secure pensions and consulting arrangements.

The potential for trouble is obvious. Usually the conflicts between management and the entity are played out in the arena of business judgment: should this or that investment be made? Should a failing division be liquidated or is there a chance it will recover? These decisions are not, in their nature, legal decisions. But the time comes when many management decisions will involve sticky legal considerations. What if the lawyer discovers that management has been paying bribes, withholding information from auditors, mulcting the entity? To whom should he turn, if anyone?

At a symposium on the question, Lewis Van Dusen suggested that where the evidence of managerial malfeasance is clear, the lawyer should talk to the directors. But suppose the directors are in on the plot or refuse to act? "It may be appropriate for the lawyer to resign his representation," Van Dusen said. But, he added: "Such a decision . . . should carry with it no duties to advise the shareholders. They are stuck with the quality of the directors they elect, and I do not think that a lawyer's duty extends to advising the shareholders that they have made a bad choice."[24]

That is a fine pickle. The lawyer's duty runs to the entity, but if one or even two groups of individuals within the entity betray it, better to remain silent (and maybe resign) than to tell someone who might be able to undo the mischief. How the shareholders will ever discover they made a bad choice is a puzzlement.

Deciding who the client is becomes at times an even more vexing problem for the government attorney. James D. St. Clair made the point when questioned about his being paid by government funds for his defense of President Nixon. St. Clair answered that it was proper for him to be on the public payroll because he represented the "office of the Presidency," and not the incumbent "individually."[25] However, the client (the entity of the presidency) spoke only through Richard Nixon. Suppose Richard Nixon had instructed the presidency's lawyer to do something injurious to the client? One might suppose that St. Clair received any number of such instructions: to delay and to dissemble, for example. These are acts which, if not unlawful or unethical when done on behalf of a flesh-and-blood client, were undoubtedly destructive of the perquisites of the Ghost of Presidents Future. Who again will believe that a president has a good faith reason for declining to turn over documents to Congress or the courts? Had Nixon resigned before the Supreme Court test, the question of the president's right to refuse a subpoena might still be open to doubt—a bad thing for the nation perhaps, but maybe useful to His Presidential Entity.

At a more earthly level, the government lawyer must always be conscious of a divided loyalty. The prosecutor's duty "differs from that of the usual advocate; his duty is to seek justice, not merely to convict," the code says.[26] This admonition provides no guidelines. The law, not ethics alone, requires the prosecutor to give the defendant any evidence that might tend to prove his innocence, but how far beyond that should the prosecutor go in aiding the defense? Must the prosecutor forgo a line of questioning because his adversary might miss its significance? Should the prosecutor calibrate his zeal by his assessment of the degree of probability that the defendant is guilty? Suppose the prosecutor thinks that there is some reason to believe a suspect did not commit the crime. Should he fail to seek an indictment or move to dismiss it?

Finding the client is equally difficult when the lawyer is on the civil side of government. Say an Internal Revenue Service lawyer discovers that his superiors have decided to promulgate a regulation unlawfully intended to make it difficult to take alimony deductions because the commissioner loathes divorce. The commissioner tells him that the decision is a "policy matter" and to keep his mouth shut. The lawyer responds that if the law gave the commissioner discretion to rule one way or another, he would accept his superior's political judgment. But in this case, he insists, there is no such discretion. What is the lawyer's responsibility? Is his client the commissioner, the agency, or the public? If the public, must he denounce his boss's action? And in what forum? Should he hold a press conference or write a letter to the president or to the *Washington Post* or to his local bar association?

In 1973, dissatisfied with the ABA code, the Federal Bar Association (comprising some 16,000 federal government lawyers) issued a supplementary code applicable to the lawyer in government service.[27] Its answer to the above series of questions is that on "rare occasions" (which ones were not specified) the lawyer's conscience will prompt a public attack. But, it says, the lawyer cannot ethically go public unless he has first resigned. That is a handy deterrent to an overactive conscience. Again, critical guidance is absent.

This absence should not astonish. According to hoary tradition, the lawyer's highest duty is to represent the fixed interests of the known client who pays for his time, the public be damned. To hint that the government lawyer has responsibilities beyond those owed to his immediate employers is to counter the deepest professional instincts. That they are no longer adequate to guide the lawyer in this uncharted territory is a clue that our legal system has evolved faster than the ethical system of those who are supposed to be its guardians.

Nowhere has this evolution been more rapid or dramatic than in the growth of the "public interest" bar. Here the two questions ("Who is the client?" "What is his interest?") come together, for the public interest lawyer has pioneered a new kind of lawsuit from which the client disappears and the lawyer himself comes to stage center.

This new type of litigation is the much lauded and much abused "class action," a procedural device that allows a court to consider the interests of people who are not formally before it. As such, the class action has been around for decades, but in the federal court system it was burdened by restrictive rules that were not liberalized until 1966. (In most states, the rules remain restrictive.) The liberalization occurred at the same time as, and was prompted by, an important change in the activists' consciousness of how to use the courts to make and enforce public policy.

Actually, the change had been brewing for a long time. As early as the 1920s and 1930s, the American Civil Liberties Union and the NAACP's Legal Defense Fund were pursuing test cases whose outcomes would have a significant impact on society and on the operations of government. The ACLU and the Defense Fund brought (or defended) cases in the name of a specific person whom they believed to have been wronged by the government. But since the cases challenged reigning constitutional interpretation or dominant government beliefs, decisions in favor of their clients had broad ramifications. Thus a suit on behalf of one black family prevented from purchasing a home in St. Louis resulted in a Supreme Court decision declaring racially restrictive covenants in land titles to be unenforceable throughout the United States.[28] In that case, a particular family had a concrete interest that it wished to vindicate. When, however, the movement for political reform through litigation caught up with such vehicles as the class action, something new was created.

Lawyers began to bring cases on behalf of vast agglomerations of people, referred to as "consumers" or "blacks" or "women" or "Indians." The naming of an individual plaintiff has become a polite fiction. The big test cases do not depend on the whim of an individual client. A court will not dismiss a case when an individual plaintiff accepts a hundred-dollar settlement from a company alleged to be defrauding millions of people. The names of several recurrent public interest plaintiffs—Consumers Union, Environmental Defense Fund, Common Cause, Friends of the Earth, and others—symbolize the near autonomy that lawyers enjoy in prosecuting such cases.

Though public interest lawyers protest that the funds available to support them are small, the impact of their work can be tremendous. Increasingly, cases are conceived, fashioned, and executed by themselves or through organizations designed specifically for the purpose of bringing innovative litigation with potentially vast reforming effect.

The ethical difficulty springs from the lawyer's transformation from adviser or advocate to actual client, from general to commander in chief. In designing suits ostensibly on behalf of large amorphous groups, the lawyer substitutes his own values for those of the group.

This profound alteration of the lawyer's role raises the question whether he has special responsibilities in pursuing his social and political ends. There can be no quarrel with his right, as a citizen, to pursue those ends. And in seeking a public interest broader than that which often results from the actions of narrow and selfish clients, there can be little question that public interest lawyers have produced social good. The question remains, however, whether as an inevitable by-product of their enthusiastic activity they are not also producing social harm.

The answer is that they may be. For when the lawyer becomes his own client, he is no longer necessarily representing known interests for known clients. Indeed, individuals within the abstractly named class may be hindered by his efforts. There is room to consider only one example, so let it be the most contentious of all: racial integration of the schools. (I follow here the brilliant exposition of Harvard law professor Derrick A. Bell, Jr.)[29]

The dominant belief among civil rights lawyers has been and continues to be that the interests of the black community are best served by total integration. "The actual presence of white children is said to be essential to [their constitutional] right in both its philosophical and pragmatic dimensions. In essence the arguments are that blacks must gain access to white schools because 'equal educational opportunity' means integrated schools, and because only school integration will make certain that black children will receive the same education as white children."[30] This belief became an accepted canon of constitutional doctrine following the Court's revolutionary decision in *Brown v. Board of Education* in 1954. So the lawyer who brings suits according to this principle might suppose himself to be acting as close to the interests of a broad class of people as would ever be possible.

But, as Bell documents in some detail, that is not necessarily the case. For once the basic principle was established, subsidiary principles had to evolve. The most controversial is school busing to produce racial balance in schools. Busing has become controversial because of considerable concern in both the black and white communities that while it may increase racial balance, busing may also reduce the quality of the education all children are receiving, black as well as white. As Bell says, "The busing issue has served to make concrete what many parents long have sensed and what new research has suggested: court orders mandating racial balance may be (depending on the circumstances) educationally advantageous, irrelevant, or even *disadvantageous.*"[31]

A serious breach in the unity of the class is thereby created. The resolution or compromise of these conflicting interests concerning schools within the black community cannot be abstractly deduced. But at least until very recently, civil rights lawyers as a group have felt compelled to push for educational equality rather than educational quality or community control. In one case that Bell cites, a federal judge in San Francisco asked counsel whether the court ought to consider a demand by many blacks "that they run their own schools" and that "they [be allowed] to have black schools." Said Bell: "When a young black attorney recruited for the case by the NAACP sought to prepare a memorandum with an affirmative response to [the judge's] question, his colleagues on the case were shocked. Subsequently, the young attorney agreed to withdraw from the case, and his position was not asserted in any subsequent proceeding."[32]

Groups such as the NAACP frequently have a vested interest in one outcome. When the civil rights attorney draws financial, moral, intellectual, and emotional support from such groups, it will be difficult for him to believe in another outcome. But the views or needs of a large part of the class he is ostensibly representing may depend on some other outcome. To argue that the lawyer is simply following the dictates of the law on behalf of clients is a naïve response. For the lawyer and his associates are instrumental in framing the cases and the theories that will be presented to the courts from which the pronouncements of law will come.

As Bell asks: "How should the term 'client' be defined in school desegregation cases that are litigated for decades, determine critically important constitutional rights for thousands of minority children, and usually involve major restructuring of a public school system? How should civil rights attorneys represent the often diverse interests of clients and class in school suits? Do they owe any special obligation to class members who emphasize educational quality and who probably cannot obtain counsel to advocate their divergent views?"

Similar questions can be asked of other areas of public interest law practice.[33] What is in "the consumer's" interest can never be stated definitively because no two people have precisely the same interests and because people so often have conflicting interests within themselves. The public interest lawyer's dilemma is, at bottom, no different from that of the corporate lawyer plying his trade in a non-adversary situation: other significant interests may go without representation. A responsible ethic must ensure that these other significant interests do not go unrecognized and unrepresented.

CHAPTER 8

The Failure of Self-Regulation

The Ethics of Enforcement

Among the less glorious chapters in the history of the American bar was the twenty-year judgeship of Albert W. Johnson of the U.S. District Court for the Middle District of Pennsylvania.[1] Appointed by Calvin Coolidge in 1925, he was under nearly constant federal investigation almost from the day he took the bench. Rumors were rife that a litigant could "fix" a case through his two lawyer sons and one non-lawyer son-in-law. It was said that Johnson ran a bankruptcy and receivership racket, through which he received a kickback for appointing various lawyers to oversee the affairs of ruined companies. After a time this was common knowledge among members of the bar; yet during a House impeachment hearing in 1945 that finally led to Judge Johnson's resignation, Estes Kefauver, then a member of the House committee, was moved to remark: "Many times we would meet lawyers who would say, 'We know it is a rotten, crooked setup from beginning to end, but do not quote us, because we have to practice law here.' "

One of the lawyers who had occasion to come before Judge Johnson's court was Hoyt A. Moore, a New York lawyer whose name is now memorialized in the firm he helped lead: Cravath, Swaine &

Moore. Moore was general counsel of the Bethlehem Steel Company. That corporate giant owned 25 percent of the stock of the Williamsport Wire Rope Company and had an exclusive purchasing arrangement with it (Williamsport bought steel for fabricating wire rope and strand). In the 1920s, Bethlehem helped Williamsport finance an expansion, but by the early 1930s, Williamsport was, so to speak, on the ropes, a barely surviving casualty of the Depression. In 1932, Bethlehem instituted bankruptcy proceedings as a creditor; the following year the steel giant decided it would acquire the company outright. Williamsport's stockholders opposed the takeover, and so did Judge Johnson. Through his cronies, Judge Johnson put a proposition to Moore: in return for a payment of $250,000, the judge would see to it that Bethlehem got Williamsport.

In the parlance of the law, that was a "solicitation of a bribe."

What did Moore do? Did he report the matter promptly to the U.S. Attorney? Did he denounce the go-betweens and stalk off indignantly? Had he done either, I wouldn't be telling this story. According to the House report, Moore himself had estimated that he would have to make a $150,000 or $200,000 payoff and that "$250,000 was not excessive and it was not objectionable to him." A scheme was cooked up by which Judge Johnson would order the sale of Williamsport's assets in return for payment of "administration expenses" that would be laundered through intermediaries.

The deal went through. Bethlehem saved $1.2 million in the acquisition of the fabricating company, and Moore began to pay out the administration expenses, keeping records on the back of a manila envelope, which he was careful not to place in the regular files of his law firm. Unfortunately for Johnson, his principal co-conspirator lied about how much he had bargained for and put the judge off for years with stories about Bethlehem's slowness in paying. In the end, Johnson and his family got virtually none of the money. A trusted crony kept most of it.

Eventually, the sordid story came out, principally through the efforts of a federal prosecutor whom the attorney general had deputized to clean up the mess in the Middle District of Pennsylvania. Johnson escaped impeachment by resigning and waiving his right to any federal pension. Because his co-conspirators refused to testify, Johnson was acquitted at his trial for bribery and conspiracy. A number of lawyers were convicted, however, including the secretary of the American Bar Association. (His conviction was later reversed because the prosecutors had leaned too heavily on his ABA connections, misleading "the jury into considering [his] professional misconduct instead of his criminal guilt." Since he was then eighty-two, no retrial was ordered.) Bethlehem was directed to disgorge the Williamsport company.

But Hoyt Moore escaped clean. He simply availed himself of the statute of limitations. Since the events took place in the early 1930s and the indictments were not issued until after 1945, the government was helpless.

The bar association was not helpless, however. Bribing a federal judge is one of the most heinous offenses in the lawyer's pantheon of scabrous acts. For just such offenses, the bar had (and has) a grievance committee. In New York, where Moore practiced, the grievance committee of the Association of the Bar conducts investigations of lawyer misconduct on behalf of the Appellate Division of the state supreme court, which has the power to disbar.

What did the bar do? Nothing. What did the courts do? Nothing. Moore went about his business, which was running the Cravath firm, until he died in 1959 at the age of eighty-eight. (In Pennsylvania, Judge Johnson also lived reasonably well. He escaped disciplinary hearings, and a local bar association even did him the honor of electing him president.)

Those were the old days, lawyers say. Surely today bar associations are far more responsible. In *Lions in the Street,* Paul Hoffman quotes John Bonomi, long-time chief counsel of the Manhattan grievance committee, to the effect that a latter-day Moore would not escape his committee's scrutiny.[2] Maybe not, but then Moore openly admitted his bribery to a House committee. That is hard to miss. The Manhattan grievance body managed to waste its time disbarring a recent president of the United States, for acts which also were hard to miss. What about less obvious cases?

Unfortunately, there is no reason to be as sanguine about even slightly less prominent cases. A 1970 report of a special ABA committee chaired by the late Supreme Court Justice Tom C. Clark began by saying: "After three years of studying lawyer discipline throughout the country, this Committee must report the existence of a scandalous situation that requires the immediate attention of the profession. With few exceptions, the prevailing attitude of lawyers toward disciplinary enforcement ranges from apathy to outright hostility. Disciplinary action is practically nonexistent in many jurisdictions; practices and procedures are antiquated; many disciplinary agencies have little power to take effective steps against malefactors."[3] For an ABA committee, this harsh language is extraordinary. But its condemnation was reasonable, perhaps even mild, under the circumstances. The failures of the disciplinary system were (and remain) so spectacular that placing the system in receivership seems the only sensible solution.

Most complaints against lawyers involve "neglect" of the client: failure to keep the client up to date on what is happening with the case or, more seriously, failure to move the case along at all. Here, for example, is a summary of one complaint that was mailed to the grievance committee in Manhattan:

> The complainant alleged that his lawyer deliberately delayed his criminal case in order to charge for several court appearances. He further alleged that he gave the attorney $1500 to obtain bail and that the attorney never transmitted the funds for that purpose. The complainant remained in jail. [The lawyer] is the subject of numerous prior complaints and had been admonished on three occasions.[4]

What did the grievance staff do? It responded that the complaint was really nothing more than a quarrel over the lawyer's bill, and that "fee disputes" do not fall within the committee's jurisdiction. The staff made the same excuse in the following civil matter:

> The attorney represented the complainant in a divorce proceeding. The divorce order had been entered and the attorney paid. The complainant alleged that the attorney had altered and falsified documents [the separation agreement], was withholding funds belonging to the complainant, was refusing to return documents belonging to the complainant, breached the lawyer-client relationship by revealing confidential information to the detriment of the complainant, had a conflict of interest, and having made an oral statement of his fee [after refusing to put it in writing] subsequently lied to the complainant about the agreed fee.[5]

Countless other examples of disciplinary committee malfeasance could be cited.

The examples just given come from an investigation of the Manhattan grievance procedure conducted by an ad hoc committee that Cyrus R. Vance, then president of the association, appointed in 1974. Although the Manhattan grievance committee has long been regarded as one of the finest in the nation, the ad hoc committee found serious flaws and recommended extensive changes. Yet even the reformers were incapable of overcoming the limitations that the fraternity of the bar imposes on its members. For in discussing fees, a major subject of complaints by the public, the committee opined: "The question of fees is obviously a source of much misunderstanding and irritation between the bar and the public. . . . The organized bar must educate the public about what lawyers do to earn their fees." Nary a word was devoted to the need to educate lawyers about what they *should* do to earn them.

Another group of complaints that grievance committees often dismiss out of hand are those in which "misconduct" is said not to be involved. What the disciplinarians consider misconduct is perhaps the most curious feature of the entire system. Advertising and solicitation are forms of misconduct. Working for many types of legal aid projects has in the past been considered to be unethical and hence subject to grievance proceedings. And before 1975 lawyers who routinely dared to charge less than the minimum fee lived in fear of a bar inquiry. But many actions that the lay public might consider wrongful and that ought to subject the errant lawyer to discipline are disregarded altogether.

Most seriously disregarded is canon 6 of the bar's own code, which enjoins a lawyer to "represent a client competently." The standards of canon 6 are so vague that one state, Georgia, refused to adopt it or any of its disciplinary rules. Grievance staffs rarely view incompetent representation as a matter for their concern. To a client who complained that his lawyer had delayed his personal injury suit by continually canceling scheduled trial dates, the Manhattan grievance staff sent a letter saying that "quality of representation is not within its jurisdiction."[6] Astonishingly, the ad hoc committee, in the face of canon 6, agreed that the staff had acted properly in failing to pursue the complaint. Of course, there are many reasons why trial dates might have had to be canceled, but the refusal to act does not square with the substance of the complaint.

Grievance committees have been no more vigorous in condemning actual defalcations by lawyers. The Clark committee found, for example, that most disciplinary bodies would let off lightly any attorney who embezzled from his client if the lawyer made restitution prior to the grievance proceeding. This liberality is akin to giving the dog his first bite—and sometimes his second or third.

No more sensible is the custom of waiting out the criminal trial. In most cases involving criminal conduct by the attorney, grievance committees will not act until the lawyer has lost his final appeal in the courts. That means that lawyers who have stolen clients' money and committed a variety of other unlawful deeds can continue practicing, sometimes for years, before the bar moves in to suspend or disbar them. In 1976, for instance, Matthew Troy, a New York City councilman and a Brooklyn power broker, pleaded guilty to federal income-tax evasion charges. The income he failed to report was money he took from his clients' accounts and "converted" to his own use. Federal law requires taxes to be paid on such money. Under state law, a lawyer who is convicted of a felony is automatically disbarred. But federal tax violations are only misdemeanors under a benevolent state law. More than one year later, as this book goes to press, Troy, whose guilty plea amounts to a confession that he stole from his own clients, still has not been censured, suspended, or disbarred.*

Because record-keeping is a chore and budgets are small, few bar committees keep adequate files or bother to check them when a lawyer is brought up for disciplining. The ad hoc committee in New York found numerous instances of lawyers who had been complained against ten or more times. In several instances, the lawyers had actually been censured formally more than once before.

The fault is not fully the staff's. It is underfinanced and must devote itself to excruciatingly boring work. So perhaps it is reasonable to expect it to forget to cross-check now and then. The fault also lies with the gray eminences who are appointed by the private bar from the private bar to oversee the staff. On the record, these lawyers evidently lack the imagination or will to guide their deputies. The default, in the end, is their default.

The failure of grievance committees to stalk incompetence is mirrored by the abysmal record of the courts. During the past several years, many judges, most notably Chief Justice Warren E. Burger, have complained that a significant number of advocates who appear before them are incompetent. Trial judges constantly swap stories about lawyers they had to rescue discreetly from a sinking case. Numerous courts have had to grapple with the serious question of whether to overturn a criminal conviction because the defendant had "inadequate assistance of counsel," a violation of the principle that every defendant is entitled to be competently represented by counsel at trial. Yet neither the Chief Justice nor the other judges have for-

---

*His trial on charges of converting his clients' funds is pending.

warded the names of obviously unskilled and incompetent attorneys
to disciplinary committees for appropriate action, nor have they imposed sanctions on their own motion.

These failures derive, according to one close study of the disciplinary system, from a gross mismatch between the public's needs and the
bar's objectives: "Clients complain chiefly about matters touching on
performance while the agencies to which they complain concern
themselves almost exclusively with misconduct."[7] To the disciplinarians, aside from obviously criminal behavior, "misconduct" means, as
we have seen, some act that will lower the bar's profits or bring
lawyers into public disrepute. In 1966, to cite only one prominent
example, the grievance committee of the District of Columbia bar
initiated an investigation of Monroe Freedman. At a class designed
to train lawyers to represent indigent criminal defendants, Freedman
advanced his theories about the proper conduct of defense counsel.
His talk was reported in the *Washington Post,* and the following day
he received a registered letter from the grievance committee, "informing me that disciplinary proceedings had been begun against me, on
the complaint of several federal judges that I had 'expressed opinions'
in apparent disagreement with the canons of professional ethics."[8]
The proceedings dragged on for four months, and finally terminated
when *Time* magazine published a piece on the episode, turning it into
a national cause célèbre. Freedman was never told the names of the
complaining witnesses who thought a professor of law could be disbarred for exercising his First Amendment right to speech.* This
same committee at the same time refused to take action against an
obviously mentally ill lawyer who, many local judges had complained,
had been found on several occasions defecating in their courtroom
stairwell.

---

*Freedman has long stated his belief that the chief complainer was Chief Justice
Burger, who has, however, denied any complicity in the affair. The committee apparently violated its own rules in Freedman's case to boot. At one point, Freedman learned
that the committee had decided against taking any action. Under the rules, the matter
should have ended. Instead, the committee bucked the case up to the federal district
court, which eventually approved the decision to let it drop.

One class of violations that grievance committees almost universally ignore are those of prosecutors. Consider, in that regard, the prosecution's conduct in the espionage trial of Daniel Ellsberg and Anthony Russo for giving the Pentagon Papers to the *New York Times*. The law requires federal prosecutors to turn over exculpatory material to the defense. The Justice Department had in its files several Defense Department reports concluding that the Papers contained little classified information and that virtually none of it was sensitive or damaging to national security. Prosecutor David Nissen knew of these reports, but he repeatedly denied that he was aware of the material. By accident, the defense lawyers stumbled onto the existence of the reports, after the trial began. The trial was interrupted, the jury excused, and J. Fred Buzhardt, then general counsel of the Defense Department, was called to testify. He admitted that the reports had actually been submitted to Nissen. Upon examining them, Judge Matthew Byrne told Nissen (who had once worked for Byrne when he was U.S. Attorney in Los Angeles): "I don't understand how you can possibly feel that you were not required to produce these documents ten months ago."

The trial was finally aborted when it became fatally linked to the spreading Watergate investigation in Washington. In April 1973 it came out that E. Howard Hunt and Gordon Liddy had burglarized the office of Ellsberg's psychiatrist. The next month the *Washington Post* reported the possibility of wiretaps on Ellsberg's telephone, a clear violation of law that the prosecution was also obligated to tell the defense. At Judge Byrne's request, the temporary FBI director, William D. Ruckelshaus, checked the files and discovered the famous wiretap on Morton Halperin's telephone. Some of the conversations were with Ellsberg. That was the final straw, and Judge Byrne dismissed the indictment; the government's misconduct had "incurably infected the prosecution." To this day, however, neither Nissen nor the other government lawyers who deliberately withheld exculpatory reports and information in violation of law and of a specific court order have ever been publicly disciplined.[9]

Judges as a class share in this immunity. As Professor Alan M. Dershowitz has said, "There is a code of honor among lawyers, especially established lawyers, not to reveal the truth about the judiciary —to cover up its scars and pockmarks so as not to cast the noble enterprise of judging, and its often not so noble functionaries, into disrepute."[10] This dereliction is a continuing one. In New York, the state legislature was finally shamed[11] into creating a Commission on Judicial Conduct, a state agency armed with subpoena power that is charged with investigating complaints of improper behavior on the bench and, if warranted, to bring proceedings aimed at censuring or removing the offending judges. Even so, staff lawyers report, many lawyers called to give testimony have been exceedingly reluctant to volunteer what they themselves heard and saw in open court. Some have even committed perjury (by lying under oath at depositions) to avoid damaging a sitting judge.[12]

The nomenclature of the disciplinary system is a further impediment to sanctions against lawyers. The bar operates a "grievance" system. In the absence of grievances actually expressed, the bar is content to do nothing. That is part of the reason why errant prosecutors are not disciplined. Judges defer to the prosecutor's superiors, who have no interest in publicly confessing the sins of their office.

This same logic applies to the upper echelons of the bar, the institutional lawyers. As the ad hoc committee put it in a burst of candor rare for the bar, "The system only catches 'small fish.' "[13] Corporate lawyers do not do the things that irritate the leadership because, as we saw, they do not need to. Their misconduct is, rather, a failure to perform their function properly. But this failure may be in the client's interests. The chairman of Bethlehem's board would have had no interest in writing a letter to tell the New York City grievance committee that his general counsel had just bribed a federal judge. Of course, journalists write about corporate malfeasance now and then, but disciplinary committees do not consider newspaper stories to be grievances. Thus, in the wake of reports on International Telephone & Telegraph's activities in recent years (involvement with the CIA in

Chile; dubious behavior in the acquisition of the Hartford Insurance Company, including the possibility that it made an under-the-table deal with the president and the attorney general to settle an antitrust suit on favorable terms), one might suppose that the bar would have summoned one or two of its lawyers for an explanation. But nothing is more improbable.

The 1970 Clark Report listed thirty-six specific recommendations for reforming this self-serving, self-protective disciplinary system. The recommendations included ways of strengthening and financing grievance committees, sharing information among the committees, and ending the obsessive secrecy in which the disciplinary sessions are held. But, concluded Bayless Manning, former dean of Stanford Law School, "The effect of this powerful report upon the bar generally has been that of a feather dropped in a well."[14] Although three-quarters of the states reacted to the report by increasing their budgets to some degree, little extra has been accomplished.[15] The California state bar spent $1.3 million on discipline in 1975–1976. Of the 5,000 complaints, only 937 got to the investigative stage. Of these, only 11 cases resulted in disbarment, 42 in suspension, 36 in censures (of which 21 were administered privately). Out of a lawyer population of 50,000, these figures seem suspect. In New York City, the ad hoc committee reported that "in virtually every category the discipline imposed has been considerably more lenient" in the five years following the Clark Report's publication.[16]

Nor does the public disciplining of several lawyers caught up in Watergate point the way toward a renascence of probity and efficiency. These cases were so notorious that an outraged public would have dismantled the self-regulatory mechanism had it taken no action. Moreover, many of the sanctions were not particularly onerous. Most lenient was the penalty imposed on Richard G. Kleindienst, once attorney general of the United States.[17] He pleaded guilty to a peculiar charge: failing to disclose information to Congress. This obscure violation was cooked up so that Kleindienst might sidestep the more serious charge of perjury. In fact, Kleindienst, then deputy attorney general, had lied to a committee of Congress holding hearings on his nomination to be chief law officer of the United States. He testified that President Nixon had not ordered him to drop an appeal of an unfavorable ruling against the government in its antitrust suit against ITT. That was untrue; Nixon had given such instructions in no uncertain terms. In the District of Columbia, Kleindienst was suspended from practice for twenty days—the length of a lawyer's vacation. The Arizona bar tapped him on the wrist with a censure. All in all, not serious sanctions and certainly no deterrent for the future. Kleindienst now has a private practice in Washington.

The Failure of the Ethical System

The ethical system, as now constituted, teaches contempt for ethical behavior. That is because the formal system cannot overcome the hypocrisies that are built in, around, underneath, and above the public platitudes.

Platitudes not only cannot overcome example, they turn the example into destructive hypocrisy. The child who is told not to lie will disregard the advice when he catches his parents lying and observes that no one has become the wiser. Worse, the child learns contempt for the principle itself. The principle becomes a cover-up. Something like that has happened with the ethical system of lawyers.

In a sense, this is perhaps inevitable. For, by virtue of his training, the lawyer is in a very special position with respect to all rules. In David Riesman's phrase, "Lawyers learn not to take law seriously."[18] The only secret that the lawyer really possesses about the law is that no one can ever be certain of what the law is. Even to speak of "the law" is a misnomer. The lawyer differentiates himself from the layman chiefly by being able to make educated guesses about how a particular case will work out. But the lawyer knows that there is no certainty, that cases can go either way, that there is rarely transcendent right on one side and transcendent wrong on the other. The lawyer is accustomed to the ways of bending and changing rules to suit his (or his client's) purposes, to dance in the shadows of the law's ambiguities. Rules hold no particular terror for the lawyer, just as the sight of blood holds no terror for the surgeon. Because he operates a system of rules, the lawyer becomes indifferent to them in the way that a doctor becomes indifferent to the humanity of the body that is lying on the operating table.

To the lawyer, rules are for the other fellow. This is the Fortas Syndrome. Abe Fortas was forced to resign from the Supreme Court because he was discovered to have been receiving an annual stipend from a litigant in bad repute. This was a clear appearance of impropriety. Fortas, it was widely said, believed himself to be incorruptible (perhaps he was, and is). He violated the rule because he did not think it really applied to him. It was for other, weaker men and women. (This syndrome traces back at least as far as Francis Bacon, who as Lord Chancellor of England was impeached in 1621 for accepting bribes, sometimes from both sides to the dispute. His defense was that he did not let bribes interfere with his impartial decision in each case.)

The lawyer's disdain for rules that apply to him cannot of course be expressed in public. Like Caesar's wife, the lawyer wishes to appear above suspicion. But his conflicting desires—to be free from rules and to appear to conform to them—set up intolerable strains that result in the hypocrisy that we have explored throughout this book.

One delicious example may summarize the point. George Beall was the U.S. Attorney in Baltimore who investigated Spiro T. Agnew and helped engineer his resignation and guilty plea in October 1973. At the ABA's annual meeting ten months later in Honolulu, Beall spoke to a large crowd. Everyone wanted to hear this dedicated public servant, especially because Richard Nixon himself had resigned just five days earlier. Beall exemplified the spirit of service that placed principle above party loyalty. (Beall's brother was Republican senator from Maryland.)

Beall talked about the ethical responsibilities of all lawyers, even if they happened to be serving as vice-president of the United States (or U.S. Attorney). In the course of his remarks, Beall posed "two moral questions which have been raised by the year of scandal in Washington. One is how much does the prevalence of behavior excuse behavior; the other is to what extent does the worthiness of an objective justify the means to achieve it." Beall noted Agnew's excuse that it was "customary" for contractors to make kickbacks to state officials, as they had done in Agnew's case. And the Nixon men frequently had justified what they had done by observing that others had paved the way. Beall condemned "the idea that the prevalence of kickbacks or dirty tricks somehow excused their own behavior." It is wrong, Beall said, "to excuse our behavior by arguing that everybody does it."

Beall's speech was hard-hitting, but it might have been forgotten had not the *Washington Post* excerpted it.[19] A few days later, Vermont Royster, former editor of the *Wall Street Journal,* noticed that large chunks of the excerpts parroted a paper he had published in the *American Scholar* the previous spring.[20] Specifically, portions of the quotations given above were plagiarized verbatim. Royster demanded an explanation.[21] An embarrassed Beall obliged him: his staff had put a few thoughts together, borrowing liberally from others, *as lawyers are wont to do.* Beall apologized for omitting the quotation marks and a citation to Royster's article.[22] But apologies notwithstanding, Beall thus justified his own behavior by the very excuse he (adopting Royster) had condemned.

To be sure, such hypocrisies are not limited to lawyers. Most of us at one time or another have no doubt condemned in public that which we do in private. By the same token, most are not licensed by the state to perform the lawyer's task.

In Beall's case, the undoing followed closely on the heels of the original wrong. Punishment (public embarrassment) was swift. This is not true, generally, of the bar. Lawyers have learned that they have little reason to fear discoveries.

At bar meetings the plaint is often heard that the public misunderstands lawyers, though who can say why? There is something wrong with the image, they groan; if only that image could be repaired. And so they go out shopping for public relations counselors.

It is entirely conceivable that the bar has come, through steady incantation, to believe its own lies. If so, its failure to see that lawyers have been engaging in their hypocrisies in full public view all along is understandable. And if lawyers do believe in the fiction that their rules are in the public interest, it is equally understandable why they find it mysterious that their reputation has sunk so low. But that does not alter the facts. It is the bar, not the public, that must bend in the end. The image cannot change until the underlying reality changes, until the lawyers come to their senses, lose their overweening pride, and devote themselves to rules that will serve the public before they serve themselves.

To some proposals toward that end we now turn.

CHAPTER 9

What to Do about It:
Twelve Proposals for Reform

The following dozen proposals for reform are practicable to varying degrees. Those that seem the most difficult to accomplish, because they require collective action by the bar, may be easier to promote than the proposals that any lawyer may individually effect. That is because it is often easier to embarrass the leadership of a professional body than its members. The experience of the American Bar Association during the past decade and a half bears this out. By and large, the leaders have led and the members have been dragged, resisting, toward positions more responsive to public needs and less protective of their own. But the leadership has seldom led out of any great enthusiasm for change. Much of the initiative has been a response to judicial decrees and legislative determinations, which the bar has concurred in out of legal necessity or an instinct for survival. Doubtless the suggestions that follow cannot be implemented unless the bar is half forced and half embarrassed into acting. But it is, I hope, not idle to ask this question of the American bar: Is not voluntary change, quite aside from public pressure, part of our ethical responsibility?

Zero-Base Ethics

The present Code of Professional Responsibility must be scrapped.

The code was rickety from the day it was promulgated; significant amendments have had to be adopted in six of the seven years of its existence. It is time to begin anew, to create something more than a pastiche of loquacious moralisms and obscure footnotes. Patchwork repairs of the old code will not suffice. A whole new structure must be thought out. It is beyond my present intention and ability to set down a draft of a new code here. Instead, I will suggest the outline of an approach to reform.

In the jargon of our times, it must be "zero based." That is, we must return to fundamental purposes. A code of ethics is not a place to recite professional folklore, manners, or etiquette. It should be a guide to *conduct:* under given circumstances, what ought a lawyer to do? Two basic considerations should guide: to help and not injure the client; and to do so consistent with some vision of the public good. Obviously there will be situations when helping a client can be construed as harming the public and vice versa. The code must grapple with these situations. Because there can never be a finally satisfactory resolution of the conflict between client and society, the code will have to decide under which circumstances client or public should come first. It must not, as now, ignore the confrontation or avoid it with weasel phrases.

To accomplish this purpose, the code should be restructured to consider separately the various functions of the four bars. The responsibilities of those who represent individual clients in their ordinary affairs of life are different from those who represent a criminal defendant, a private institution, or the public generally. The role of the government attorney differs from that of the lawyer who privately represents a slice of "the public interest." These distinctions must be made explicit. The negotiating, advising, and lobbying functions must be brought out from their hiding places.

No less important, self-serving provisions must be excised. It is no business of a code of ethics to prescribe means by which a profession can enrich itself at the expense of the public. To the contrary. Excision will not be easy, however, because various interlocking provisions that help to maintain the closed guild are useful individually. Thus rules against advertising and solicitation may continue to have a place, so long as they are intended to prevent lawyers from preying on the unwary. What is unacceptable is the continuation of overkill: the notion that because regulation is difficult, any act that may conceivably fall within the dangerous area must be proscribed. It is the lawyer's business to make distinctions. It is time for lawyers to be less repressive toward their own professional freedoms, so long as those freedoms serve the public and do not constitute a license to deceive and defraud.

The new code must clarify a number of duties that at present remain obscure. Among these, in no particular order of importance, are five that I single out here for special mention:

Duty to articulate interests of clients. The present code gives no guidance on how to recognize the client's interest or how to weigh his various interests when they conflict. The code should consider recurring patterns of representation; for example, the long-run versus the short-run interests of institutional clients. The lawyer must be compelled to articulate the variety of interests consciously, to himself and to the client.

Duty to advise client to behave responsibly. The professional tradition has always held that the lawyer may decline to carry out the wishes of his client if they are morally repugnant. This is a necessary rule. Otherwise the lawyer could escape responsibility for harmful acts simply by pleading: "My client instructed me to do it." But the code has never articulated the premises of client responsibility; it has never set forth any concept of client ethics. Such a concept ought to be an integral part of any code, not to bind the lawyer but to give him a point of reference against which to argue with his client. Thus, if a slumlord says, "Draft me the most unconscionable lease you can think of so I can stick it to all those poor slobs who will someday rent apartments in my buildings," the lawyer ought not jump to the task. The lawyer should be duty bound to remonstrate with his client, to give him a hard time, to force him as much as possible to desist from acts that are unconscionable.

This is, I grant, treacherous territory. Some would argue, for example, that any tobacco dealer who markets cigarettes is acting unconscionably, and no lawyer ought to help him do so. A candid tobacco dealer, agreeing that there are dangers, could legitimately retort that smoking does not give everyone cancer, especially if indulged in moderately, and besides smoking is pleasurable. Hence the ultimate risk ought to be for the smoker, not for the dealer or his lawyer. Until society chooses to ban tobacco sales outright, the lawyer has no obligation to act as though it had. On the other hand, it is no less legitimate to argue that the dealer has a responsibility to point out the dangers of using tobacco. The dealer who avoids alerting the public to potential harm is acting unconscionably. Under a new code, the lawyer's duty should be clear: he must refuse to aid the client unless the potential harm is made manifest.

Duty to avoid unconscionable conduct. Some lawyers justify as part of their duty to zealously advance their client's interests certain things that ought to be prohibited outright. The present code prohibits them in a roundabout way by calling on the lawyer to avoid fraud, deceit, and misrepresentation. But it would be sounder for a new code to enumerate situations that are unlawful or deceitful and that, nevertheless, many lawyers knowingly engage in. In other words, explicit limitations should be placed on the lawyer's duty toward client, in order to avoid the kinds of problems that Monroe Freedman has so graphically raised. The present code may arguably require the lawyer to help his client commit perjury; this logic should be explicitly rejected in the new one.

Duty to list unrepresented interests. One recurrent problem is the absence of representation for one or more persons. Only in a fully contested lawsuit are both parties represented. Even then witnesses will be without counsel, and outside the courtroom significant interests frequently go unrepresented. For the benefit of judges or other officials, the code should require lawyers to list the interests that will be affected but not represented. This requirement would mean, for example, that when a consumer advocate presses the FTC to adopt a tough set of anti-fraud rules, he must advise the Commission that there are other consumer interests; for instance, that which would want less restrictive rules to prevent the cost of products from increasing markedly. The duty to list unrepresented interests would also mean that a company appearing through counsel before a congressional committee would have to advise the committee what significant groups it ought to invite in opposition. This ought to be a minimal duty. It would certainly be appropriate for the drafters of the new code to go further and consider a rule requiring the lawyer for one interest to help in securing counsel for the unrepresented interests.

Duty to advise client concerning potential conflicts. The code now requires lawyers to advise their clients about potential conflicts of interests, but it does not at all make clear what the lawyer should say to the client or how he should say it. New rules should give guidance concerning the degree of candor desired. In a sense, the code might require "Miranda warnings" for all clients where any possibility of conflict exists. The rules must also make much more explicit the meaning of informed consent, a concept now implicit but not defined. The code should also narrow considerably the lawyer's discretion to take on potentially conflicting interests. Thus lawyers should be prohibited from accepting a commission for placing title insurance policies.

The zero-base code need not consist solely of high-flown, empty phrases. The drafters should incorporate examples to illustrate the spirit of the abstractions that they concoct.

Who should the drafters be? The code of ethics has legal force only when adopted by court rule in each state. To ask the courts of each state to appoint their own committees to draft a new code would be counterproductive, because too many contradictory standards would emerge. To call on the American Bar Association to appoint still another committee to redraft the code would be, however, a futile gesture. The private association cannot overcome the conflict of interest inherent in balancing self-interest against public and client interest. The situation calls for a national group with a less direct stake in the outcome than the ABA. I suggest that some national body, probably the Judicial Conference of the United States, appoint a committee consisting of non-lawyers as well as lawyers (including philosophers and other non-lawyer professionals) to draft a new code. This code would still be subject to approval by the state courts. Complete uniformity among all the states is not likely, but there is not complete uniformity now, and each state bar court would be under considerable pressure to explain changes.*

*In August 1977, William B. Spann, Jr., the incoming ABA president, in effect threw in the towel on the current Code of Professional Responsibility. In announcing the formation of a special committee to evaluate professional standards he charged it with the task of drafting a new code (the informal target date is 1979). There is considerable subterranean hostility toward the committee on the part of some members of the Committee on Ethics and Professional Responsibility, who continue to believe that the current code is sufficient. This tension is a reflection of the difficulties that any radical draft will have in gaining passage by a leadership that is still relatively conservative. Whether the draft will be a radical departure from the CPR remains to be seen, but the membership of the new committee is clearly more diverse than the 1960s committee that drew up the CPR. As first appointed, the special committee consists of: Robert J. Kutak (chairman), a private practitioner in Omaha and a member of the Standing Committee on Ethics and Professional Responsibility; Thomas Ehrlich, former dean of Stanford Law School and now president of the Legal Services Corporation in Washington; Marvin E. Frankel, a scholarly federal district judge in New York and formerly a professor at Columbia Law School; Jane Lakes Frank, deputy secretary to the President's cabinet and, as chief counsel to the U.S. Senate Constitutional Rights Subcommittee, a leading critic of the ABA; Howell T. Heflin, a progressive former chief justice of the Alabama Supreme Court, now in private practice; Robert B. McKay, now president of the Aspen Institute and formerly dean of New York University Law School; Robert W. Meserve, a private practitioner in Boston and former president of the ABA; Richard H. Sinkfield, a private practitioner in Atlanta; and Samuel D. Thurman, a professor at the University of Utah Law School. Serving as reporter to the committee is L. Ray Patterson, dean of the law school at Emory University and author of books on the professional responsibility of lawyers.

Public Takeover of Lawyer Discipline

The bar has failed to clean its own house. Through its grievance committees the bar has proven incapable of rooting out behavior that all concede to be improper. The solution is to dismantle the bar-appointed and bar-operated disciplinary system and replace it with one operated by and for the public.

Lawyers will dispute the need for "another bureaucracy." They will say that it will stifle the independent practice of law. Their most telling argument, which the Arizona Supreme Court made in the *Bates* case, is that the ethics of the legal profession is too complex and delicate a matter to be entrusted to the lay public. But this confuses lack of legal training with dullness and unsophistication. Lawyers are not the only creatures capable of making sensible judgments about the propriety of conduct under rules. For one thing, many if not most of the complaints and disagreements do not concern terribly complex matters. For another, lawyers regularly laud a system of justice whereby amateurs, usually the more ignorant the better, are given power to decide matters far more complex than professional ethics. I refer to the jury system.

In response to criticisms, the grievance committees in many states have taken on one or more so-called "public members." For the most part, these lay members are named by bar leaders, not by judges or other public officials. But even if governors were to appoint public members, the system would still be defective, for as constituted at present, the boards would only hear (or review) cases that come to them through complaints. Practices that require intensive investigation could still be protected by a bar unwilling to buck the political establishment or to stop a lucrative form of business. Thus in New York rumors have long been rife of a widespread practice called "sewer service," whereby summonses and complaints are never actually served; instead, the process server, perhaps at the behest of his employer, a lawyer, swears that he has made proper service. It is also known that lawyers make payments to court clerks to gain (usually minor) favors. But the Association of the Bar has sat "sphinx-like."[1] Adding non-lawyers to the grievance committee would not change the bar's propensity to overlook these practices.

In announcing the release of the ad hoc committee's report in 1976, chairman Leon Silverman justified his committee's continued reliance on a lawyer-run grievance system by asserting that, unlike the governors of New York State, the presidents of the city bar association "have been men of impeccable character *who have no constituencies.*"[2] Cyrus Vance, then president of the association, agreed with Silverman. "I do not feel obligated to any special constituency," he said.

In his misperception lies the problem. Bar presidents are elected by members of their private associations, not by the public at large, which, consequently, has no voice or means of exerting control.

The bar promises that if it is only allowed to regulate itself it really will, honest, take stern action against the miscreants in its midst. This fable must no longer engage our credulity. The conflict of interest is too large.

Yet lawyers continue to deny that it is. The Arizona Supreme Court rejected the argument that it was wrong for Bates and O'Steen to be haled before a disciplinary panel composed of competing lawyers. The court majority said that the particular grievance committee members would not significantly increase their "pecuniary interest" by ruling against these two lawyers. This is too smug a conception of conflicts of interest. Obviously the disciplinarians will not be enriched by keeping Bates' and O'Steen's salaries low; there are too many lawyers in Arizona to have any such direct effect. But the established practitioners will continue to profit by preventing the development of an alternative method of delivering legal services.

In the end, self-regulation always comes to control of private economic behavior rather than professional conduct. That is not properly a duty or right of the private bar. Disciplining wayward lawyers is a public necessity, not a private one. It should be undertaken to prevent injury to the public, not to forestall injury to the bar's reputation or perquisites. To accomplish the public object, a public agency is essential.

A disciplinary agency need not be limited to policing the work of lawyers. Other professionals have equally or more serious ethical problems. Medical discipline, for example, has deteriorated more than the bar's. The ideal agency would be one that monitors complaints against all professionals and ferrets out unprofessional conduct wherever it can. This agency would have a staff, and the prosecutors (or "complaint counsel") would probably themselves be lawyers. This ought to allay fears that lawyers will be inappropriately brought to task.

But it is not my purpose here to lay out a blueprint. I wish merely to assert the compelling need for comprehensive reform. In the meantime, dozens of recommendations in various studies ought to be undertaken promptly: openness rather than secrecy in disciplinary proceedings, initiation of proceedings in advance of or contemporaneous with criminal proceedings against a misbehaving lawyer, independent investigations into probable areas of lawyer abuse, subpoena power, larger budgets and staff, publicizing the existence of the grievance system (through free television advertising, for example), and more. To the extent that reforms within the power of the bar itself to make are not forthcoming, the need for a complete public takeover will only be underscored.

Make Ethics Committees Representative

The ABA's ethics committee and those of most state bars are grossly unrepresentative of the bar as a whole. Lewis Van Dusen freely concedes that this is so, and he thinks that this is a necessary and even good thing.

The president of the ABA appoints the members of the national committee. The appointees tend to come from a narrow class of practitioners. "With eight members," asks Van Dusen, "how could [the committee] be representative? It is difficult to get a solo practitioner to serve. [The job] requires a peculiar kind of fellow; he* must have time, interest, knowledge, and an intellectual approach." The net is a committee that, while it may be conscientious, is often trapped by its preconceptions.

If it were possible, election of members might be a solution. Van Dusen argues that direct election would be impossible, and he is probably correct. It is difficult to arouse enthusiasm among the 200,000 ABA members over a contest for president. Still, the bar could rather easily broaden the selection procedure. That there are no judges, law professors, public interest lawyers, government attorneys, and others of varying backgrounds, ought to be remedied at once.

Let Legislators Judge

Every great once in a while, a public eruption pushes the lawyers who run state legislatures to enact a law or two that cut against the interests of the private bar. But the laws often meet an unkind fate at the hands of judges who claim sole power to regulate the bar. (Thus the Arizona Supreme Court said that the legislature could not overturn the court's decision prohibiting realtors from filling in blanks on real estate contracts.) This is pernicious jurisprudence. In a democracy, the legislature has the authority to determine what constitutes injurious conduct and how to prevent or remedy it. No one would seriously entertain the notion that only hospital administrators should fix standards for the practice of medicine. Judges obviously have an interest in lawyers who actually come before them, but courtroom conduct scarcely exhausts the nature of the lawyer's work. Legislatures should not automatically delegate to courts the power to set standards, for the assumption then erroneously springs up that the

*There is at present one female committee member, Betty B. Fletcher of Seattle.

legislature may not alter the standards once announced. Courts are not necessarily the best agency to govern professional conduct, and legislatures ought not to be intimidated into thinking so.

Establish Unnecessary Practice of Law Committees

The bar considers the problem of "unauthorized practice of law" so grave that it has established a formidable apparatus, separate from the ethics-discipline structure, to control the evil. In New York, for example, the Association of the Bar has an arrangement with a rival organization, the New York County Lawyers Association. The former operates the discipline system, the latter prosecutes cases of unauthorized practice (against both lawyers and non-lawyers).

These unauthorized practice committees should be put out of business. If people are violating the law, public law enforcement agencies should be charged with the task of prosecuting.

Since numerous lawyers, now discharging their felt obligation to engage in public service by prosecuting competitors, will then have a lot of free time, I suggest that the bar create a new mechanism that can legitimately be private: the Unnecessary Practice of Law Committee. This group would not have prosecutorial powers. Its role would be advisory. But it would have jurisdiction to consider in the name of the bar any facet of law or law practice and would be charged with making proposals to eliminate those wasteful, unnecessary facets of practice that I have earlier said contribute to the lawyers' penchant for inconspicuous production. This suggestion is not made frivolously. There is a crying need for simplification in the law, a need which the bar as a private entity now largely ignores. Let this be one of its central concerns. Let us judge how devoted the bar is to the public good by how far it goes in trying to reduce its own power and money-making capacity.

Encourage Independent Paralegals

Ceasing harassment of other professionals and semi-professionals whose work encroaches on the lawyers' turf is not sufficient, however. The bar must actually encourage the development of a new professional class that can take over the routine work at low cost. Such a class—the paraprofessional—is beginning to emerge, not only in the law but in other professions as well.

But so far the paralegal aide remains just that: an assistant to the lawyer, whose time and billing are udner the lawyer's control. This monolithic use of the paralegal's time must change. As in medicine, which has many subclasses of practitioners, like nurses, the bar should face up to the desirability of developing independent paralegals, licensed to do a host of routine tasks on their own. At a minimum, the paralegal should become the pharmacist of the profession: not licensed to prescribe but to fill the prescriptions. Again, it will be a measure of the bar's genuine concern for the public good if it takes the lead rather than resists.

Draft Lawyers

As we have seen, the lawyer's obligation to serve those in need is only a moral one. In a free society that is as it should be. But it is worth serious consideration whether there ought to be an apparent exception to the general rule.

Law school training has rarely fitted any graduate for immediate practice; many years of on-the-job training are essential to the making of a skilled lawyer. That is why so many law school graduates go to prosecutorial and legal aid offices, government agencies, and large law firms for their first jobs. Therefore, we ought to consider requiring every lawyer, as a prerequisite to obtaining a license, to serve for a time those too poor to pay for their legal needs.

All lawyers ought to understand the needs and be able to cope with the problems of this large segment of the population. Without such training, comparable to the medical internship, the lawyer will have too narrow a mind and too shallow a legal experience to cope with future, "more important," problems. At present the prospect for a lawyer draft is utopian, but the idea is worth discussing and the debate should begin.

Monitor Judges

Bar associations fund committees to examine the qualifications of lawyers named to judgeships (though their standards are often perverse, witness the ABA's endorsement of G. Harrold Carswell's nomination to the Supreme Court in 1971). But just as the bar concerns itself only fitfully with the qualifications of lawyers who are already in practice, so it is remiss in failing to monitor the performance and conduct of judges once on the bench. Some states, like New York, have public agencies designed for the purpose. But these are few, underfunded, and bound by rules of secrecy that cover up most judicial misconduct.

Though it would cost money, it would not be conceptually difficult for the bar to establish private monitoring committees that periodically inspect the courtrooms of every sitting judge in the country. The committees need but randomly send in observers unannounced, and publish a report of their findings. Of course, the committees could sit to receive complaints and to investigate these, but the *in terrorem* effect of the anonymous monitoring could go a long way toward improving the conduct of judges.

Keep Public Servants at Public Jobs

Whether or not courts or agencies would enforce the rules, the bar should proclaim emphatically once and for all that full-time public officials, whether serving in a legislative or executive capacity, and whether or not allowed by law, may not ethically carry on a private law practice.

Preach Ethics

Whenever members of a private organization demand that the body as a whole take a public stand on a political or social issue, others bemoan the partisanship. If I join a bar association, I have reason to protest if the leaders decide to condemn the modern novel or endorse a candidate for public office. But in the nature of things, private associations must and do take stands on matters relevant to the professional concerns of their members on which there may be a reasonable difference of opinion. Bar associations support or condemn and lobby for or against laws they believe will affect their members.

But on some important issues, notably unethical professional conduct, the bar often remains mute. As a whole, the bar did not speak out to condemn the Southern lawyers for their reprehensible conduct during the battle for the integration of American society. Until the lawyers' antics passed the point of buffoonery in Washington during the Watergate years, the bar did not speak out; and when it finally did, it did so largely because a national president, Chesterfield Smith, could no longer stomach what he saw. (Judging by the vituperative response to his public pronouncements during 1973–1974, many members of the bar would have preferred to pretend that nothing was amiss.)

It is time for the bar to develop a means of considering and preaching against the violations of law and professional conduct in which lawyers periodically and collectively engage. If the bar is to become a moral force, it must go public. Morality gains weight only when it is active. It is not depleted but nourished by repetition.

Teach Ethics

Three years after the resignation of Richard Nixon, legal ethics has found its way into the curriculum of every law school. New, and good, casebooks have been published. Law students are discovering that the problems they will face in practice are formidable and that there are no easy answers. Is this enough? I do not believe that it is.

For years the cliché ran that by the time a person enters law school he is either ethical or he is not. Whatever was true about the cliché before 1974 remains true. The teaching of legal ethics will surely heighten the sensitivity of the forming "lawyer mind" to the pitfalls that await him, but it will not necessarily dispose him to a more sensitive awareness of his moral responsibilities in the modern world. Nor should it. That is not the function of the law school. But it is, I think, the function of our educational system generally.

The teaching of ethics must begin at a much earlier age. Like English and mathematics, it ought to accompany the student straight through school, from the earliest grades to and including college. This is not a call for indoctrination: the teaching of ethics should not be instruction in dogmatism but an opening of the mind to the dazzling range of ways in which human beings interact and affect one another. This is not a task exclusively for the bar, but the legal profession pretends to some expertise in the subject, and it ought to join with others to explore ways of restructuring the educational curriculum.*

---

*How to do this is a subject that I must leave to another book.

Renounce Wealth

In the final analysis, it is impossible for any body of professionals to live an ethical life so long as one of the chief reasons for pursuing the profession is to make large amounts of money. The bar itself has mouthed this perception from time to time. Its denunciation of ambulance chasing and contingent fee arrangements has always invoked the spirit of lost altruism. The practice of law is not simply a technical skill that enables its possessor to suck in wealth. It is a calling and a trust, for without law—and law for all of us—we are no civilization at all.

But it is a startling irony that a high proportion of those who have reminded us of the obligations of the lawyer are among the wealthiest members of the profession. A few of these, because they are wealthy enough, devote much of their time to good works. Many institutional lawyers today have served without fee in the representation of indigent people and their causes. But have most lawyers devoted enough of their time?

I do not mean to suggest that lawyers should be forced to be poor. Freedom is more precious still. But freedom presupposes an ability to renounce large earnings that come from the practice of law. There is nothing to make them devote their legal skills to non-monetary ends, but neither is there anything to stop them from doing so. There are other ways to make money.

A vow of poverty is not the imprimatur of ethical conduct, but a renunciation of riches gathered from the practice of law would be a vow worth making. It will not create saints, but we have never demanded sainthood of lawyers. If lawyering is truly a public profession, it is no more seemly for the members of the bar to live lives of luxury than it was for the clergy of old. If lawyers continue to do so, a new Reformation must somehow come into being.

From practical reforms to improbable Reformation, the prospects are uncertain. But unless lawyers themselves begin to make the necessary changes in their professional lives and relationships, more will be lost than the right to call lawyers ethical. Their continuing neglect will damage not only themselves but the whole nation, for this time around public reform in the face of lawyer recalcitrance must lead to the end of the private bar. Not merely the lawyer's freedom, but that of all, hangs in the balance.

Notes

Chapter 2. The Bar as Unindicted Co-Conspirator

1. Henry S. Drinker, "Some Remarks on Mr. Curtis' 'The Ethics of Advocacy,' " 4 *Stanford Law Review* 349 (1952).
2. *Legal Ethics* (New York: Columbia University Press, 1952).
3. Drinker, "Some Remarks," p. 349.
4. Quoted in Jerold S. Auerbach, *Unequal Justice* (New York: Oxford University Press, 1976), p. 127.
5. Charles P. Curtis, "The Ethics of Advocacy," 4 *Stanford Law Review* 3, 8 (1951).
6. *Id.*
7. Drinker, "Some Remarks," p. 351.
8. Curtis, p. 7.
9. Samuel Williston, *Life and Law* (Boston: Little, Brown, 1940), p. 271.
10. EC 7–23; DR 7–106(B). See Murray Teigh Bloom, ed., *Lawyers, Clients, and Ethics* (New York: Council on Legal Education for Professional Responsibility, 1974), case 2, pp. 14–22.
11. Drinker, pp. 350–51. See also Formal Op. 208, ABA Committee on Professional Ethics and Grievances (1953).
12. George V. Higgins, *The Friends of Richard Nixon* (New York: Ballantine, 1976), pp. 88–89.
13. Barbara Levy, *Legacy of Death* (New York: Prentice-Hall, 1973).
14. Interview with the author, July 22, 1976.
15. *New York Times*, April 2, 1971, p. 37.

Chapter 3. Writing the Ten Commandments

1. David J. Brewer, "The Ideal Lawyer," 98 *Atlantic Monthly* 596 (Nov. 1906); quoted in Auerbach, p. 51.

2. *Lawyers and the System of Justice* (St. Paul: West, 1976), p. 19.

3. Stat. 4 Henry IV c. 18 (1402).

4. See Lawrence M. Friedman, *A History of American Law* (New York: Simon & Schuster, 1975), pp. 20–21.

5. Samuel L. Knapp, *Biographical Sketches of Great Lawyers and Statesmen*, 1821; quoted in Charles Warren, *A History of the American Bar* (Boston: Little, Brown, 1912), p. 224.

6. Quoted in Maxwell Bloomfield, *American Lawyers in a Changing Society, 1776–1876* (Cambridge: Harvard University Press, 1976), p. 40.

7. Daniel J. Boorstin, *The Americans: The Colonial Experience* (New York: Vintage, 1958), p. 196.

8. Quoted in Bernard Schwartz, *The Law in America* (New York: McGraw-Hill, 1974), p. 3.

9. See Boorstin, p. 197.

10. Quoted in Bloomfield, pp. 39–40.

11. Warren, p. 214.

12. *Id.*

13. Noted in Charles Francis Adams, *Three Episodes of Massachusetts History;* quoted in Warren, p. 215.

14. From Diary of John Quincy Adams, *Massachusetts Historical Society Proceedings*, 2d ser., vol. xvi (1902); quoted in Warren, p. 220.

15. Quoted in Warren, p. 217.

16. Boorstin, p. 196.

17. Quoted in Schwartz, p. 2.

18. Boorstin, p. 205.

19. Roscoe Pound, *The Lawyer from Antiquity to Modern Times* (St. Paul: West, 1953), pp. 227, 231.

20. Quoted in James Willard Hurst, *The Growth of American Law: The Law Makers* (Boston: Little, Brown, 1950), p. 281.

21. Quoted in J. Young, *The Medical Messiahs* (Princeton: Princeton University Press, 1967), p. 19.

22. Hurst, p. 286.

23. 2 *Trial of Queen Caroline* 8 (J. Nightingale ed., 1821); later remarks quoted in William Forsythe, *Hortensius* (London: 3rd ed., 1879), p. 389; reprinted in Elliott E. Cheatham, *Cases and Materials on the Legal Profession* (Brooklyn: Foundation Press, 2d ed., 1955), p. 241.

24. *Felix Frankfurter Reminisces* (New York: Anchor, 1962), p. 276.

25. Quoted in Friedman, p. 562.

26. Quoted in Pound, p. 256.

27. See Walter B. Jones, "Canons of Professional Ethics, Their Genesis and History," 7 *Notre Dame Lawyer* 483 (1932).

28. 31 *ABA Reports* 716 (1908).

29. William H. Harbaugh, *Lawyer's Lawyer: The Life of John W. Davis* (New York: Oxford, 1973), p. 268.

30. Quoted in Auerbach, p. 33.

31. 29 *ABA Reports* 600 (1906).

32. George Sharswood, *An Essay on Professional Ethics* (Philadelphia: T. & J. W. Johnson & Co., 2d ed., 1860), p. 75.

33. Auerbach, p. 42.

34. W. A. Purrington, "The American Bar Association's Proposed Code and Oath," *Bench and Bar,* June 1908, p. 107.

35. Mellinkoff, pp. 934–47, 865–925.

36. John F. Sutton, Jr., "Revision of the Canons of Ethics of the American Bar Association," 21 *Record of the Bar of the City of New York* 472–78 (1966).

Chapter 4. *"Keeping It for Ourselves": The Bar vs. the Public*

1. EC 2–26.

2. Stephen B. Oates, *With Malice toward None: The Life of Abraham Lincoln* (New York: Harper & Row, 1977), p. 101.

3. See J. K. Lieberman, "New Ways to Cut Legal Fees," *New York,* Feb. 14, 1976, p. 83.

4. Chesterfield Smith, speech, Public Interest Practice Session, ABA annual meeting, Aug. 7, 1976, Atlanta, Georgia.

5. See Charles Fried, "The Lawyer as Friend: The Moral Foundations of the Lawyer-Client Relation," 85 *Yale Law Journal* 1060 (1976).

6. See Formal Opinion 8 in *ABA Opinions of the Committee on Professional Ethics* (Chicago: American Bar Foundation, 1967), p. 243.

7. Private conversation with author, Aug. 8, 1976.

8. See *Business Week,* Feb. 14, 1977, p. 84. See also ABA Formal Op. 305 (1962).

9. *United Mine Workers* v. *Illinois State Bar Assn.,* 35 Ill. 2d 20, 219 N.E. 2d 503 (1966).

10. 389 U.S. 217 (1967).

11. *Brotherhood of Railroad Trainmen* v. *Virginia ex rel. Virginia State Bar,* 377 U.S. 1 (1964).

12. DR 2–103(D)(5).

13. *United Transportation Union* v. *State Bar of Michigan,* 401 U.S. 576 (1971).

14. See J. K. Lieberman, *How the Government Breaks the Law* (New York: Penguin, 1973), pp. 95–96.

15. *Business Week,* March 24, 1975, p. 139.

16. *Los Angeles Daily Journal,* March 14, 1974.

17. I did write a brief story on an aspect of what he said; a photographer was dispatched to Handler's office and his picture was run as well: *Business Week,* June 14, 1976, p. 44.

18. See 45 *U.S. Law Week* 3498 (1977).

19. Personal conversation with the author, Dec. 4, 1975.

20. *Jacoby* v. *State Bar of California,* 19 Cal. 3rd 359, 562 P. 2d 1326 (1977).

21. 4 *District of Columbia Bar Report* 5 (May 1976).

22. "The Organized Bar: Self-Serving or Serving the Public?" Hearings before Subcommittee on Representation of Citizen Interests of the Committee on the Judiciary, U.S. Senate, 93rd Congress, 2d sess., Feb. 3, 1974, p. 10.

23. *Consumers Union* v. *American Bar Assn.,* 427 F. Supp. 506, 519 (E. D. Va. 1976).

24. DR 2–102 (A)(6).

25. Monroe H. Freedman, *Lawyers' Ethics in an Adversary System* (Indianapolis: Bobbs-Merrill, 1975), p. 117.

26. Mellinkoff, pp. 330–38.

27. *Consumers Union* v. *American Bar Assn.,* 427 F. Supp. 506 (E. D. Va. 1976).

28. *Id.,* p. 519.

29. *Id.,* p. 522.

30. *Bates* v. *Arizona State Bar,* 97 S. Ct. 2691, 53 L. Ed. 810 (1977).

31. In re Cohn, 43 App. Div. 2d 405, 352 N.Y.S. 2d 461 (1st Dept. 1974).

32. "Advertising, Solicitation, and the Profession's Duty to Make Legal Counsel Available," 81 *Yale Law Journal* 1181, 1184 (1972).

33. *NAACP* v. *Button,* 371 U.S. 415 (1963).

34. Freedman, p. 121; see also Andrew L. Kaufman, *Problems in Professional Responsibility* (Boston: Little, Brown, 1976), pp. 447, 456–59.

35. Personal interview, June 21, 1976.

Chapter 5. The Ethics of Fees: The Bar vs. Its Clients

1. Joseph C. Goulden, *The Superlawyers* (New York: Dell, 1973), pp. 106–7.
2. EC 2–17.
3. DR 2–106.
4. Olavi Moru, ed., *Digest of Bar Association Ethics Opinions* (Chicago: American Bar Foundation, 1970), no. 4723, p. 517.
5. EC 2–18.
6. Formal Op. 28, 1967 ed., p. 271.
7. Formal Op. 302, 1967 ed., p. 661.
8. J. Cameron Hall, *Ethics, Fee Problems, and Office Management* (Ann Arbor: Institute of Continuing Legal Education, 1964), pp. 35–36 (emphasis added).
9. 59 *ABA Journal* 1435 (1973).
10. *Goldfarb* v. *Virginia State Bar*, 421 U.S. 773, 783 (1975).
11. *Business Week*, April 13, 1974, p. 97.
12. Formal Op. 331, Dec. 15, 1972.
13. Resolution, Board of Governors, May 1972 meeting (Adopted as ABA's official position in congressional testimony).
14. "The Proper Role of the Lawyer in Residential Real Estate Transactions," ABA Special Committee, May 22, 1974, p. 8 (emphasis added).
15. See J. K. Lieberman, *The Tyranny of the Experts* (New York: Walker, 1970), chap. 6.
16. *New York Times*, Jan. 6, 1977, p. 22.
17. "Unauthorized Practice and Pro Se Divorce," 86 *Yale Law Journal* 104, 153–54 (1976).
18. *State Board of Arizona* v. *Arizona Land Title & Trust Co.*, 90 Ariz. 76, 366 P.2d 1 (1961).
19. Quoted in Mellinkoff, p. 418; 49 *ABA Journal* 162, 164 (1963).
20. *Wall Street Journal*, Sept. 3, 1976, p. 1.
21. *Id.*, p. 19.
22. *Id.*
23. Matter of Bates, 555 P.2d 640, 647 (Ariz. 1976) (concurring opinion).
24. *Surety Title Insurance Agency, Inc.* v. *Virginia State Bar*, 431 F. Supp. 298 (E. D. Va. 1977).
25. *New York Times*, Feb. 7, 1977, p. 26.
26. DR 7–109 (C).
27. *Person* v. *Association of the Bar*, 554 F. 2d 534 (2d Cir. 1977).
28. Joseph C. Goulden, "The World of the Superlawyers," *Washingtonian*, Nov. 1975, p. 126.

29. Dietrich Rueschenmeyer, *Lawyers and Their Society: A Comparative Study of the Legal Profession in Germany and in the United States* (Cambridge: Harvard University Press, 1973), p. 128.

Chapter 6. The Ethics of Doing Harm: Clients vs. the Public

1. Richard Wasserstrom, "Value and Conflicts in the Professional Role," 3 *Learning and the Law* 45, 48 (1976).

2. Potter Stewart, "Professional Ethics for the Business Lawyer: The Morals of the Marketplace," 31 *Business Lawyer* 463, 467 (Nov. 1975).

3. *Los Angeles Times*, July 2, 1974. A documentary history of the case is reprinted in Stuart Charles Goldberg, *Professional Responsibility* (New York: New York Law School, 1976), chap. 1.

4. *Albany Times Union*, June 21, 1974, p. 11.

5. Arthur Powell, *I Can Go Home Again* (Chapel Hill: University of North Carolina Press, 1943), pp. 287–92; Powell, "Privilege of Counsel and Confidential Communications," 6 *Georgia Bar Journal* 333 (1944); noted in Kaufman, p. 182.

6. Kaufman, p. 182.

7. Drinker, *Legal Ethics*, p. 137.

8. *Los Angeles Times*, July 2, 1974.

9. New York State Public Health Law, sec. 4200(1).

10. This situation is taken from ABA Consortium for Professional Education, *Dilemmas in Legal Ethics*, part 2, "Counseling," 1976 (videotape transcript).

11. DR 4–101(C)(3); EC 7–15; DR 7–102(A); DR 7–102(B)(1).

12. Address to the Symposium on Private Investments Abroad, Southwestern Legal Foundation, Dallas, June 16, 1976.

13. *SEC* v. *National Student Marketing Corp.*, pretrial brief of White & Case, Civil Action No. 225–72, U.S. District Court, District of Columbia, Jan. 17, 1977, pp. vii, viii, ix–x. See *SEC* v. *NSMC*, 360 F. Supp. 284 (D.D.C. 1973). See also Burt Schorr, "White & Case on Trial," *Juris Doctor*, March 1977, p. 15; James Sargent, "The SEC and the Individual Investor: Restoring His Confidence in the Market," 60 *Virginia Law Review* 533, 572 (1974).

14. *Ernst & Ernst* v. *Hochfelder*, 425 U.S. 185 (1976).

15. A. A. Sommer, Jr., "The Emerging Responsibilities of the Securities Lawyer," 1974–1975 *Federal Securities Law Reporter* par. 79, 631.

16. *New York Law Journal,* May 6, 1977.

17. Freedman, p. 28.

18. *Id.,* pp. 30–31.

19. *Id.,* p. 35.

20. *Id.,* p. 38.

21. Anne Strick, *Injustice for All* (New York: Putnam, 1977), chap. 5.

22. The technique was demonstrated in the popular, though stylistically flawed, 1976 film *Lipstick.*

23. "Standards of Conduct for Prosecution and Defense Personnel: A Symposium," 5 *American Criminal Law Quarterly* 8 (Fall 1966).

24. *Id.,* pp. 14–15.

25. *Id.,* p. 26.

26. *Id.,* p. 29.

27. Freedman, p. 48; "Professional Responsibility of the Criminal Defense Lawyer: The Three Hardest Questions," 64 *Michigan Law Review* 1469, 1474 (1966).

28. *Id.*

29. EC 7–4; DR 7–102(A)(1)

30. Personal interview, June 23, 1976.

31. Personal interview, Aug. 12, 1976.

32. See Marvin E. Frankel, "The Alabama Lawyer, 1954–1964: Has the Official Organ Atrophied?" 64 *Columbia Law Review* 1243 (1964).

33. Murray Schwartz, ed., *Law and the American Future* (Englewood Cliffs, N.J.: Prentice-Hall, 1976), p. 11.

34. Quoted in Mark J. Green, *The Other Government* (New York: Grossman, 1975), p. 138.

35. *Id.,* p. 69.

36. "Judicial Control of Antitrust Cases," 23 *Federal Rules Decisions* 417–20 (1959).

37. EC 7–6.

38. Freedman, p. 60.

39. Jerome Carlin, *Lawyers' Ethics: A Survey of the New York City Bar* (New York: Russell Sage, 1966), p. 46.

40. DR 7–102(A)(8).

41. H. Freeman and H. Weihofer, *Clinical Law Training,* p. 122; quoted in Alvin B. Rubin, "A Causerie on Lawyers' Ethics in Negotiation," 35 *Louisiana Law Review* 577, 581 (1975).

42. M. Meltsner and P. Schrag, *Public Interest Advocacy: Materials for*

Clinical Legal Education (1974) p. 232; quoted in Rubin, *id.*

43. Derived from ABA Consortium for Professional Education, *Dilemmas in Legal Ethics,* part 3, "Negotiation," 1976 (videotape transcript).

44. Rubin, p. 589.

Chapter 7. In the Best Interest of the Client: The Problem of Conflicts

1. *New York Times,* June 13, 1976, p. 26.

2. DR 9–101(B).

3. DR 5–105(D).

4. Formal Op. 342, Nov. 24, 1975.

5. See Josh Fitzhugh, "D.C. Bar Panel Softens Conflict Rule," *New York Law Journal,* Nov. 26, 1975, pp. 1,3.

6. Opinion No. 889, 31 *Record* 552 (Nov. 1976).

7. *Id.,* p. 570.

8. *E.g.,* S. 555, 95th Cong., 1st Sess. (1977).

9. See *Outside Counsel, Inside Director: The Directory of Lawyers on the Boards of American Industry* (New York: Law Journal Press, 1976).

10. *Business Week,* March 29, 1976, p. 100.

11. *New York Law Journal,* Feb. 17, 1977, p. 1.

12. *New York Times,* Dec. 19, 1976, p. E1.

13. *Outside Counsel, Inside Director,* p. 42.

14. See *Business Week,* Aug. 9, 1976, p. 74.

15. EC 5–1.

16. EC 7–9.

17. F. Raymond Marks, *The Lawyer, the Public, and Professional Responsibility* (Chicago: American Bar Foundation, 1972), p. 260.

18. Stephen B. Oates, *With Malice Toward None,* p. 101.

19. Victor S. Navasky, "Right On! With Lawyer William Kunstler," *New York Times Magazine,* April 19, 1970, p. 30.

20. 56 *ABA Journal* 552 (June 1970).

21. Joseph A. Califano, "The Washington Lawyer: When to Say No," *Verdicts on Lawyers,* Ralph Nader and Mark J. Green, eds. (New York: Grossman, 1976), p. 192.

22. *Id.*

23. EC 5–18.

24. Lewis Van Dusen, "Who Is Counsel's Corporate Client?" 31 *Business Lawyer* 474–75 (Nov. 1975).
25. *New York Times,* March 13, 1974, p. 1.
26. EC 7–13.
27. C. Norman Poirer, "The Federal Government Lawyer and Professional Ethics," 60 *ABA Journal* 1541 (Dec. 1974); cf. Kaufman, p. 208.
28. *Shelley* v. *Kraemer,* 334 U.S. 1 (1948).
29. Derrick A. Bell, Jr., "Serving Two Masters: Integration Ideals and Client Interests in School Desegregation Litigation," 85 *Yale Law Journal* 470 (1976).
30. Bell, pp. 478–79.
31. *Id.,* p. 480.
32. *Id.,* pp. 483–84, fn. 41.
33. See "The New Public Interest Lawyers," 79 *Yale Law Journal* 1069 (1970).

Chapter 8. The Failure of Self-Regulation

1. Joseph Borkin, *The Corrupt Judge* (New York: Potter, 1962), pp. 141–86.
2. Paul Hoffman, *Lions in the Street* (New York: New American Library, 1973), p. 143. Bonomi has since resigned to enter private practice.
3. ABA Special Committee on Evaluation of Disciplinary Enforcement, *Problems and Recommendations in Disciplinary Enforcement* (Chicago: ABA, 1970), p. 1.
4. Ad Hoc Committee on Grievance Procedures, Association of the Bar of the City of New York, Jan. 26, 1976, p. 29.
5. *Id.,* p. 30.
6. *Id.,* p. 28.
7. F. Raymond Marks and Darlene Cathcart, "Discipline within the Legal Profession: Is It Self-Regulation?" 1974 *Illinois Law Forum* 193, 225.
8. Freedman, p. viii.
9. The story is told by Victor Rabinowitz, Ellsberg's defense counsel, in "The Prosecutor: The Duty to Seek Justice," *Verdicts on Lawyers,* pp. 231–41.
10. Alan M. Dershowitz, book review of Richard Harris, *Freedom Spent, New York Times Book Review,* Nov. 28, 1976, pp. 42–43.
11. Jack Newfield, "The Ten Worst Judges in New York," *New York,* Oct. 16, 1972, p. 32.

12. Personal interview with staff lawyer.

13. Ad Hoc Committee report, p. 38.

14. Bayless Manning, "If Lawyers Were Angels: A Sermon in One Canon," 60 *ABA Journal* 821 (1974); see also Sharon Tisher, Lynn Bernabei, Mark Green, "The Conspiracy of Silence," *Juris Doctor,* July/Aug.1977, p. 12, based on Tisher, Bernabei, Green, *Bringing the Bar to Justice: A Comparative Study of Six Bar Associations* (Public Citizen, Inc., 1977), chap. 5.

15. Eric H. Steele and Raymond T. Nimmer, "Lawyers, Clients, and Professional Regulation," 1976 *American Bar Foundation Research Journal* 919, 941–42.

16. Ad Hoc Committee report, p. 49.

17. See Kaufman, pp. 315–20, for unpublished concurring opinion in decision of *Board of Governors, State Bar of Arizona* v. *Kleindienst* (1974).

18. David Riesman, "Toward an Anthropological Science of Law and the Legal Profession," in *Individualism Reconsidered* (Glencoe: Free Press, 1964), p. 450.

19. *Washington Post,* Aug. 22, 1974 (editorial page).

20. Vermont C. Royster, "Public Morality: Afterthoughts on Watergate," *American Scholar,* vol. 43 (Spring 1974), p. 249.

21. *Washington Post,* Aug. 29, 1974, p. 1.

22. *Id.,* Aug. 30, 1974, p. C1.

Chapter 9. What to Do about It: Twelve Proposals for Reform

1. Ralph Nader, "An Overview," in *Verdicts on Lawyers,* p. ix.

2. Press conference, Feb. 3, 1976 (emphasis added).

INDEX